Perception

PERCEPTION

Irvin Rock

**SCIENTIFIC
AMERICAN
LIBRARY**

An imprint of Scientific American Books, Inc.
New York

Library of Congress Cataloging in Publication Data:

Rock, Irvin.
  Perception.

  Bibliography: p. 236
  Includes index.
    1. Perception. I. Title.
    BF311.R556   1984   153.7   83-20104
ISBN 0-7167-5001-5

Printed in the United States of America

Book design by Malcolm Grear Designers

Scientific American Library is published by
Scientific American Books, Inc., a subsidiary
of Scientific American, Inc.

Distributed by W. H. Freeman and Company,
41 Madison Avenue, New York, New York 10010.

1 2 3 4 5 6 7 8 9 0 KP 2 1 0 8 9 8 7 6 5 4

To David, Lisa, and Rayna

CONTENTS

PREFACE

Natural science begins with and depends upon perception, but perception itself has not aroused the universal curiosity that other subjects of science have. Scientific exploration began with things most distant from us—the stars—and only much later moved inward, toward man himself. It required a sophisticated self-consciousness to appreciate that perception itself constitutes one of the greatest and most difficult scientific problems of all.

Even today few people recognize that the way the world looks to us is a remarkable achievement that calls for explanation. Whereas many individuals have some understanding of the phenomena and concepts of the natural sciences, with respect to the field of perception few have gone beyond the knowledge that the eye functions like a camera and yields a "picture" on the retina. Our perception of a world of objects and events, however, cannot be explained adequately by simply referring to processes within the eye or to the transmission of information into the brain about the retinal image. The usefulness of the analogy of the eye to a camera ends with the formation of that image; the problem of perception then begins.

This book explores the perception of the properties of objects (such as size and shape), their distance from us, and their motion. It focuses on problems such as are posed by the achievement of constancy of perceived object properties despite an ever-changing retinal image. Given the similarity of the eye to a camera, the mystery of our perception is how we manage to transcend the inadequate, distortion-prone, ambiguous, two-dimensional images established on the retina and achieve the rich, constant, usually correct, three-dimensional representation of the world that we do. The book also investigates cases in which perception fails to achieve correct representation, namely, illusion.

There is a problem in writing a book such as this on a still young and controversial field. One wants to present the body of knowledge and theory concerning which there is a high degree of consensus in order to represent most accurately the state of the art. But, when there is much disagreement even about what are the important facts, that is difficult to do. Moreover, a theoretically neutral book presenting either no speculation at all or all sides of every issue can make dull reading. I have thus tried to steer a middle course: Describe the perceptual phenomena that most investigators consider important, discuss the major theories that have been proposed to explain them, and give my own point of view and the evidence supporting it. When I advance a somewhat idiosyncratic theory or speculation, I say so.

I must call to the reader's attention the fact that this book has little to say about mechanisms in the brain that have been or might be uncovered by way of explanation of perception. Instead, I discuss, in nonphysiological language, theories of perception that describe the kind of process that might be assumed to occur when we have various perceptions. By analogy to computers, one might say that the first step in explaining mental events is to describe them in terms of the kind of processing that occurs (software) rather than in terms of the neurophysiological structures that can carry it out (hardware). The reasons for taking this approach are set forth in Chapter 1.

Also neglected in this book are topics closely related to sensory physiology. Thus I do not discuss color vision because explanation in this area of investigation, at least thus far, has tended to center around the question of the kind of cells in the retina that are predominantly responsive to one or another wavelength of light. But I do discuss the perception of various shades on the white-gray-black (or achromatic) continuum because these perceptions cannot be adequately explained in terms of specialized cells in the retina or, in my opinion, any other mechanism confined to the retina or the eye. Similarly, I do not cover topics such as adaptation to light and dark, visual acuity, and the like because the focus of interest in these topics is not that of perceiving objects and events among objects. Instead, I presuppose that these more peripherally determined processes are successfully carried out so that information about the outside world is sharply focused by the cornea and the lens as an image on the retina and is transmitted into the brain. This kind of sensory information can be thought of as constituting the raw material from which perception is constructed.

The book also has little to say about senses other than vision. One can hardly do justice to *visual* perception in a short introductory book. The choice of vision is dictated not only by my particular area of interest but by other considerations as well. Certain kinds of perceptual experience, such as those of shape, of motion, of pictures, and of the third dimension of space, are either exclusively visual or are far better realized in the domain of vision. Moreover, various theoretical controversies, such as the Nativist-Empiricist debate over the origin of form and depth perception, have historically centered around phenomena of visual perception. As an introduction to all of the field of perception, vision is thus a logical choice.

For those interested in sensory processes, neural and brain mechanisms underlying perception, and auditory perception, sources of information are given in the Selected Readings. Also recommended there are books on visual perception by way of antidote for whatever biases, prejudices, and possible errors exist in this book.

There remains the pleasurable task of thanking various people without whose contribution this book either would not have been completed or would not contain whatever may be clear, well illustrated, and meritorious in it. It was Linda Chaput, Editorial Director of the Scientific American Library, who suggested the idea for this book and steered it through the various stages of publication. It was Jonathan Cobb who so intelligently, skillfully, and diplomatically edited it, acquiring knowledge of the field of perception along the way in order to do so, ably aided and abetted in the process by Heather Wiley. It was my friends Carl Zuckerman and Charles S. Harris who once again sacrificed their time and energy to help me by reading the various drafts of the manuscript and suggesting needed revisions. It was Sylvia Rock who typed much of the manuscript, often under the pressure of deadlines, and who kept our family afloat during the long periods when I was too immersed in writing to be of much use to anyone else.

I R
Highland Park, New Jersey

Perception

1 THE WORLD OF PERCEPTION

In the painting reproduced on the facing page, we instantly identify the objects depicted. To create the impression of verisimilitude in the viewer, the artist followed the rules of perspective. He painted the doilies and the top of the plant pot in the shape of ellipses, and he painted the tops of the tables and the windows of the buildings seen from the cafeteria in the shape of trapezoids, the lengths and directions of lines and the actual shape given to each object depending on where it was located in relation to him.

The rules of perspective explain what the artist did. But why does the resulting painting create the impressions in us that it does? How, for example, do we come to perceive a circular doily out of the image of an ellipse? Why are we able to perceive the table's shape as rectangular when what meets the eye is the contour of a trapezoid? If we saw a photograph of the scene, the same discrepancies between what actually meets the eye and what we spontaneously perceive would be evident, and the same questions could be asked. Perception of pictures differs from perception of the three-dimensional world, but, even if we had looked at the scene itself from the artist's vantage point, close attention to the image our eyes received would have revealed many of the same discrepancies: Trace on a transparent surface held in front of one eye the outline of a plate resting on a table across the room, for example, and it comes out as an ellipse, not a circle. In short, whether we look at a painting, a photograph, or the world around us, how does it happen that the image the eye receives is transformed into the quite different impression that characterizes what we spontaneously perceive?

Edward Hopper, Sunlight in a Cafeteria, *1958.*

The image of an object as it is focused on the film of a camera.

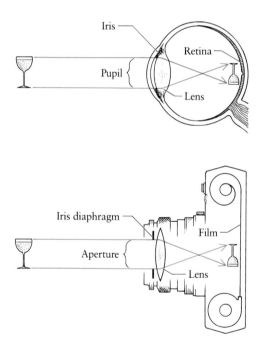

Similarity of eye and camera.

The Eye as a Camera

As schoolchildren, most of us learned a simple and appealing explanation of why things appear to us the way they do, based on the analogy of the eye as a camera. According to this "theory," the eye takes "pictures" of the scenes before it. Light reflected from objects in the scene is focused by the lens inside the eye onto the retina, the "film" at the back of the eye, to form images. These images are then transmitted to the brain, generating mental representations of the scenes—our perceptions.

The analogy itself is a good one up to a point: The image of a scene focused on the retina resembles that focused on the film in a camera or, for that matter, a faithful rendering of the scene by an artist. The eye has a lens just as a camera does, and as in a camera, the lens changes its focus. The eye has an aperture (the pupillary opening) that varies in diameter to admit more or less light, as does a camera. The image formed on the retina is upside down and reversed left to right, just as is the image that appears on photographic film.

The theory based on the camera analogy, however, leaves everything about perception still to be explained. This becomes evident as soon as we compare the way the world appears to us with the images of it projected on our retinas. I have already noted the discrepancy between the shape of the object's image and its perceived shape. In addition to that, however, the image of an object projected on the retina changes continuously as we move and as our position with respect to the object changes, yet we tend to perceive the properties of objects as constant under most viewing conditions. In watching people walking toward or away from us, for instance, we don't see them physically enlarging or shrinking, even though the image on the retina does exactly that. If we tilt our heads to one side in gazing at a building, it doesn't appear to tilt, even though its retinal image does so. As we go from dim, indoor illumination to bright sunlight, the intensity of light reaching the eye can vary by a factor of thousands. Nevertheless, white surfaces look white even in dim light, and black ones look black even in intense light. How can we explain these constancies in our perception? The camera theory would lead us to predict continuous change.

Even when the retinal image remains the same, the camera theory cannot explain the way objects appear to us. For example, the moon appears to be larger at the horizon than when it is elevated in the sky, yet the size of its retinal image remains essentially the same. Similarly, the photograph on the facing page can be seen either as a vase or as the profiles of Prince Philip and Queen Elizabeth, although the image on the retina remains the same. If perception is like picture-taking, how can we explain the fact that a single picture can yield two or more distinct perceptions?

The camera analogy is of equally little help in explaining other puzzles of perception. The eyes are in constant motion. If we scan the vase in the photograph, many separate images of it are formed on our retinas, yet we still perceive it as a unified whole. How do we integrate these successive retinal images? Obviously, a camera cannot unify the successive pictures it takes. In fact, a camera cannot give even a *single* picture coherence. None of the different segments of line of the emblem on the vase belongs *a priori* with another segment or with the background. How, then, do we come to perceive each part of, say, the figure of the unicorn as "belonging" to its other parts and not to the background? Such organization can only be achieved by a perceiving organism. With no one looking at a picture, with no brain behind a retinal image, there is no such separate entity as a unicorn within the picture or image.

Perception as a Mental Construction

Initially, the camera theory seems a congenial explanation of why we see the world as we do. It seems to fit so well with our tendency to presume that our visual perceptions, as well as our perceptions based on our other senses, are direct recordings of reality. Philosophers refer to the belief or unconscious assumption that the world that we perceive is identical with a real world that exists independent of our experience of it as *naive realism*. If that real world is simply identical with the world that we perceive, it is understandable why one might think that all we need do to perceive it is to take a picture of it. To understand perception, however, we must discard this assumption. Only by doing so can we appreciate that the mind does not simply record an exact image of the world but creates its own "picture."

Knowledge derived from physics informs us that the world from which we obtain sensory information is very different from the world as we experience it. We know that the universe consists of electromagnetic fields, atomic particles, and the empty spaces that separate atomic nuclei from the charged particles that spin around them. The picture the brain creates is limited by the range of stimuli to which our senses are attuned, a range that renders us incapable of perceiving large segments of the electromagnetic spectrum and matter at the atomic scale.

If we had the sensory apparatus of some other of the earth's organisms, "reality" would seem quite different. Honeybees and snakes respond to frequencies of light to which we do not. Bats can navigate around thin obstructions by means of echolocation. Fish respond to sound frequencies and odors that have no perceptual reality for us, while the sensory world of the amoeba is so primitive and so foreign to our own that it defies characterization.

Reversible vase created for Queen Elizabeth's Silver Jubilee in 1977. We see either a vase or two profiles depending on how we organize the visual pattern.

The perceptual world we create differs qualitatively from the physicists' descriptions because our experience is mediated by our senses and constructed internally as a representation of the world. Thus we perceive colors, tones, tastes, and smells—perceptions that either have no meaning in the world of physical reality or have a different meaning. What we perceive as hues of red, blue, or green the physicist describes as surfaces reflecting electromagnetic waves of certain frequencies. What we experience as tastes and smells the physicist refers to as chemical compounds. What we experience as tones of varying pitch the physicist describes as objects vibrating at different frequencies. Colors, tones, tastes, and smells are mental constructions, created out of sensory stimulation. As such, they do not exist outside of living minds. The philosopher asks, Does a sound exist when a tree falls in the forest if no creature is near enough to hear it? We can assume that the fall would cause vibrations in the air. They would exist, to be sure. But there would be no sound because a sound, by definition, implies the sensation evoked in a living being by such vibration.

Even though our perceptions are mental constructions rather than direct recordings of reality, they clearly are neither arbitrary nor mostly illusory. Members of every species must correctly perceive, however differently, certain aspects of the external world. If they did not, they would never be able to obtain the necessities of life or to avoid its dangers and would die. We are no exceptions. Within the range of stimuli to which our senses are attuned, our perceptions of the sizes, shapes, orientations, stabilities, and lightnesses of things turn out to be not simply different from the images formed on our retinas but remarkably correct, or, as students of perception say, *veridical*. Philosophers rightly point out that we have no direct access to what is "really" there in the world other than through our senses. But by *veridical* is only meant that our perceptions correspond with the properties of things considered objectively and independent of viewing conditions, such as can be ascertained by measurement. Thus our perception of a shape such as a circle can be said to be veridical if we know or can easily determine by measurement that the object has equal diameters in all directions.

Surprisingly, the correctness of our perceptions is seldom affected by our knowledge of the world, at least the kind of knowledge that can be imparted by hearing or reading a factual statement. Illusions, for instance, do not disappear merely because we discover that they are illusions. Even though we know intellectually that the moon remains stationary as we look at it, it still appears to be moving when we see it through a thin cloud passing in front of it or see it next to a moving cloud. (In subsequent chapters, I will document many other instances of the independence of perception and factual knowledge.) To the extent

that our perceptions are independent of our factual knowledge about the world, they should be distinguished from the domain of knowledge and thought. Our perceptions arise through the processing of sensory information in a manner largely independent of other cognitive processes.

If the source of our visual information about the world is filtered through a distorted and highly variable retinal image, how, then, do we come to construct the world more or less veridically? This is the central question of the science of visual perception.

Turn the book upside down and the "mounds" in this photograph of the moon are transformed into craters. The perceptual question is, Why do we perceive the picture quite differently depending on the location of the shadows?

Perception as a Science

All scientific inquiry begins with perceptions. It is through our perceptions that we arrive at the facts to be explained, whether these be the orbits of planets, the colors of foliage, the reactions of chemicals, or the behavior of baboons.

The study of perception, however, differs from other fields of scientific inquiry in certain crucial respects. In other fields of science, the goal is to separate facts from illusions and to explain the objective properties or behaviors of things. The goal of the science of perception, by contrast, is to understand the act of perception itself, to discover how and why things appear the way they do. In this, illusions are as important as correct percepts and have equal status as facts. Once the existence of moon craters is known to the astronomer, for example, the fact that this discovery was made by a perception, by looking through a telescope, is of no further consequence. What is of interest is how the craters were formed. To the student of perception however, the appearance of the crater is of direct interest. How do we perceive its depth? Why does a crater look like a mound when a picture of it is inverted?

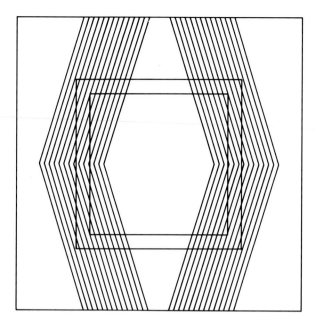

Investigation of perception of figures such as the one above reveals a striking fact: We still experience the illusion that the vertical lines are bowed even after we have convinced ourselves that they are in fact straight.

In the heyday of the Behaviorist movement in psychology, it was argued that perception is not a proper subject for scientific investigation because perceptions are subjective states. In other disciplines of science, it was said, the facts are open to public observation, whereas the contents of mind are not in themselves directly observable. We can all look at craters and confirm one another's observation of them. But no one can look at anyone else's perception of craters. Thus, we cannot directly observe the facts to be explained.

It is true that no one else can look at my perception of an object. Suppose I experience the illusion that the vertical lines in the illustration above are curved, although they are in fact straight. If I report the fact that the lines seem curved, no one can confirm that I have seen what I report. But others can confirm the perceptual phenomenon for themselves, and they can also report on their own perception of the lines. Thus, while we cannot observe peoples' perceptions per se, we can confirm or disconfirm their generality and *infer* whether or not they actually occur.

In other respects, perception, as well as other mental processes, have long since been established as suitable for, and susceptible to, scientific investigation. As we shall see, we can isolate one factor at a time and study its effect; such isolation is the very essence of scientific method. We can also make reasonably rigorous predictions about what will be perceived in a given situation and design experiments that can confirm or refute these predictions. The potential for disconfirmability is another hallmark of scientific method. We can repeat observations both in the same observer or in different observers. We can repeat experiments. Thus, observations or conclusions about perception are subject to the test of reliability and verification, just as are those of other sciences.

Many people, including many psychologists, believe that explanation of a mental event consists exclusively of the discovery of how the brain works in generating such an event. I think that this is a mistaken belief. It is true that many secrets about the workings of the visual nervous system have been uncovered that clarify some facts about perception. We now know, for example, how patterns of light reflected from objects in the world trigger neural discharges of the densely packed cells on the retina, and how these neural "signals" are transmitted through various relay stations to the visual cortex. We know from relatively recent discoveries that the eyes are in a constant state of very rapid oscillation, or tremor, and that such motion is crucial for vision because it causes the image to be continuously shifted over the retina. Visual cells respond more to the onset and cessation of stimulation than to steadily maintained stimulation. The stabilization of the image on the retina by various methods will thus eliminate visual perception of contours. We know from the recording of single cells in the visual system that, in some species, neurons exist that discharge rapidly only when a certain stimulus pattern is present in the appropriate region of the retina. These neurons can be considered to be detectors of such features as spots, contours, or edges. We also now know that light stimulation of corresponding regions of the two retinas transmits signals to one region in one hemisphere of the brain and yields singleness of vision and that stimulation of slightly noncorresponding regions by a similar pattern yields depth perception.

Such knowledge has enabled us to clarify some of the problems of the perception of objects and events, but it does not explain them. Because scientists have discovered that the information the visual cortex receives reflects the nature of the retinal image, for example, we know that size and shape constancy cannot be explained on the basis of the central cortical registration of the size and shape of the image in the brain. In other words, if the retinal image is not a faithful picture of the outer object, then neither is the pattern of projection of that image to the visual cortex. Therefore, scientists are still far from identifying the neural mechanisms of constancy.

Nor does this accumulated knowledge about the workings of the visual nervous system explain the other facts about perception outlined in the preceding pages: How we achieve veridicality, how the same image can yield now one perception and now another, how organization of the pattern of stimulation occurs such that we perceive distinct and segregated things, or why a changing image does not necessarily give rise to a changing perception.

The difficulty with concentrating solely on neural mechanisms is not simply that we still know so little about the brain. Ultimately, we may discover the neural mechanisms underlying a mental or behavioral fact,

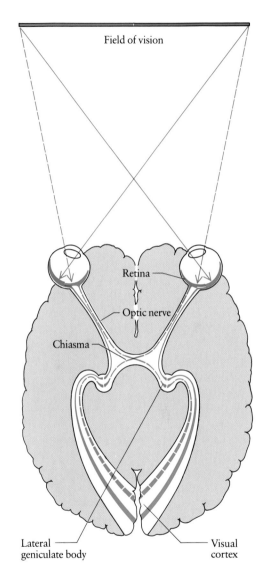

Field of vision

Retina

Optic nerve

Chiasma

Lateral geniculate body

Visual cortex

Projection of neural fibers from retina to visual cortex. Note that fibers from the left side of both retinas—representing the right side of the visual field—project to the left hemisphere and that fibers from the right side of both retinas—representing the left side of the visual field—project to the right hemisphere.

but this understanding would be incomplete without intervening levels of explanation.

The need for several levels of explanation arises in all science. Darwin's principles, for example, can be said to explain the evolution of species, but they tell us nothing about the underlying mechanism of evolution. Suppose we discover how to describe the mutation of an organism in biochemical terms. Would this description have any meaning to us without Darwin's principles? The evolutionary effect of the mutation only makes sense within the context of the organism's adaptation to an environment and its competitive chances for survival. Thus, while reduction to more fundamental levels of analysis is desirable, higher levels of analysis retain their usefulness and are often required first.

In perception, before we can hope to understand an event in the brain that underlies a percept, we must possess an idea of the process that leads to the percept's formation. Suppose we want to know why a picture of a crater looks like a mound when it is inverted. In the absence of any understanding of the process of perception, we would have no idea what to look for in the brain. Suppose, however, that through experimentation we discover that, when people are shown pictures of an enclosed region with a shadow at the top, they perceive it as a hole or indentation, whereas, when they are shown the same picture with the shadow at the bottom, they perceive a mound or elevation. Now at least we know a general principle about the perception. We can try to penetrate the problem further by asking about the origin of the principle. Since light in our environment almost always comes from above, a hole will tend to be shadowed at its top. Thus the principle might be one that is learned. If we discover the principle is learned, we will know that the kind of brain event we should expect to find to explain the shadow effect will be one encompassing the storage of a learned principle. If we finally do find the neural correlate of this effect, we would still retain the principle as part of the explanation. If we discarded the principle, the brain event, couched solely in the language of neural discharge, would have little meaning.

I believe that only in rare instances do we have an inkling of the physiological brain event underlying perception. In the chapters that follow, therefore, I will not be talking very much about brain mechanisms but instead will explore explanations of perception couched in functional terms—namely, what *kind* of process can be occurring that would explain the type of perception in question.

Explanations of Perception

In exploring what kinds of processes lie behind our perceptions, we need to draw on work in the three major, and frequently conflicting, traditions of thought that inform contemporary investigations of perception. These traditions are the Inference Theory (usually closely associated with the empiricist perspective), the Gestalt Theory (associated with the tradition that emphasized innate tendencies of mind), and the Stimulus Theory (associated with the tradition that searches for correspondences between physical and sensory variables and thus sometimes referred to as the psychophysical approach).

THE INFERENCE AND EMPIRICIST PERSPECTIVE   Theories about perception originated with philosophers concerned with the problem of knowledge, or epistemology. How do we come to know anything, they asked, and how valid or reliable is such knowledge? The early British empiricists, such as Hobbes, Locke, and Hume, argued that knowledge is acquired solely by sensory experience and association of ideas. The mind at birth is a blank slate, a tabula rasa, upon which experience "writes" through sensations received. In particular, as regards perception, the philosopher Bishop George Berkeley argued in his famous essay in 1709 that what vision directly gives us is inadequate for correctly perceiving the world. In order to achieve correct perceptions, we must learn how to interpret visual sensations. We do this through a process of association. For example, in theorizing about the perception of distance, Berkeley reasoned as follows. The third dimension cannot be directly given by vision since the retina is only two-dimensional. In order to see the world three-dimensionally, we must learn to associate certain sensations given by looking at an object with its actual distance from us, the knowledge of which we must obtain through other means. Specifically, we can ascertain how far away from us an object is by grasping, touching, or otherwise moving toward it. When we do this, certain signs (or *cues,* as they came to be called) become available to us, such as the degree of thickening of the lens in the eye. We directly sense this thickening by the degree of strain on the muscles attached to the lens. We associate this sign (in this instance, the degree of strain on the ciliary muscles) with the distance to reach the object. In subsequent experience, the sign tells us how far away the object is.

During the second half of the nineteenth century, the great scientist Hermann von Helmholtz developed a similar theory, but worked it out more systematically than had Berkeley. Helmholtz contributed to our knowledge about almost every topic in the fields of sensory processes and perception and systematized this knowledge in his epic volumes on physiological optics. He argued that perception was based upon a process of inference, in which, through past experience, we infer from the sensations we receive at a given time the nature of the object or event that they probably represent. Because we ordinarily are not aware of drawing such

a conclusion, Helmholtz described the process as one of unconscious inference, *unbewusster Schluss:* "The sensations of the senses are tokens for our consciousness, it being left to our intelligence to learn how to comprehend their meaning."

Suppose, for example, you are looking at a black object in bright sunlight. How can you identify its color? Despite the fact that the object reflects only a small proportion of the light it receives, a great deal of light falls on it. The sensation produced by the black object would thus be one of high intensity. However, cues from the surrounding scene, whose significance you would have learned from experience, would also tell you that the object is in bright light. You therefore take those cues into account and interpret the sensation as standing for a dark surface color.

THE GESTALT PERSPECTIVE   An entirely different theoretical perspective on the problem of perception has come down to us from René Descartes in the seventeenth century and Immanuel Kant more than a century later. Descartes held that mind was far from the tabula rasa that the British empiricists described, but rather possessed innate ideas about form, size, and other properties of objects. Kant explicitly took issue with the empiricist view that "there is no conception in man's mind which hath not at first . . . been begotten upon the organs of sense," as Hobbes had written in the previous century. Instead, he argued that the mind imposes its own internal conception of space and time upon the sensory information it receives. If we did not have an innate predisposition to localize things in separate spatial positions and to order events successively in time, then how could we profit at all from sensory experience?

The principal heirs of this tradition of thought were the Gestalt psychologists of the early decades of this century. The central Gestalt concept was that of perceptual organization. Whereas sensations are logically separate and unrelated, our perceptions are of whole units or things. It is difficult to maintain that we begin life with a chaotic amalgamation or sum of sensations and somehow learn to organize them into distinct and segregated units such as objects with specific shapes separated from a background. It is far more plausible to believe that the perceptual world is organized to begin with on the basis of innately given laws that govern unit formation and the emergence of a figure on a background.

The whole units we perceive—for example, a melody or an object form—are not only the result of a process of organization that unifies some elements of the world rather than others. The elements of these units are related to one another in such a way as to create a configuration that has properties that do not reside in the parts at all. A melody, for instance, is not simply a sum of separate tones; it is a quality based on the interrelation of all the tones. Thus the famous Gestalt dictum: The whole is qualitatively different from the sum of its parts. That is why one can alter all the tones by transposing the melody in octave or key and still preserve the melody. The melody remains the same because the tonal relations and rhythms remain the same.

By the same token, the Gestaltists emphasized the relations of elements as the basis of other kinds of perceptual phenomena. As we shall see, the Gestaltists argued that the preservation of such relations in the face of certain absolute changes in stimulation could account for constancy as well as for various illusions.

Underlying these psychological principles were thought to be brain processes unlike those in which impulses travel only along neuron pathways. Rather, the brain was thought of as a solid electrical conductor in

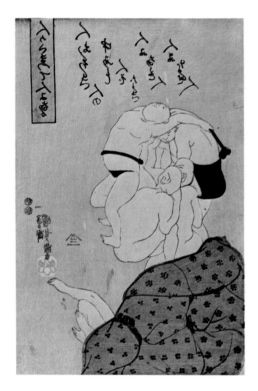

Kuniyoshi Ichiyusai, A Person Made of People, *Late Edo era. The configuration of the whole in this illustration is clearly qualitatively different than the sum of its parts.*

which currents spread through the tissue along paths of least resistance. Thus, when asked why the world looks the way it does, the Gestaltist gives an answer that is quite different from that of the Helmholtzian. To the Gestaltist, our perceptions are the result of spontaneous interactions in the brain to which sensory stimulation gives rise; to the Helmholtzian, they are the result of the unconscious interpretations we make of sensations, based on past experience.

THE STIMULUS PERSPECTIVE   The Empiricist and Gestalt theories assume that the stimulus the eye receives is inadequate, ambiguous, or impoverished and thus cannot provide an adequate explanation of our perceptions. However, researchers working in the psychophysical tradition, the third major theoretical perspective, argue that all the information necessary to explain our perceptions is present in the environment, waiting to be picked up by the moving eye of the observer. For each type of perception—whether it be of color, shape, size, depth, motion, or whatever else—there is a unique stimulus or type of stimulus information. Thus there is no need to postulate such mechanisms as unconscious inference or spontaneous neural interaction to explain perception.

Clearly, the stimuli we receive are integral to the mental pictures of the world our brains create. Our perception of color is based on different wavelengths of light, our perception of tonal pitch on frequency of sound vibration, our perception of brightness on amplitude of light waves, and so on. The program of psychophysical investigators of the late nineteenth century, who are often credited with founding scientific psychology, was precisely one of correlating subjective sensations with physical stimuli.

In visual perception, the psychophysical approach lost its appeal when stimulus correlates could not be found for many perceptual phenomena. However, beginning in the 1940s, James J. Gibson of Cornell and his associates began to suggest stimulus correlates for many of those properties and events that previously had resisted psychophysical investigation. Gibson argued that perceptions such as those of planes in depth and constancy of size are based on more abstract features of the stimulus than earlier workers in the psychophysical tradition had considered. For example, it was maintained that the stimulus correlate of our perception that the plane of the ground recedes into depth is a gradient in the texture in that plane, not the appearance of separate objects located at different distances from one another on that plane. In the photograph on the facing page, the density of the elements on the ground increases from the bottom of the picture (representing the foreground) to the top (representing the more distant ground). This texture-density gradient is the stimulus for the plane of the ground, and the steepness of the gradient is the stimulus for its apparent slant.

A gradient of texture density. The projection of the stones on the beach is increasingly dense from the bottom to the top of the picture.

The program of those who share this theoretical perspective, then, is to discover what the higher-order features of the stimulus are for every kind of perception. By essentially considering a perception as a response and the features of the input as a stimulus, they attempt to sidestep assumptions about the mind in much the same way as the Behaviorists do.

In my opinion, none of the major theoretical perspectives, at least in the manner in which they have been formulated, constitutes an adequate, unified theory of all the phenomena of perception. An explanation that would encompass all such phenomena would have to do justice to a wide variety of perceptions and to the specific facts now known about them. Moreover, certain ideas intrinsic to each of these perspectives are already known to be incorrect. Therefore, before we can reach any conclusion about the correctness of a major perspective, it is essential that we explore in more detail the various kinds of perception of objects and events.

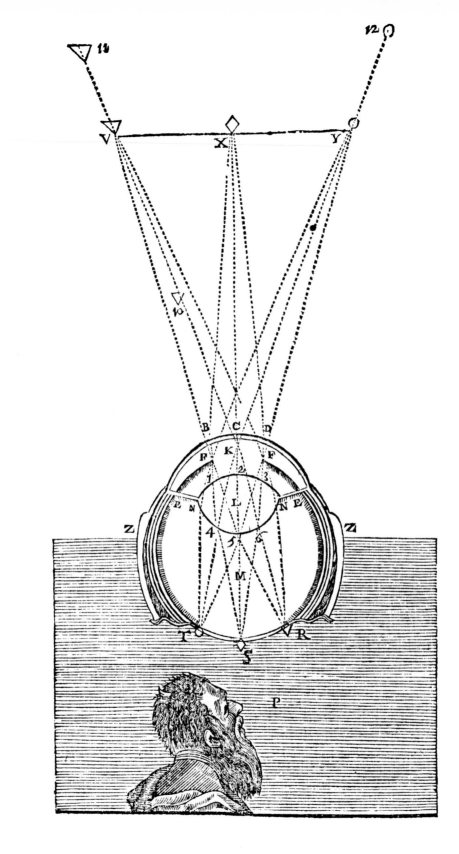

2 CONSTANCY

In the opening years of the seventeenth century, the French philosopher René Descartes described an experiment that would reveal the visual image as it appears on the retina of the eye. One could remove the eye of an ox and place it in a frame, scraping the back of the eye to make it translucent, he said. By looking at the retina, one could see how the world was projected on it. To understand perceptual constancy—our tendency to see the properties of objects as unvarying despite ever-changing retinal stimuli—and most other aspects of perception, we first must know how scenes actually are represented on the retina.

The drawing on the facing page that illustrates such an experiment shows us the essentials of how the lens of an eye—or any convex lens—creates an image. The lens, when it is shaped for optimal focus, bends, or refracts, all the rays of light emanating from the same source to focus them at a single point. From point Y in the drawing, the three rays designated by the dotted lines are all focused by the lens on point T on the retina. Similarly, the rays from point V are all focused by the lens on point R. In this way, rays emanating from the outline of an object are focused on the retina so as to form a corresponding outline although, as we shall see, that outline will be different from the object's outline—distorted, one might say—and will be different from time to time as well.

Because we are concerned with perceptual constancy in this chapter, not the sharpness of an image (which affects acuity), we can disregard variations in the shape of the lens and the action of the cornea, the eye's transparent outer covering which cooperates with the lens to focus light, and assume that only one ray of light emanates from any point of an object. For our purposes, then, the image on the retina is equivalent to that formed on a screen in a camera obscura. A camera obscura consists of a pinhole opening, instead of the larger, variable aperture of the eye or

A procedure described by Descartes for directly viewing the image formed on the retina of an animal's eye.

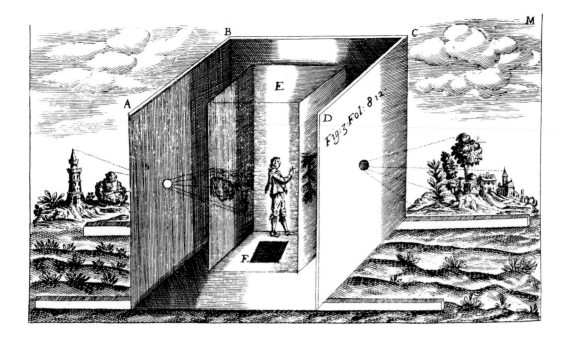

Camera obscura. In this version, drawn in 1646, small openings on two of the walls yield inverted pictures of the scenes outside. To see pictures in a camera obscura clearly, the entire room must be dark.

an ordinary camera, and a screen for direct viewing, rather than the retina or the chemically treated, light-sensitive surface of film. Because the pinhole is small, for all intents and purposes we can say that only one ray of light passes through it from any point in a scene. Thus, the problem of focusing does not arise. The shape of the screen of the camera obscura is flat, not spherical as it is in the eye. However, this difference does not affect the formation of an image or the problem of constancy under discussion.

Geometrical Optics

What a scene looks like in a camera obscura, on the retina, or through a camera is a function of geometrical optics, the propagation and projection of light on a surface. All that we need to know about geometrical optics to understand the formation of the image derives from two simple principles: (1) light travels in straight lines, and (2) the angle formed by the two rays of light from any two points in the scene as they enter the eye is proportional to the angle between the rays as they are projected on the retina. Thus, the size of the image cast on the retina is determined by the *visual angle*—the angle formed by the incoming rays. How these principles determine the precise image formed on the retina depends on whether or not the object viewed is in the frontal plane—that is to say, in a plane perpendicular to the line of sight—and also on the object's distance.

If an object is seen in the frontal plane, the relative proportions between points on it are maintained within the image, as shown in the top figure on the facing page. The visual angle, and consequently the size of

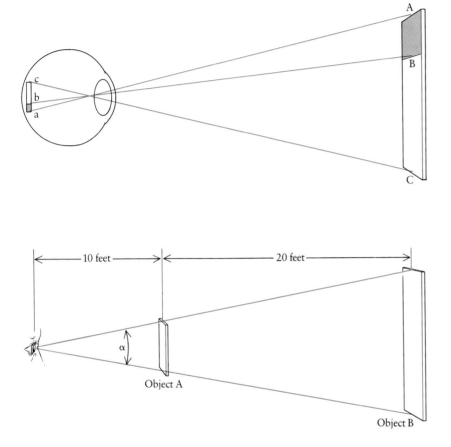

(Top) Retinal image formed by object in a frontal plane. The relative proportions between points within the object are maintained within the image. (Bottom) Objects of different sizes may subtend the same visual angle if they are located at different distances.

the image, will vary systematically not only with the size of the object viewed but also with its distance from the viewer. For example, a book held at different distances in your line of sight will cast retinal images of different sizes, the size of the image (or the visual angle that produces it) being inversely proportional to the book's distance from the eye. This fact is sometimes referred to as Euclid's law of the visual angle.

If the book is not held in the frontal plane, the angle formed by the rays from its endpoints will be compressed, the retinal image of this surface of the book will thus be smaller, and its shape will be distorted. The more the orientation of the object departs from the frontal plane, the more its shape on the retina will be distorted. In the language of perspective, this compression is termed *foreshortening*.

These same principles explain why roads, railroad tracks, and other parallel lines in the environment that are not in the frontal plane will

Perspective foreshortening. The projection of the widths of the doors is compressed because they are in a plane slanted away from the observer.

yield projections to the eye that converge. They also explain why an image of pebbles on a beach or some other uniform texture on a surface becomes increasingly dense with receding distance. In these cases, the visual angles subtended by objects and by the separation of spaces between objects become increasingly small as distance increases.

We can attend to the actual visual angles subtended by objects in the world by assuming a special attitude of the kind taken by artists. Usually this requires some effort on our part. However, in instances in which objects are seen at great distances or are extremely foreshortened, we often become spontaneously aware of the sizes of these angles. Thus, in driving down a road, we see the road's edges as parallel, yet we are often aware at the same time that its sides converge toward the horizon. Later in the chapter I will discuss the significance of this subsidiary awareness we sometimes have of the actual visual angles formed by objects. However, although we *can* perceive objects as an artist does, these perceptions are not the central or most salient aspect of the way the world looks to us. That most salient aspect is constancy.

Now that we know something of geometrical optics, it can be easily understood why and in what respects the retinal image is a distorted representation of a scene. In the discussion that follows, we can use a photograph or a photographically accurate drawing of a scene as a reflection of the essential geometry of the retinal image because these renditions are effectively the result of light from the scene projected on a plane, just as is the retinal image. Indeed, photographs and drawings are comprehensible to us precisely because they more or less resemble the image of a scene as it appears on our retinas.

Despite great variation in the images on the eye that represent a given object in the world, the object looks much the same to us. It appears to be about the same size despite the changes in the size of its images (*size constancy*), to have much the same shape despite changes in the shape of its images (*shape constancy*), and to have much the same orientation (tilted, upright, upside down) despite changes in how its images are oriented on the retina (*orientation constancy*). It also appears to be located in much the same direction in relation to ourselves and other objects despite where on the retina its image is located (constancy of direction or *position constancy*), and much the same lightness, or shade of gray, despite changes in the intensity of light reaching the eye from its surfaces (*lightness constancy*).

How does the brain construct from these varying images a visual world that is characterized by constancy? Currently, there are two, apparently conflicting, answers to this question entertained by students of perception, the stimulus-relation theory and the taking-into-account theory. The former derives from the psychophysical tradition and the latter primarily from the work of Helmholtz and other Inference theorists. Let us first consider the explanations for constancy of size.

Size Constancy: The Stimulus-Relation Explanation

Despite the increasing or decreasing size of the retinal image (or visual angle) of an object as a function of distance, its apparent size remains more or less the same. If all the brain had to go on in determining the size of the object was its visual angle, constancy would never be achieved. To the contrary, size perception would vary with every change in an object's distance.

Normally, however, we see objects not alone but in the context of other objects and against some background. According to the stimulus-relation theory, size perception and size constancy can be explained by the ratio of the visual angle of one object to that of other objects. For example, if we see a man standing next to a house, his height bears a definite size relation to the height of the house. That relation will not change no matter from how far away we view the man. Or consider the size relation of an object to a uniformly textured background. An object on a lawn will cover a given number of units of the grass texture. Viewed from a different distance, the object will cover, or occlude, the same number of units. In instances such as this, the late James Gibson argued, constancy can be explained by the unvarying size ratio of objects in a scene, without having to refer to distance at all.

Do our perceptions of size depend on such stimulus relations? In an attempt to answer this question, Sheldon Ebenholtz and I carried out the

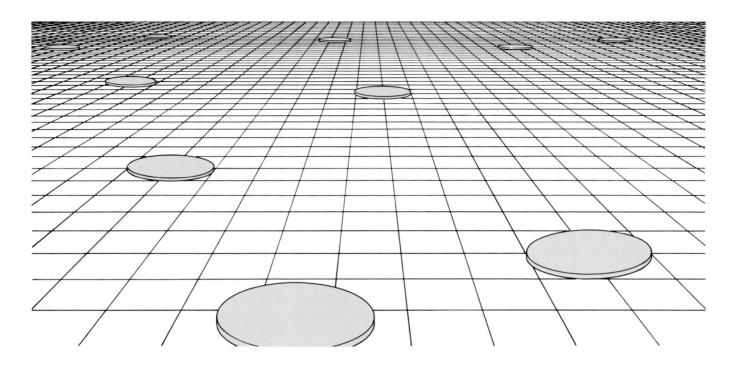

following two-part experiment. In one part, an observer sat midway between two luminous vertical lines in an otherwise dark room. One line, the standard, was 3 inches high, and the other was a line whose length could be varied by the subject. The observer was asked to look back and forth and to indicate when the length of the variable line matched the standard. In this, the control part of the experiment, subjects were able to match the standard line's length almost exactly, selecting on average a line 3.1 inches long.

In the second part of the experiment, the observer was again asked to match the lines, but this time they were surrounded by luminous rectangles—actual frames of reference—as shown at right. The standard line was enclosed in a rectangle 4 inches high, making it three-fourths the height of the rectangle, and the variable line was enclosed in a rectangle three times larger, or 12 inches high.

Although the room was dark except for the luminous lines and rectangular outlines, in one condition employed the observer could see that the two rectangles were equally far away because binocular vision was permitted. Binocular vision—vision with both eyes—as we will see in Chapter 3, yields two of the clues, or *cues*, that we use to perceive distance. Thus the observer could be expected to match the two lines for length correctly unless the proportionality of line to rectangular context is indeed a determinant of size perception.

Whereas subjects were quite accurate in matching the lines in the control condition, when only the lines were visible, they selected, on average,

One theory of size constancy: Because the background is uniform, the equal-sized disks, although diminishing in visual angle with distance, occlude an equal number of units.

In the experiment on size perception in a dark room, the observer is asked to select a luminous line on the right that appears equal in length to the line on the left.

The effect of context on the interpretation of size. Cover the man and the fish is pan size. Cover the hand and the fish is a rather respectable catch.

a 6.5-inch-high line in the experimental condition. Thus the rectangle context produced a very powerful illusion in which a line that was more than twice as long as the standard looked equal to it. If proportionality were the only determinant of our perception of size, however, the line selected should have been three-fourths the height of the large rectangle, or 9 inches high. Instead, the result was a compromise.

Size relations, the results of this experiment suggest, are important in affecting or modifying our experience of the sizes of things in daily life. Witness, for example, how we interpret the size of a fish in the photograph above, depending on whether the hand or the man is covered. Or consider the shock we experience in watching a puppet show when the "giant" puppeteer comes on stage at the end. Size-contrast effects such as this are often important in the arts.

Nevertheless, size proportionality is probably not the major explanation of either size perception or size constancy. In the examples just cited, for instance, the dramatic effects are primarily the consequence of our interpretation of the picture and our interpretive acceptance of an altered scale rather than the consequence of our actual perceptions of size. In examples more typical of daily life, our perceptions of size change only slightly with varying contexts. Furthermore, the results of the proportionality experiment, impressive as they are, are not good enough to explain constancy. Further experiments have established that, if the difference in the size of the rectangles is greater than the 3:1 value described above, the result departs even more from the proportionality prediction. Yet when one compares a scene such as a person next to a house viewed from 1000 meters with that scene viewed from, let us say, 10 meters, the difference between visual angles of the house is equivalent to an experiment with frames of reference that differ by 100:1. While full constancy might well occur in such a real-life comparison, the result of an experiment on line matching with two rectangles that differ by 100:1 would depart appreciably from a proportionality prediction. As for Gibson's theory, it maintains that constancy does not simply depend upon the occlusion by objects of an equal number of units in the texture of the plane. It also requires that the plane is perceived to be receding in depth with textured units that are perceived as equal and everywhere equidistant from one another. Naturally, if that is true, objects at different distances that cover an equal number of texture units are, almost by definition, equal in size. If, however, the textured surface does not look like a receding plane, the effect does not occur.

The major reason for rejecting the stimulus-relation explanation of size constancy, however, is that constancy can be achieved in instances where stimulus relations are not applicable. For example, in a dark room with only a single luminous object visible, constancy will hold as long as distance information is available, such as is provided at near distances by *accommodation*—the tendency of the lens to accommodate for the distance of an object until sharp vision is achieved—and by *convergence*—the tendency of the two eyes to converge on an object in order to maintain single vision of it. Yet if the subject is required to view the object with one eye through a tiny pinhole—or artificial pupil, as it is called—thus eliminating such cues to distance, constancy fails. Under these conditions, the object's size appears to be indeterminate—that is, to have no definite objective size at all—and two such objects will be matched on the basis of visual angle alone.

Size Constancy: The Taking-into-Account Explanation

Because of the weaknesses in the stimulus-relation explanation of size constancy, some investigators have rejected it in favor of an inference explanation, in which distance is taken into account in size perception.

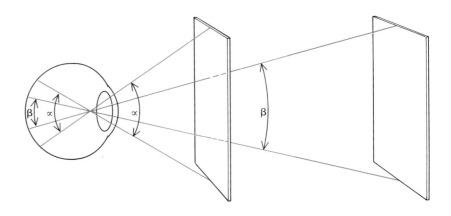

An object of the same size seen at two different distances. Size constancy is achieved if the distances are correctly taken into account.

According to this theory, the perceptual system—the system in the brain that is concerned with perception—engages in an operation of computation that includes both an object's visual angle *and* its perceived distance. (The actual cues we use to determine an object's distance will be discussed in Chapter 3.)

Suppose, for example, that the object shown on the left in the figure above is 12 inches square and seen at a distance of 10 feet. If perceived size were governed only by visual angle, the square viewed at 30 feet would appear to be one-third the size of the one at 10 feet, or a square of 4 inches to a side, because visual angle is inversely proportional to distance. If distance is taken into account, however, then we have

Perceived size = perceived distance × visual angle

Perceived size of near square = 10 × visual angle

$$\text{Perceived size of far square} = 30 \times \frac{\text{visual angle}}{3}$$

$$= 10 \times \text{visual angle}$$

Thus, the diminution of an object's visual angle with distance would be exactly compensated for by the increase in its perceived distance, as long as the latter is perceived accurately.

This kind of computational process, suggested by Helmholtz as an explanation of constancy, is beyond conscious knowledge or control and occurs very quickly. Helmholtz referred to it as unconscious inference. It depends upon sensory information about distance, not merely upon what

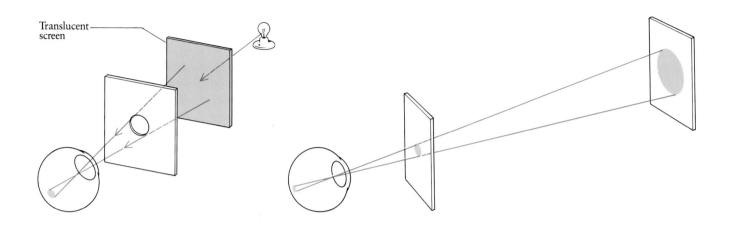

we may think an object's distance is. If Helmholtz's theory is correct, certain illusions should occur when the ordinary relation of size to distance does not hold. The perceived size of an afterimage and the perceived size of the elevated moon relative to that of the moon on the horizon are cases in point.

AFTERIMAGES AND EMMERT'S LAW   An *afterimage* is a percept lasting only a few seconds that is caused by the fatiguing of those retinal cells that have been stimulated by the light from an object. To achieve this effect, briefly view, while keeping the eyes stationary, a highly contrasting region such as a small hole cut out of cardboard placed in front of a light. Then look at surfaces at varying distances from you. You should see a visual "thing" that is the same shape as the object that created it, located at the distance of whatever surface is now viewed, as shown above. Notice that, if the afterimage is viewed on a paper held at arm's length, it will appear relatively small. If it is viewed farther away, however, as on a distant wall or billboard, it will appear much larger, even though the size and shape of the retinal image remain the same. The perceived size of the afterimage varies directly with the distance of the surface on which it is viewed. This relation is an instance of a more general perceptual relation known as Emmert's law: The perceived size of an image of a particular visual angle is directly proportional to its perceived distance.

The illusion of afterimages appearing to vary in size despite a constant retinal image is precisely what we must predict if perceived size is governed not only by visual angle but also by distance. The two seemingly different facts, that images of the same size lead to perceptions of differ-

(Left) Forming an afterimage. (Right) Projecting the afterimage to differing distances. The perceived size of the afterimage illustrates Emmert's law.

The moon's diameter in the photograph at right is two-thirds that of the horizon moon shown at left, simulating the magnitude of the moon illusion obtained in the experiments described in text.

ent size (Emmert's law), and that images of different size lead to perceptions of the same size (constancy), in fact illustrate the same principle: Distance is taken into account in computing object size from image size. This leads to illusions such as in Emmert's law when the image remains constant and to veridicality (or constancy) when the image diminishes with distance. This principle also helps explain a common illusion of size in viewing the moon.

THE MOON ILLUSION   Since antiquity, it has been observed that the moon appears much larger when it is over the horizon than when it is high in the sky. Through the ages, many writers have speculated that the illusion has a physical basis, locating its source variously in the horizon moon's relative dimness, or redness, or some process of magnification based on refraction because, when the moon is at the horizon, the light rays pass through more of the earth's atmosphere. A little thought will make clear, however, that explanations of this kind make little sense. To the contrary, measurements of photographs of the moon in different locations in the sky reveal no illusion. In fact, the image of the moon at the horizon is actually slightly smaller, not larger than its image high in the sky because the moon is closest to the observer at its zenith. Therefore, the illusion must be perceptual in origin.

The visual angle that the moon forms at the eye remains essentially the same regardless of its location, but our perception of its size varies. The taking-into-account theory could explain this illusion if distance cues cause us to see the moon as farther away at the horizon than when it is high in the sky. We would then perceive its size to be greater at the horizon because, according to Emmert's law, perceived size is directly proportional to perceived distance.

Do we perceive the distance to the moon to be greater at the horizon? When seen over the terrain, the moon seems to be located roughly at the distance of the horizon. Therefore it must look as large as an object on the ground at the horizon whose visual angle equals that of the moon. The terrain provides information about distance so that, over a relatively flat landscape, the horizon may appear to be very far away indeed, and consequently the moon appears very large. Contrary to widespread belief, the moon illusion does not require comparison of the moon with familiar objects on the ground, such as houses or trees. The illusion is quite compelling on the ocean or a desert.

What can we say about the apparent distance of the elevated moon? Because the elevated moon is seen through empty space, within a homogeneous surround, the only possible sensory cues we have as to its distance would derive from the tendency of the eye to accommodate for the distance of an object until sharp vision is achieved and from the tendency of the two eyes to converge on an object in order to maintain single vision of it. However, the cues to distance of accommodation and convergence are ineffectual beyond short distances, a few feet and several yards, respectively. Therefore, based on such information, the perceptual system might localize the elevated moon as relatively nearby even though we know it is faraway.

If the moon at the horizon appears farther away than the elevated moon, then, because the visual angle formed by the moon remains essentially constant regardless of the moon's location, we would perceive its size as larger. This is the argument that various thinkers have advanced over the centuries in attempting to explain the illusion, and it is consonant with what we know now as Emmert's law.

What appears at first to be a telling objection to this explanation may have occurred to the reader: How can it be maintained that the moon at the horizon looks larger—because it appears to be farther away than it does in elevation—when the fact is that it appears to be nearer at the horizon? The late Edwin Boring, the first psychologist to do formal experiments on the moon illusion, and many others have made the same objection. Boring supported this objection by asking a sample of observers whether the horizon moon or the elevated moon appeared to be closer to them. All of the observers said that the horizon moon appeared closer. This led Boring to reject the apparent-distance explanation and to conduct experiments that seemed to show that differences in the perceived size of the moon could be attributed to differences in the degree of elevation of the observer's eyes in the head. Boring's own theory can be dismissed because the apparent size of the elevated moon remains the same even when it is viewed lying down, staring straight ahead, and the horizon moon the same even when viewed with head tilted forward and eyes elevated. But what about his objection and his findings about distance?

There is an explanation of Boring's findings about distance, and perhaps the reader's own observations, that still allows us to consider the apparent-distance theory seriously. When asked in which position the moon appears to be closer, the observer is comparing moons that already appear to be different in size. Because relative size is a cue to distance and because we tend to believe that objects appear to diminish in size as they recede into distance, the observer may conclude from the fact that the moon appears larger on the horizon that it also appears closer. This conclusion about distance is not so much the result of a genuine perceptual cue as it is a product of a thought process or judgment. A test of the reasoning is to modify Boring's observation about the apparent distances to the moons by eliminating the moons from view. Observers were asked which region of the *sky* appeared to be farther away. Virtually all said it was the sky at the horizon.

Because the objection of Boring and others could be met in this way, and because Boring's own theory was implausible, it seemed proper to reopen the investigation of the taking-into-account theory as an explanation of the moon illusion. In the early 1960s, Lloyd Kaufman and I developed a set of experiments to test this theory. The basic idea behind our initial experiments was quite simple, namely to create artificial moons that, optically speaking, would be far away from the observer, just as the real moon is. To make immediate comparison possible, and thus avoid the possible inexactitude caused by the long delay typical in observing the moon in its different celestial locations under natural conditions, we created two such artificial moons. To make measurement of the illusion possible, we designed the disk of light simulating a moon so that its size could be varied.

The apparatus used is shown in the figure on the facing page. Light rays from the lamp pass through a circular aperture in the rotatable drum and are reflected into the eye by the partially reflecting front-surface mirror. But the observer sees this disk *through* the mirror on the real sky. Between the disk of light and the front-surface mirror, we placed a collimating lens, which makes the rays of light parallel, so that the eye reacts to them as it does to rays from an infinitely distant object. This eliminates the unwanted impression that the disk is located nearby, between the eye and the sky. The observer looked through one device at a disk located at the horizon. He or she was told that this was the standard and asked to compare it to the size of the disk located in the elevated sky that could be seen through an identical apparatus. By rotating the drum, the observer could select a disk that appeared to be equal in size to the standard. If a moon illusion occurred—that is, if the horizon disk looked larger—the observer would select an elevated disk larger than the horizon one to

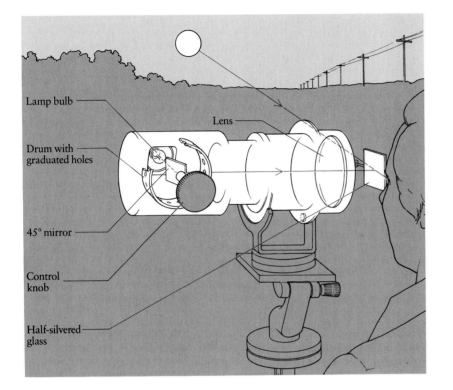

Labels on figure:
Lamp bulb
Lens
Drum with graduated holes
45° mirror
Control knob
Half-silvered glass

Apparatus used to simulate a moon in the sky. The observer looks through the half-silvered glass and sees a reflected disk of light against the sky.

match it. The amount by which it is larger is a measure of the illusion for that observer. The reverse condition was also tested, in which the elevated disk was used as the standard. In that case, the illusion was revealed by the observer selecting a smaller horizon disk as the one that appeared to match the elevated disk. As is typical of laboratory experiments on perception, and particularly of experiments on the constancies, each observer was asked to go through several trials with each disk as a standard, the average of all trials was computed, and then the average of these averages for all observers was computed.

The results of various experiments using this apparatus and method suggest that the moon illusion is created just as the taking-into-account theory predicts: The apparent size of the moon is computed from its perceived distance; as its apparent distance increases, its size is perceived to grow. It was shown that, when a scene was used that permitted a greater apparent distance to the horizon or when cloud cover was present that added a "ceiling" to the sky in addition to the "floor" ordinarily

In an experiment using mirrors that reversed the moon illusion, observers viewed an artificial moon overhead against a vertically rising terrain, and an artificial moon in a horizontal direction against an homogeneous sky.

provided by the terrain, for example, the moon illusion increased. Under such conditions, the magnitude of the illusion, expressed as a ratio of the perceived size of the horizon moon to the elevated moon, was approximately 1.5 to 1.

If the apparent-distance theory is correct, the moon illusion should disappear when sight of the terrain is entirely eliminated. This is precisely what happened when we occluded sight of the terrain with cardboards or when we asked observers to view the moon in the dark in the Hayden Planetarium. In a further experiment, mirrors were used to create the impression of a terrain for the elevated "moon," so that, in looking upward, the observer saw the ground rising in a vertical direction. Similarly, mirrors were used to eliminate the sight of the terrain ordinarily visible below the horizon moon, so that, in looking straight ahead, the observer saw only sky. Under these conditions, the illusion was reversed: The elevated moon appeared larger. The moon illusion, then, like the afterimage illusion, can be explained on the basis of the same principles that explain veridical size perception and constancy.

Other Spatial Constancies

The taking-into-account theory also offers the best explanation of other spatial constancies, such as constancy of shape and orientation. In the case of our tendency to see the shapes of things as constant, the relevant factor taken into account is the slant of the object. If a rectangle is slanted away from the frontal plane, its retinal image is trapezoidal. If there is information about the angle slant, the perceptual system can take this into account to compute that the shape of the object is rectangular.

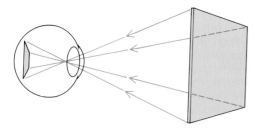

Shape constancy results if the observer correctly takes into account the slant of the object's surface.

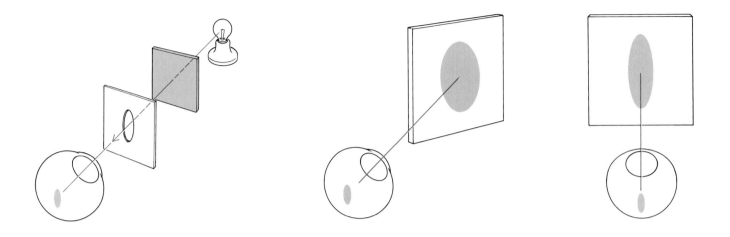

The taking-into-account process is not as simple here as in the case of size because it includes computations based on the differential distances of parts of the object. For example, if, because the slant is accurately perceived, one part is seen correctly as farther away, the size of that part can be veridically perceived as a result of size constancy. That part yields a smaller visual angle than closer parts do, but, if it is seen to be the same size as the near part of the object, the perceived shape would have to be rectangular rather than trapezoidal. Note that this analysis suggests that shape constancy can be derived from size constancy.

Certain illusions are again predictable in terms of the theory. If one views an afterimage of an ellipse by projecting it on a surface slanted backward by, say, 45 degrees, the elliptical image will yield a circular shape percept, as shown in the illustration above. The object *cannot* look like an ellipse because this retinal-image shape is interpreted on the basis of the apparent slant in space of the object producing it. This is analogous to Emmert's law of size perception. Of course when projected on a surface in a frontal plane, the same image will look like an ellipse.

The perceived orientation of things in the environment—that is, whether they are vertical, oblique, or horizontal—remains constant regardless of our own orientation. Even when we tilt our heads, which results in a tilting of the retinal image of contours in the scene, for example, we continue to perceive veridically how things are oriented. In the case of orientation constancy, the relevant fact that our perceptual system takes into account is our own position. It determines this by sensing the direction of gravity. However, there is good reason to believe that stimulus relations are also important in orientation constancy, as we shall see in Chapter 8.

Analogue of Emmert's law for shape perception. An afterimage of an ellipse is first formed (left). When that image is projected on an appropriately slanted surface it will yield an impression of a circle. When the same image is projected on a surface in the frontal plane it will yield an impression of an ellipse.

Lightness Constancy

What determines our perception of neutral (or achromatic) color—the shades of lightness, from white to black? The answer that often springs most readily to mind is that our perception of these shades is determined by the specific intensity of light reflected by a surface to the eye, referred to as *luminance*. After all, everyone knows that white surfaces reflect more light than do black surfaces, which is why one wears white clothing in the summer to reflect sunlight and dark clothing in the winter to capture the sun's warmth.

The luminance of a white surface is indeed far greater than that of a black one—at least for any given illumination. The qualification points to the difficulty with the absolute-luminance explanation. Illumination varies from place to place and from time to time. A black part of a whitewall tire in bright sunlight can reflect light to the eye that is thousands of times stronger than that reflected by the tire's white part in a dimly lit garage. Were luminance the explanation of lightness perception, the black part of the tire in sunlight should look much lighter than the white part indoors. But it doesn't. Constancy prevails.

Can lightness constancy be explained by a taking-into-account theory? Helmholtz thought so. The perceptual system, he argued, takes account of the conditions of illumination. The process would have to go somewhat as follows: The degree of luminance of a region on the retina is registered, and the amount of prevailing illumination is perceived. The perceptual system then computes (or infers) the shade of the surface by taking into account the illumination. If both the luminance and the illumination are high, the surface lightness could then be perceived as dark because the strong illumination would produce the high luminance in the region of the retina representing the object.

Few if any contemporary investigators accept this theory of lightness constancy, however, primarily because its logic is flawed. We generally do not, or need not, see the source of light itself. We also see many different surfaces, each one of which reflects light to the eye. The strength of such reflected light is a joint function of the reflectance character of the surface and the amount of light falling on it. Therefore we have no unambiguous source of information about illumination, although that is precisely what we must have if we are to take it into account in computing surface lightness.

The stimulus-relation theory in this case offers a simpler and more consistent explanation of how we perceive the lightness of things and why constancy prevails. We generally see an array of surfaces of varying values on the achromatic scale. There is a particular ratio between the luminance of one shade and that of any other shade. For example, a

The most deeply shadowed regions of the church's white siding project luminances to the eye almost equal to the luminances projected by the black shingles in the direct sunlight. Yet they look very different.

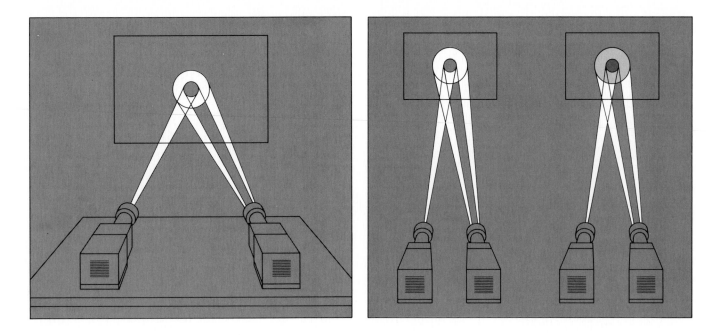

Dark-room experiments on lightness perception. (Left) By varying the intensity of light (or luminance) in the projection of the ring, the disk inside it will appear to vary in lightness from white to black. (Right) Experiment demonstrating that the ratio of luminances of adjacent surfaces determines perceived lightness. In the illustration the disks do not appear to be the same shade of gray because the regions surrounding the rings and disks also affect our perception of the shades.

white surface reflects about twice as much light as a nearby middle gray surface, while a black surface reflects only about one-eighth of the light that the middle-gray surface does. According to the stimulus-relation theory, when a particular ratio of luminance values from neighboring regions in the field is given, we will perceive a particular color in the white-gray-black continuum.

This hypothesis was tested by Hans Wallach of Swarthmore College in the following way. In a dark room, one slide projector produced a disk on a screen and another projector produced a ring around the disk, as shown in the figure at left above. Everything else was masked out on each slide. When Wallach held the intensity of the disk constant and varied only the intensity of the ring, observers perceived the lightness of the disk to vary all the way from white to black. It looked white when the luminance of the ring was about one half that of the disk, it looked gray when the luminance of the ring was about twice that of the disk, and it looked black when the ring-to-disk ratio was about 30 to 1.

This last effect is astonishing when one considers that the disk is not a dark surface but a white screen illuminated by a single projector. With the ring turned off, the disk looks like a bright, luminous source of light.

Based on this experiment, we can conclude that light-intensity ratios yield the varying shades of lightness. But what about the problem of constancy? The reader may have already anticipated that the ratio hypothesis also elegantly explains constancy. When the prevailing illumination changes, it affects the absolute luminance of every surface but it does not affect the ratios among them. To test the hypothesis rigorously, Wallach introduced a second ring-and-disk pair, as shown at right above. Suppose the absolute values in the first pair are Ring: 2 and Disk: 1, where the values are arbitrary units and where the disk appears to be a

particular value of gray. Suppose the absolute value of the ring in the second pair is 8. The observer is now given the task of adjusting the luminance in the disk of the second pair until it appears to have the same color as the disk in Pair 1. The result, averaging for all subjects over many trials, was a setting very close to 4, meaning that observers selected a disk whose luminance was 4 times as great as that of the disk in Pair 1 to which it was being matched. More importantly for our purposes, the result is quite close to the predicted value of 4 based on the ratio of 2 to 1 in Pair 1. Thus the hypothesis is confirmed.

It follows that whatever may interfere with ratios in daily life (or in the laboratory) will affect perceived color. This gives us some insight into visual contrast, such as is represented in the centuries-old illusion illustrated above. The inner squares are all equal shades of gray, but they look different. Since the ratios of squares to surrounding regions all differ, we should expect the squares to look different. But the thoughtful reader may object that the contrast effect is not as great as we should expect, given the very different ratios. The objection would be well taken and can be explained by pointing out that there are other ratios to consider in a case like this. The ratio of each square to the white page surrounding all the squares is the same, not different. So one might look upon the contrast effect as resulting from a conflict among various ratios: the immediate ones, squares to surrounding regions, all differ; the more remote ones, squares to page, are all the same. The latter ratios prevent what would otherwise be a more drastic effect, as in Wallach's experiment.

Most students of perception believe that the relational explanation of perceived lightness, lightness constancy, and contrast is essentially correct. From the discussion so far, it appears that the problem of lightness

Lightness contrast: The inner squares appear to vary in shade because the lightness of the surrounding squares varies.

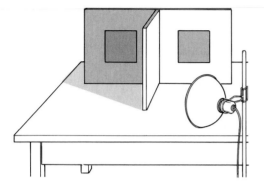

Arrangement typically used for experiment on lightness constancy. Observer must match standard gray square on one side with comparison square on other side in very different illumination. The match is usually to the shade of gray of the standard.

constancy is much better dealt with by a theory based on stimulus relations than by a taking-into-account type of theory, although, as we shall see, there is more to lightness constancy than stimulus ratios.

There are certain parallels worthy of mention between the perception of lightness and the perception of chromatic hues—the colors of the visible spectrum. Color constancy occurs if light of predominantly one frequency is used as the source of illumination. Then, a colored region will no longer reflect light to the eye of the same frequency that it would when receiving white light. Nonetheless the region will continue to appear in its normal color. Just as in the case of lightness constancy, the explanation concerns the fact that the chromatic illumination also falls on the area surrounding the colored region so that the *relation* between the two is unchanged in certain respects. There is also a parallel with respect to the *shades* and *tints* of colors. Colors are said to vary along three dimensions: the hue itself (based on the frequency of the light), the saturation or pureness of color of a given hue (based on the extent to which it is mixed with white light), and the degree of lightness (based on the lightness or darkness of that white-light mixture). If lightness is based on ratio, and it seems that it is, then the appearance of a color should be affected by variations in the lightness or darkness of a neighboring or surrounding region. For example, an orange disk can be made to appear brown simply by increasing the intensity of white light in a surrounding ring. Few people realize that brown is simply a shade of orange.

Is Constancy Learned or Innately Determined?

How do we come to possess spatial and lightness constancies? Almost all beginning students of perception assume that constancy is learned as we develop and move around in the environment. In doing so, we discover that distant objects that appear small are actually quite large, that slanted things that look like ellipses and trapezoids are in fact circles and squares, and so forth. This belief is consistent with the popular but erroneous camera theory of perception, discussed in Chapter 1, and, like it, rests on the assumptions that perception corresponds with the picture the eye "takes" and that what is referred to as constancy is a matter of knowing about things, not a matter of how things appear to us.

If constancy were a fact of knowledge rather than perception, the appearance of things ought to be governed by their retinal stimuli, and the achievement of constancy should be a corrective added by our reason. If appearance were governed by the retinal image, different objects of equal luminance should *look* as if they are the same shade. In the photo-

A duplicate drawing of the woman and man in the background of the Capitol's corridor has been placed in the foreground. Despite the equality of the visual angles the couples subtend, they look different in size.

graph on page 33, however, the luminance of the black shingles in bright sunlight and that of the white siding in shadow are almost the same, but they hardly look alike; furthermore, the white siding in shadow does look like the siding in sunlight, although its luminance is quite different. And, in the illustration above, the visual angle of the woman and man in the left foreground is the same as that of the same woman and man in the background, but they do not appear to be the same in size. In both these instances, if we saw the objects in life rather than in pictures, the differences would appear even greater.

Studies of many animal species also suggest that constancy is not a matter of reason but of perception. In experiments on size perception, the animal subject typically is first trained to discriminate between two objects equally far away on the basis of their different sizes. For example, the animal learns that choosing the larger object is always rewarded. Then, in the critical test, the larger object is placed farther away, so that its visual angle is now smaller than the visual angle of the smaller object. If the animal's perception of size is governed by visual angle, it should go to the nearer object. But if its size perception is similar to ours and it perceives the more distant object to be larger, the animal should continue going to it. In all species tested—including primates, other mammals, chickens, and fish—size constancy prevails.

Analogous experiments indicate that many species are able to achieve lightness constancy. In one experiment, for example, fish were first trained to push the darker of two buttons seen under equal illumination. Then, the darker button was placed under brighter illumination than the lighter button. Thus, under these conditions, the luminance of the darker button was greater: It reflected more intense light to the eye than the lighter button. Nevertheless, the fish continued pressing at the darker button. One may therefore infer that the fish continued to perceive that shade as darker and expected to receive food as a consequence of pushing it.

If animals with mental capacities as limited as a chicken behave as we do in terms of constancy, it is most unlikely that they do so on the basis of what they know and not of how things look to them. But even if we can safely assume that many species achieve constancy as we do, this does not rule out the possibility that constancy is developed through experience. Infants initially might actually perceive the same object located at varying distances as objects of different sizes. Through experience, they might develop constancy so that they now would actually perceive the object located at varying distances as the same in size. In other words, instead of having learned to think about a similar perception in a new way, their perception itself would have changed. A specific example may help to make this possibility clear. The drawing at left *looks like* a three-dimensional object. Thus there can be no question that we *perceive* the drawing as three-dimensional. It is not just a matter of knowledge. Yet, in my opinion, it is probable that this perception is governed by past experience—probably with real boxes, cubes, and the like.

How can we determine whether or not the achievement of constancy depends on prior experience? If the basis of constancy at issue is some stimulus relation, as is probable in the perception of lightness, there is no problem: Dependency on experience seems unlikely and, in fact, gratuitous. Given a certain stimulus basis for a perception, such as is surely true for the chromatic hues, what need to invoke a learning hypothesis? By the same token, if lightness is directly given by ratio of luminances, it seems quite plausible that lightness constancy is a direct outcome of determination by such a ratio. What little evidence there is on this question confirms this reasoning.

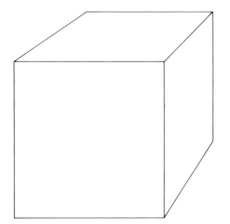

We perceive this two-dimensional drawing to be three-dimensional, probably because of our past experience with real boxes and similar structures.

If, however, a constancy is based on an inference process, as is probably the case in size perception, experience may play a role in its genesis. To determine whether or not the constancy of a perception is innate, experiments must be constructed that rule out experience as a factor. One way of doing so is to test animals or infants at birth or shortly thereafter; a more drastic way is to test more mature animals that have been prevented from learning about the visual world, usually by eliminating their vision or pattern vision at birth. Both methods have inherent difficulties: At birth, infants and many animals are not mature enough to test since they are not capable of locomotion or of learning to discriminate between objects of differing sizes or lightnesses, while early deprivation of vision may cause severe deterioration of the visual nervous system and prevent normal maturation.

The issue is further complicated by the fact that a capacity may not be present at birth but still be innate. By the term "innate" psychologists mean that a particular behavior, trait, or perceptual achievement is genetically determined or "wired in," the result of evolutionary adaptation. But the function may not manifest itself until later in life, a consequence of normal maturation in a suitable environment. For example, certain aspects of sexual behavior are surely innately determined in various species but are not displayed until the animal has matured. Similarly, the visual nervous system, the maturation of which is innately determined, requires exposure to light or, more importantly, patterned light to mature normally. Given these complexities, it is not surprising that we do not as yet have definitive evidence on the question of the role of experience in the genesis of size and shape constancy.

The most interesting available evidence comes from studies of 6-to-12-week-old human infants conducted by T. G. R. Bower of Edinburgh University. In experiments on size constancy, illustrated on the following page, Bower conditioned infants to turn their heads slightly in response to a 12-inch cube at a distance of 3.3 feet, using as a reward a peek-a-boo appearance of a hidden experimenter. Bower then moved the cube farther away, to 9.9 feet, to test for the presence of constancy in the infants. Bower's method thus circumvented the difficulties alluded to above of doing experiments on perception with very young infants. The infants were not required to move around in the environment and not required to learn a difficult size-discrimination problem.

Based on a well-known fact about conditioning discovered by Ivan Pavlov, Bower reasoned that, if the cube continued to look much the same to the infant, the conditioned response should remain in full force; to the extent that it looked different, the response should be weak or absent. Bower found that infants indeed continued to respond vigorously when the same cube was tested at the greater distance, although its visual

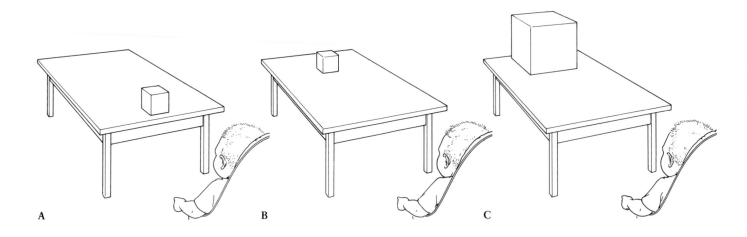

A   B   C

Experiment investigating size constancy in infants. A. The 12-inch cube to which infant was conditioned. B. The same cube placed at a distance three times greater than in A. C. A 36-inch cube placed at the greater distance, yielding the same visual angle as the conditioned cube.

angle was thereby reduced to one-third its initial size. They responded only weakly, however, when a cube three times larger, 36 inches in size, was placed at such a distance (9.9 feet) that its visual angle remained the same as that of the initial object. The results imply that infants perceive size much as we do, on the basis not of visual angle alone but of constancy.

Unfortunately, variations of Bower's experiments conducted in Australia have failed to confirm his findings that young infants respond primarily to objective size rather than to visual angle. Bower's findings may simply be incorrect. But there is another possibility. Infants may be so sensitive to changes that, when the object is placed farther away, the conditioned response may decline not because the object's size looks different but because its *distance* looks greater to the infant. Thus not only was the responsiveness to the 36-inch cube at 9.9 feet reduced in Bower's experiment but the greater responsiveness to the 12-inch cube at that distance was not as great as to that cube when it remained at the original distance of 3.3 feet. We will have to await further research for clarification of this issue.

Using a similar experimental design, Bower also performed experiments on constancy of shape in which the conditioned stimulus was a rectangle at a slant. The infants responded strongly when the rectangle was oriented to the frontal plane, suggesting that it looked much the same, but they responded only weakly to a trapezoidal shape in the frontal plane that generated the same retinal shape as the rectangle. These findings were confirmed by the Australian investigators. Thus shape constancy appears to be present in the perception of very young infants.

Even if all of Bower's findings are substantiated, they would not rule out the possibility that constancy is an achievement based on experience. Infants could develop constancy in the first several weeks of life.

An experiment on size constancy in rats conducted by Don Heller at Yeshiva University supports this possibility that some experience is necessary. The animals were reared under conditions of complete darkness until they were 34 days old. (Unlike many other animals, rats, being nocturnal, do not seem to suffer impairment of the visual system when confined to darkness in early life.) Then, while still kept in the dark, they were trained to run down an alley that led to the larger of two equidistant luminous circles. The rat could only view the circles when it stood directly behind a glass partition in front of the two alleys (see the illustration at right, below). The weight of the rat in this position turned on a switch that made the circles visible. Thus, during training, the rat had no opportunity to view the same object at different distances and perhaps develop constancy from such experience. Even as the rats ran down the alleys, the circles were not visible to them.

In the critical test, also conducted in the dark, the larger circle was placed farther back so that it subtended a visual angle equal to the smaller circle. If the rats already possessed the ability to perceive constancy of size, the larger circle, farther away, should look larger. However, the rats equally often ran to the small circle as to the large circle. In another variation, the larger circle was moved so far away that its visual angle was the smaller one; in these trials, the rats chose the other, objectively smaller circle (the visual angle of which was larger).

Apparatus used to test size perception in rats reared in the dark.

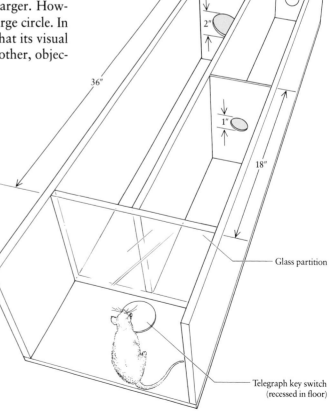

36"

2"

1"

18"

Glass partition

Telegraph key switch
(recessed in floor)

A control group of rats reared in daylight and then given the same training and test in the dark consistently chose the objectively larger circle. These results indicate that the rats reared in daylight had already achieved constancy and that the rats raised in the dark did not misperceive size because of inadequate distance cues in the dark alleys. Finally, the experimental animals were placed back in lighted cages for a week. They were then retested in the experimental alleys and found to behave like the normally reared rats: They displayed constancy. Thus, during the single week of relatively restricted locomotion in a small cage (and perhaps during a much shorter period of time), something happened to alter perception from nonconstancy to constancy of size. This experiment suggests two things: Size constancy—at least in rats—is a consequence of experience, and size constancy may be a result of exposure to dynamic change of visual angle, that is, experience of objects moving toward and away from them and experience of their own motion toward and away from objects.

Infants, even before they are able to crawl and move about, may achieve constancy in a similar way. They may achieve it through frequent early perception of moving objects. Particularly relevant might be the movement of people toward and away from the crib. In order to investigate this possibility, researchers have attempted to isolate this factor of a change of size of the stimulus by projecting patterns on a screen in front of the subject and then zooming the lens so as to cause the pattern to enlarge or shrink. The phenomenon has been referred to as the "looming effect."

Adult observers experience such expanding or contracting patterns as objects approaching or receding, as everyone knows from viewing movies, television, animated cartoons, and the like. Substantial evidence indicates that monkey and human infants as young as two weeks of age experience these patterns in the same way. The experiments on this issue make use of the fact that an object perceived to be rapidly approaching and on a collision course with the observer will produce an alarm reaction. When, however, the projected pattern rapidly shrinks, simulating recession of an object, or when it expands but is not on a collision course with the observer, the alarm reaction does not occur. Thus the presence of this reaction makes it quite probable that the looming effect is innately determined and does not require prior experience. If we assume that the expanding image pattern appears to the infant the way it does to us, as a thing approaching (rather than simply as a thing at one distance expanding in size), we can conclude that size constancy is innate under dynamic conditions. The innate basis of constancy under dynamic conditions might then be the vehicle by which infants learn about constancy under static conditions.

Although, as we have seen, the data on the origins of constancy are somewhat contradictory at present, the following conclusions seem warranted: (1) shape constancy is present in very young infants; (2) size constancy may or may not be present at birth but most probably is by a very early age; (3) size constancy (and possibly other constancies) under *dynamic* conditions is probably present in infants without benefit of any prior experience; and (4) lightness constancy, because it is a function of stimulus ratios, is innately determined.

Failure of Constancy

In many instances in daily life, objects located at very great distances appear extremely small. Consider, for example, the striking smallness of houses viewed from a plane traveling at an altitude of 20,000 feet or the size of people on the street when viewed from a skyscraper. Students of perception have used such expressions as "the falling off of constancy" and "underconstancy" in describing these instances.

The logic behind this terminology is straightforward. Constancy can be no better than the sensory information on which it is based. Because our sensory capacities are limited, we are not always able to achieve full constancy. With respect to size constancy, for example, one might say that the maximum distance that can be detected perceptually is on the order of hundreds or, at most, thousands of yards. We can thus hardly expect that the distance to, say, the moon, which is 250,000 miles away, will be perceived accurately. Instead we should expect the moon over the horizon to appear to be about the size of a house or other terrestrial object of the same visual angle on the horizon. Since the moon is roughly 2000 miles in diameter, one might say that we have here a considerable departure from constancy. But it is important to note that the failure does not lie with the perceptual apparatus responsible for constancy but with the information available to it.

In past studies, particularly those conducted in Europe in the first decades of this century, subjects were found to underestimate consistently the size of objects located at great distances from them, the more so the greater the distance, as you might suspect from your own experience. The accepted explanation of this phenomenon was that distance perception did not keep pace with objective distance because such cues as accommodation and convergence were ineffective beyond short distances. Thus, the size of a distant object was underestimated, because size perception is a product of visual angle and distance. Thus it seemed to make sense to speak of "underconstancy" and "the falling off of constancy."

Often failure or partial failure of constancy is to be explained in just this way. For example, an airplane in the sky looks smaller than it would if constancy prevailed, and surely this is a consequence of poor cues to distance (see the earlier discussion of the elevated moon). The same explanation of underregistration of distance information has also been invoked for objects on the ground, where more distance cues are available. For example, when the airplane is seen on the ground from roughly the same distance as when it was airborne, it undoubtedly will look larger than it would in the sky, but it will also undoubtedly look much smaller than it would if seen close up. However, in experiments conducted in recent decades, researchers have found that observers report very distant objects to be even larger than they objectively are—an observation referred to as *overconstancy*—and that constancy often holds at very great distances, when distance cues are available. How can we make sense of these contradictory findings and explain why objects at great distances often look diminutive in everyday life?

We typically do not take measurements of perception in everyday life, so investigators assume that their facts are to be trusted more than casual observations. However, my view is the opposite. We must start from observations in daily life and, if experiments yield different results, we should re-examine our experiments. Overconstancy is a case in point.

Overconstancy does not appear to be a phenomenon of perception, but an artifact of the instructions sometimes given to research subjects. When subjects are instructed to select a size from among the nearby comparison objects that *is equal to* that of the distant standard, judgment about the probable objective state of affairs is emphasized, not perceptual appearance. Subjects then reason that, because distant things usually look small, they had better select a match that takes account of this fact, and in doing so they overcompensate. By contrast, when instructions emphasize projective matching—that is, taking the attitude of an artist who strives to achieve accurate representation of the visual angles of things—underconstancy occurs. When instructions simply emphasize how things *look*, however, constancy more often than not holds up. If this last finding is the least biased and most valid one, why, when distance cues are available in daily life (as contrasted with formal experiments), do very distant objects look diminutive? I would suggest an explanation in line with an observation I made earlier, that there are two modes of visual perception. In addition to the salient mode, in which constancy prevails, there is another, the proximal mode, in which perception does correlate with, or conform to, relations within the retinal image. For example, at the same time we see a plate on a table as circular, we are aware that we see it from such an angle that it is visually foreshortened along one axis and projects as an ellipse. Similarly, we cannot help but notice that a far-off person fills very little of our visual field compared to the extent that a nearby person does. In this sense, we see

In Mlle. Charlotte du Val-d'Ognes *(c. 1800), attributed to Constance Marie Charpentier, the two figures seen through the window look small because the cues to their distance from the woman in the foreground are poor. Thus we are more likely to notice how little of the visual field they fill compared to the artist's main subject.*

the person as "ant-like" while also perceiving him or her as a full-sized person. According to this interpretation, then, there may be many instances in which distance is not registered incorrectly and constancy does not fall off but in which we are most struck by the smallness of the visual angle compared to our veridical perception.

If this description of dual modes of perception is correct, it is no wonder that experiments can lead to varying or contradictory results. Subjects are caught in a potential conflict. If they match on the basis of constancy, they fail to take note of one facet of perception; if they match on the basis of visual angle (which is very difficult to do), they fail to take account of the *most* central facet, namely, constancy. Such an explanation sheds a different light on the evidence of individual differences in constancy experiments and the development of constancy.

INDIVIDUAL DIFFERENCES IN CONSTANCY   In constancy experiments, subjects consistently differ from one another. Some tend to match on the basis of constancy regardless of conditions or the kind of constancy tested. Others tend consistently to stray from full constancy.

The fact that experimental observers are consistent in their patterns of matching would seem to suggest that some characteristic of the individual is responsible rather than just random variation in the face of a difficult task. Yet there is no convincing evidence that such differences occur in daily life. When several people are together, do they not typically agree about the strikingly huge size of the horizon moon, the strikingly diminished size of houses, trees, and cars seen in the valley from a very distant mountain, and other such perceptual phenomena?

Experiments may bring out differences that are not really present in perception. One such reason might be the conflict, to which I just alluded, between the two modes of perception. If a conflict does indeed exist, it may become a matter of judgment in deciding what the experimenter really wants and thus how to resolve it. Naturally, then, different people may come to different conclusions. Artists and some others may be more sensitive to or more aware of the proximal mode of perception. We would expect this to influence their matches in the direction away from constancy more so than it does for other individuals. But even if this is true it would not mean what the quantitative results seem to imply—namely, that they are poorer in achieving constancy.

The same reasoning could also explain some puzzling results of experiments on the development of size perception in children. Some studies seem to show that the extent of perceptual constancy increases with age. These findings would make perfect sense if the testing of young infants revealed no sign of constancy, but, as we have seen, such studies suggest that perceptual constancy is present in the early months of life.

Given the early appearance of constancy, how can we explain the fact that some studies indicate that constancy perception increases with age? It could mean that constancy is approximated in an infant and becomes refined with age. Or it could mean that young children understand the instructions in an experiment less clearly or differently than adults do. They may be more aware than adults of the conflict between the two modes of perception or, alternatively, adults may be clearer that the constancy mode is the one to focus on.

The best available evidence on size perception is that children of 5 or 6 years of age only show some partial failure of constancy at a considerable distance, beyond 50 feet. Since, as we shall see in Chapter 3, it is most probable that the cues to distance beyond that range are based primarily on the kinds of information artists make use of—perspective, shadows, and the like—the deficit in children, if any, may be attributed to lack of sensitivity to such cues rather than to an immature capacity to achieve constancy.

The Explanations of Constancy Reconsidered

One might conclude from our survey of constancy that both the taking-into-account theory and the stimulus-relation theory are correct, at least with respect to some of the facts. Since these theories can be extended to cover many other phenomena of perception and not just the constancies, it is important to consider them more carefully.

The stimulus-relation theory is an offshoot of a simple stimulus theory that asserts that all we need do to explain a particular kind of perception is to isolate the relevant stimulus impinging on the sense organ. The role of the mind for such a theory is little more than a center for picking up the neurally encoded sensory signals. This could be true for the luminance-ratio theory of lightness constancy, except that the stimulus consists of a ratio. For this type of theory, no active, interpretive mental processes need be assumed.

Another interpretation of constancy is similar to the simple stimulus theory—namely, that ratios and other stimulus relations govern perception. However, they are believed to do so because interactions in the brain are the neural processes that determine perception. Here we see an example of the thinking of the Gestalt psychologists. In other words, both approaches would regard ratios, proportions, and other stimulus relations as the basis of constancy. But whereas the stimulus theory has it that these are the higher-order stimulus correlates of perception, the Gestalt theory has it that such stimulus relations yield constancy percepts because of the neural interaction to which they give rise.

Another approach, stemming from the thinking of Helmholtz's contemporary Ewald Hering, also emphasizes the role of neural interactions. It is a fact of the visual nervous system that the discharging of impulses in one neuron inhibits the discharging of impulses in adjacent neurons. This *lateral inhibition*, as it is called, might be thought to explain contrast, the inhibition causing one region to look darker when an adjacent region is "bright." Lateral inhibition has also been invoked to explain lightness constancy, although the explanation is more complicated. The reduction of the ratio principle to a physiological mechanism has given it great appeal to many investigators. Despite the underlying difference in the view of the mind in these approaches, they share the belief that constancy is based on such stimulus relations as ratios.

The taking-into-account theory of constancy, by contrast, implies mental computation. To infer that an image whose visual angle is small but whose source is far away represents a large object is a process somewhat like thought. It would require knowledge, albeit unconsciously represented, of how visual angle depends upon distance. Thus, perception for this kind of theory depends upon a much greater, active role of the

When viewing scenes such as that shown in Edward Hopper's Sun in an Empty Room (1963), we perceive the walls in differing orientations to be of uniform color even though their luminances differ.

mind. In that respect, the theory can be said to have its roots in a very different tradition of philosophy. Perception would thus be much more the result of mental reconstruction than of a passive monitoring of stimulation or of spontaneous neural interaction.

From the discussion so far, it would seem that the facts about lightness perception favor the first theory and that those about size, shape, and orientation favor the second theory. However, certain difficulties for the ratio theory of lightness perception and certain recent findings put this theory in a rather new light. Consider, for example, a room such as the one shown in the painting above, in which the walls are painted a uniform shade but have differing orientations to the source of light. Where any two walls pictured meet at a corner, one wall almost always receives more light than the other. The walls at the corner will thus yield adjacent retinal images of differing luminance. According to the ratio theory, they should look different from one another. For example, one wall should look much lighter than the other. But more often than not adjacent walls in such a scene will appear to be the same color, although one may appear to be in dimmer illumination than the other. Lightness constancy occurs when, according to the ratio theory, it should not.

By a simple experiment, the corner where the walls meet can be "flattened out" perceptually so that the walls look like surfaces in the *same* plane, and in this way constancy can be abolished. To perform this experiment: (1) close one eye, (2) hold the head still, and (3) hold up cardboards to block from view the regions where the corner meets the ceiling and floor. The change will be dramatic: The two surfaces now will look like different shades of gray. The results of this experiment suggest that if and only if the two regions that differ in luminance appear to be in the same plane does the ratio between them lead to differing lightnesses. If this is true, it is clear that luminance ratio does not so automatically determine lightness perception as has been implied.

Experiments by Alan Gilchrist at Rutgers University have now established that, when the regions that form luminance ratios are in different perceived planes, even parallel planes, those ratios will have little bearing on lightness perception. Yet, when these regions are perceived to be adjacent and in the same plane, the ratios do govern such lightness perception. How can we make sense of these facts?

These findings appear to be but a special case of a broader principle. That principle concerns how the edge between regions is perceived. Recent evidence suggests that the perceptual system only picks up the information about luminance difference at the edge between regions and then "assumes" that the difference at the edge applies throughout a region until another edge occurs. The evidence furthermore suggests that the perceptual system sorts the various edges in a scene into two categories: those in which the luminance ratio is based on lightness differences and those in which it is based on illumination differences. Once the two types of edges are sorted out, only the ratios from the entire set of regions between which there are surface-lightness edges enter into the determination of specific lightness values. The illumination edges do not enter into this computation.

How does the perceptual system distinguish luminance edges from illumination edges? We do not yet have a complete answer to this question, but the perceptual system may make use of several kinds of information available to it. The best known is the gradual transition from dark to light that usually accompanies illumination edges, namely the *penumbra* around cast shadows. A penumbra occurs because the sun, an incandescent bulb, or another source of light is an extended region, not a single point. Another probable indicator is a difference in the orientation

The penumbra at the edge of a cast shadow serves as cue that the darkened region is shadowed. When the penumbra is ringed by a border, the shadow looks like a dark-gray or black region.

of neighboring planes, such as the corner walls discussed earlier, it generally being the case that the illumination will be unequal across such corners. Given the tendency to interpret a luminance difference at a corner as based on illumination, we can now appreciate why constancy occurs in such cases but not when we perceptually "flatten out" that corner. A third possible indicator is the magnitude of the luminance ratio at an edge. A lightness edge can be no greater than about 30 to 1 because that is what we get from a white with a reflectance value of 90% and a black with a reflectance value of 3%. But an illumination edge often yields a very high ratio because the only constraint on its magnitude is light indirectly reflected back on the unilluminated surface by all other surfaces.

The theoretical picture now looks very different than the one outlined earlier as characterizing a stimulus theory. If the perceptual system makes use of depth information or the like in arriving at "decisions" about whether regions of particular luminance values result from reflectance properties of surfaces or from illumination, a process of computation must occur that takes account of the whole array of relevant edges in leading to "assignment" of lightness values. This process is very different from the direct determination of a color percept by a specific luminance ratio between two regions. The entire process depends much more on cognitive decision and inference, although admittedly unconscious, than has been thought to be the case. While constancy is still to be understood in terms of unchanging ratios of luminance with changing overall illumination, it is now clear that a good deal of mental processing lies behind this seductively simple formulation.

The two theories of constancy thus are perhaps not very different after all. Both involve quasi-cognitive operations. In the cases of spatial constancies, such as those of size and shape, the important retinal-image information is given absolutely (visual angle and shape of image), and this is assessed by the perceptual system in terms of other relevant information (distance and slant). While information concerning stimulus relations contributes to our perception of objects, it is not a sufficiently reliable indicator of size or shape because a given thing can be seen in any context and can change its context from moment to moment. Thus what matters most for arriving at a perception of an object's size or shape is its distance or slant, and the visual nervous system has evolved adaptively to allow taking these into account.

In the case of the perception of lightness, however, the important retinal-image information is given relativistically. By definition of physical reflectance, a white surface is one that reflects most of the incident light falling upon it, and a black surface is one that absorbs most of that light. Therefore, given several such surfaces, what we need to know is something relative—namely, how much more or less one surface reflects light than another. That information is quite reliable if we can discount cases in which that relative difference is based on an illumination difference. The first step in the achievement of lightness constancy, then, is the extraction of such information from the retinal image. But, beyond this first step, the achievement of both kinds of constancy seems to depend upon computation and inference.

In this chapter, we have had occasion to discuss the perception of distance and depth several times, particularly in connection with the phenomenon of size constancy. But, to do justice to this topic, it would have been necessary to go off on lengthy tangents at the expense of making an already difficult discussion all the more so. With this gap in mind, I turn now to a consideration of how we arrive at our impression of the three-dimensionality of objects and of their distances from us.

3 THE MANY PATHS TO THE THIRD DIMENSION

The seemingly infinite distance and expanse over the sagebrush and buildings and on to the fields and mountains beyond is immediately apparent in the Ansel Adams photograph reproduced on the facing page. What is it in the photograph that yields such a striking sense of distance? If we viewed the scene ourselves rather than merely the picture of it, what other factors would enter the equation to add to the powerful impression of depth?

We take the three-dimensional world in which we find ourselves so much for granted that we seldom think of our ability to perceive how far away things are from us and from each other as an achievement calling for explanation. If we possessed a three-dimensional retina and a mechanism that registered the distance of a thing by its location in such a retina, our ability to perceive depth might be less remarkable. But the human retina is effectively a two-dimensional surface. Thus the puzzle of depth perception is how we gain information about distance, and how we make use of this information to reconstruct a three-dimensional perceptual world.

For animals, including humans, successful navigation through the world and survival itself depend upon accurate distance perception. For centuries, philosophers and natural scientists were split into two camps with respect to the question of the origins of the perception of the third dimension. The Nativists maintained that space perception was an innate faculty of the mind (or, in more modern terminology, that the perceptual system was programmed or prewired for three-dimensional perception). The Empiricists maintained that such perception in the adult was the end result of past experience in infancy and early childhood. The controversy was carried on mainly with logical arguments. Only in recent years have experimental techniques begun to resolve the issue, as we shall see.

Many of the cues to distance and depth that we use in viewing real scenes are present in pictures as well.

For both sides of the question, the problem remains: What information is available to the perceptual system that enables us to achieve adequate impressions of distance and depth?

In the photograph, perspective, the partial covering of objects in the background by objects in the foreground, shadow, and, possibly, our familiarity with the usual sizes of sagebrush, buildings, and other objects in the scene seem the obvious cues that yield the impression of depth. In everyday life, binocular vision—vision with two eyes rather than one—is often said to be the basis of our perception of the world as three-dimensional. How can we tell whether or not these factors are crucial and what others may also yield information about distance? After all, the fact that binocular vision, for example, is not necessary for depth perception can be seen simply by closing one eye and looking at surrounding objects. Similarly, familiar size cannot be crucial, because our perception of distance is often veridical even when the objects viewed are unfamiliar.

Cues to the Third Dimension: An Overview

We can bring the problem of depth perception into scientific focus by eliminating all sensory information about the distance of an object. The laboratory procedure for doing this can easily be recreated at home by viewing an object with one eye and with the head held still in a completely dark room. The object should be luminous—for example, coated with luminous paint—and should not have a characteristic size. A rectangle or circle will do.

Under such conditions, the exact distance of the object cannot be determined with any accuracy or certainty. A rather interesting consequence of the indeterminacy of the object's distance is the indeterminacy of its size. This is exactly what we should expect, given what we know about the dependence of perceived size on perceived distance.

One investigator, Walter Gogel of the University of California at Santa Barbara, believes that, even though subjects may have no usable information in such a dark-room experiment, they nonetheless have a tendency to localize the object at some specific distance from themselves, roughly between 6 and 8 feet. Although Gogel presents evidence for the existence of such a "specific-distance tendency," as he calls it, the fact remains that objects viewed under the conditions of the dark-room experiment are difficult to localize with any certainty or precision and are subjectively indeterminate in size.

What potential sources of information about distance have we eliminated in this experiment? By making use of a similar procedure in the laboratory, investigators have isolated several different cues. Some of these cues are inherent in our eyes themselves and in the structure and

Right eye view

Left eye view

The disparity between the left eye's and the right eye's view of a small square in front of a larger one.

functioning of the visual nervous system; others are inherent in the characteristics of the objects viewed and in the manner in which they project images to the eye.

RETINAL DISPARITY   By closing one eye, we have eliminated whatever information might be provided by the simultaneous utilization of the two eyes together. Investigators distinguish two separate factors here, retinal disparity and convergence. When we view objects with both eyes open, the images of the objects projected on each retina are slightly different, or disparate, because the eyes are in slightly differing positions with respect to the scene, roughly 2.5 inches apart on the average. The information that this disparity yields concerns the *difference* in distance between two or more points, since only when points differ in their distance from us will the two images differ. I will refer to this aspect of perception as *depth*. If only flat objects in one plane are viewed, there is no retinal disparity. The achievement of depth from binocularly disparate images is referred to as *stereopsis*.

CONVERGENCE   The other factor based on binocular vision, convergence, is the angle formed by the two eyes looking directly at, or fixating, a given point in space. The gaze of each of our eyes normally tends to converge on the same point.

If the eyes behaved independently of one another, an object's image would fall in entirely different positions on each retina, which would result in double vision. Singleness of vision depends upon the imaging of the same objects on corresponding points of the two retinas. The reason for this is that the light-sensitive cells in the retinas, the rods and cones that are in such corresponding places in each eye, give rise to neural signals that travel along fibers that ultimately end up in roughly the same region of the visual cortex of the brain.

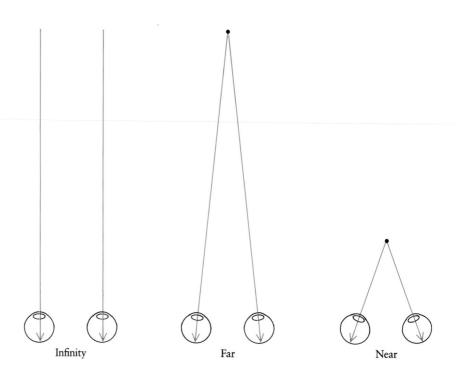

Infinity   Far   Near

Angle of convergence of the eyes at infinite,
far, and near distances.

When the eyes converge, the directions of gaze of the two eyes form a particular angle with respect to one another, a kind of triangulation. If the object is near, this angle will be relatively large; if the object is far, the angle will be more acute. At infinity, the directions of gaze would be parallel and the angle would be zero, as can be seen in the illustration above. Thus, the convergence (or, more generally, just vergence) angle of the eyes could be a cue to distance if the perceptual system receives information about the degree of convergence of the eyes and can interpret it appropriately. This kind of information concerns the *absolute* distance of a single object from us. I will refer to this aspect of perception as *distance*.

ACCOMMODATION   One potential source of information is *not* eliminated in our dark-room experiment. The lens of the eye reflexively changes its thickness in order to achieve sharp focus for objects at differing distances. Logically, if the brain "knew" about the state of accommodation of the lens, it could use such information as a clue to the object's distance. It could also gain information from the fact that objects farther or nearer than the object focused on will yield blurred images, the more so the farther away they are from the plane upon which the eyes are focused. Accommodation and convergence are often termed *oculomotor cues* because they depend on movements of (or within) the eye.

Accommodation, as we shall see, is considered to be a weak source of information about depth. Therefore, it was not deemed necessary to eliminate it in our experiment. We could have eliminated this cue as well by simply viewing the object through a pinhole, or artificial pupil. The

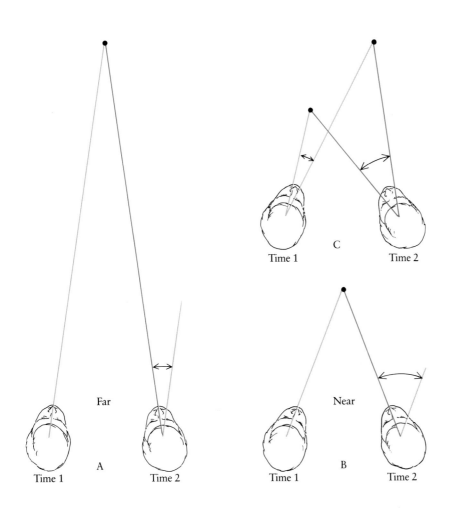

Motion parallax as a cue to distance and depth. The direction of near objects (B) changes considerably with movement of the observer whereas the direction of far objects (A) changes little. The change in the angular direction of the images of two or more objects with respect to one another (C) can also be a cue to depth.

reason why a pinhole eliminates accommodation as a distance clue is easy to grasp. The pinhole allows only a single ray of light (or a very narrow beam) to reach the eye from any point in space. Thus a lens is not needed to focus the light. A sharp picture of a scene would be produced regardless of the distance of the objects in it.

MOTION PARALLAX   Still another possible source of information about depth that is eliminated in the dark-room experiment is motion parallax—motion on the part of the observer. The nearer an object, the more its direction (with respect to the observer) changes when the observer moves, as can be seen in the illustration above. When many objects are visible at differing distances, observer movement also yields a change in the direction of things relative to each other, which could be a source of depth information.

PICTORIAL INFORMATION   Finally, our dark-room experiment eliminates the kind of information that artists have made use of at least since the Renaissance. This includes perspective, shadow, and the partial covering (or occlusion) of one object by another object in front of it. Some investigators would also include the familiar sizes of things as a cue to distance. Collectively, this kind of depth information is called *pictorial*, because it is captured by pictures, be they drawings, paintings, or photographs. Pictorial information depends upon how the objects in a scene and the surfaces upon which they rest appear, rather than on physiological mechanisms, observer motion, or the use of both eyes. Pictorial information can be obtained by a stationary observer using only one eye, even if viewing through an artificial pupil.

In considering this list of potential distance and depth cues—retinal disparity, convergence of the eyes, accommodation of the lens, motion parallax, and pictorial information—many questions immediately arise. Is each of these factors equally important in perceiving the distance of a thing from us or the depth between different things? Are there limits on the range of effectiveness of these factors? What is the origin of depth perception? That every cue except the pictorial ones would have the potential of delivering up an impression of distance and depth by virtue of innate mechanisms of mind seems intuitively plausible. Are all these cues innate and the pictorial cues learned? In what ways do the cues interact to yield an impression of depth?

   To prove that a given cue can, by itself, yield an impression of where an object is in the third dimension, we must isolate its effect from that of all other cues. This can be done by creating situations in which all other cues are eliminated, are held constant, or work against the perception of depth. Alternatively, we can create situations in which no factors are operating and artifically create the one cue whose effects we want to test. Once we know the independent effects of each cue, we can explore how the perceptual system might integrate information from all the cues to yield the impression of a three-dimensional world that we typically achieve.

Retinal Disparity

To demonstrate that retinal disparity is indeed a cue to depth, we must show that the combination of the slightly different images each eye receives can alone yield an impression of depth. In 1838, Charles Wheatstone came up with an ingenious idea. He created the disparity artificially by means of a *mirror stereoscope*, a device he invented that can present the two eyes with slightly different pictures, pictures that differ in the

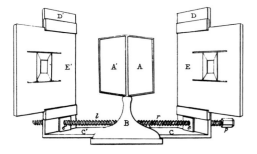

Wheatstone's mirror stereoscope. Each eye can view a separate figure even while the two eyes converge at the distance of the figures. A and A' are mirrors through which the pictures on E and E' are seen.

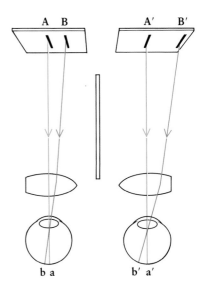

Diagram of Brewster's refracting stereoscope. The half-lenses allow the directions of gaze of the two eyes to remain parallel so that each eye can view a different figure.

same way that the retinal images do when one is viewing an actual scene. By using two-dimensional objects, he was able to prove that the resulting depth perception must be the consequence of the disparity between the two views; by using simple geometrical pictures, he was able to prove that the crucial factor was the disparity and not pictorial information. Normally, the two eyes will naturally converge on one of the two pictures, and the eyes will also tend to be appropriately accommodated to that distance. For each eye to aim separately at only one of the two pictures, together they would have to be converged either at a very great distance or to be crossed and converged at a distance nearer than the pictures. In either case, however, the lenses would then be inappropriately focused, leading not only to blurred images but to a strong reflexive tendency to change convergence. Wheatstone's device made use of two mirrors that allowed the eyes to converge at about the true distance of the pictures while still seeing one picture with one eye and the other with the other eye.

Wheatstone's contemporary, Sir David Brewster, invented another method of achieving stereoscopic vision of separate pictures, this time using lenses. Brewster's stereoscope, the principle of which is shown at right, above, is still in use today because it is so compact and simple a device. The half-lenses in front of the eyes serve to collimate the incoming light (i.e., to render the rays parallel as if they were coming from a great distance). Thus, accommodation relaxes, and the directions of gaze of the two eyes can be parallel as if they are viewing a very distant object. Each eye can then view its own picture by looking straight ahead.

The two sets of figures at right illustrate the logic of stereograms. Suppose that the smaller square in the upper set of figures is in front of the larger square and that you are looking at them head-on. To the left eye, the projected image would appear as figure A; to the right eye, it would appear as figure B. These two patterns, when combined, create the impression of depth. If the smaller square were *behind* the larger one, they would appear to the two eyes as in the lower set of figures. Notice, therefore, that depth can be reversed stereoscopically simply by transposing the left and right stereogram patterns. Inverting or reversing the left-right orientation of the patterns will have the same effect.

The impression of depth from the stereograms that appear in this book may be achieved by using the viewer inserted inside the back cover. A depth effect may sometimes also be achieved without the aid of a stereoscope by imagining that you are looking *through* the two pictures, at a point far beyond, while blocking the view of one of the two pictures from each eye. This can be done by using a sheet of cardboard or paper, as shown in the drawing on the following page. Or it can be achieved by fixating an imaginary point *in front* of the two pictures by crossing your

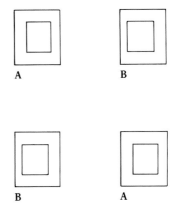

Viewed as stereograms, the upper set of figures will appear as a small square floating in front of a large square, and the lower set of figures will appear as a large square floating in front of the small one.

(Left) Procedure for viewing stereograms without the aid of a stereoscope. (Right) Hand-held stereoscope. This instrument was first developed by Oliver Wendell Holmes in 1861.

Vlajimir Tamari, Palestinian Still-life, 1977. Stereograms composed of paintings or photographs often yield a greater sense of depth than do simple geometric ones because they contain other depth cues.

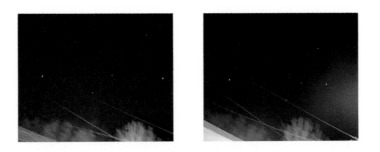

Stereogram of Jupiter, Saturn, Mars, and some of the stars in Virgo. To achieve disparity, the second photograph was taken a month after the first, during which time the earth had traveled approximately 50 million miles in its orbit around the sun. However, this kind of sparse stereogram does not yield a vivid depth impression.

Stereogram consisting of two photographs of the same scene. These pictures were taken 66 feet apart rather than 2.5 inches apart, which is the approximate distance between the eyes. As a result, even objects in a scene that is 15 miles away yield a stereo depth effect. A similar technique has been used in aerial reconnaisance. Other uses of stereoscopy include: the viewing of X-ray stereograms, the viewing of slides through binocular microscopes, and the detection of counterfeit money by the depth effect produced when a counterfeit and a genuine bill are compared.

eyes. In this method, the stereo depth will be reversed. Still another method is to view a picture with superimposed red and green components through red and green filters. However the disparity is achieved, some people have only a weak impression of depth from stereopsis, while a few are stereo "blind."

A recent discovery makes dramatically clear just how powerful a cue retinal disparity is by itself. In 1960, Bela Julesz at the Bell Telephone Laboratories developed two patterns of random dots that, when viewed as a stereogram, will fuse in such a way that a figure appears to be floating in the foreground or background. In the illustration on the following page, for instance, a triangle appears in front of the background. Where does the triangle come from? Directly from the binocular fusion going on inside the head. The effect is an interesting illustration of psychological construction, since the triangle perceived has no existence either in the two figures or in their retinal images.

Random-dot stereograms developed by Bela Julesz. When the two views are fused, a triangle is seen floating in the foreground.

If one looks at the illustration with the aid of a magnifying glass, one will see that the two patterns are almost identical. But there is a difference. The dots in the center of the right-hand pattern, inside the region of the "triangle," are shifted a bit to the left in relation to those in the left-hand pattern. On an almost microscopic scale, the necessary disparity between left and right is indeed present. The Julesz discovery shows, then, that the perceptual system can simultaneously process many minute differences between two retinal images and that in so doing it can construct an overall pattern or shape.

Stereopsis is perhaps the most important source of information that allows us to create a vivid, almost tangible and realistic impression of space between things. This is all the more true the closer the viewer is to the objects. In fact, one might think that stereopsis would be increasingly ineffective the farther away the object, because the more similar will be the images to the two eyes. To be more precise, the disparity between the two images decreases with the square of the distance. If perception followed this geometry, the impression of depth within an object based on retinal disparity should then become, let us say, one-ninth of its magnitude at 3 feet when it is viewed at 9 feet. But in fact the impression of depth may decrease little. Hans Wallach and Carl Zuckerman, then at the New School for Social Research, have shown that the perceptual system takes account of the fact that the object is farther away, and thus it interprets the smaller disparity as signifying more or less the same depth. The process seems to be very similar to that of size constancy, and it is therefore referred to as *stereoscopic depth constancy*.

Despite this constancy process, however, information about depth from retinal disparity surely becomes increasingly less important at greater distances, unless the distance between objects is very great, as, between trees several hundred yards apart, for example. Stereopsis is hardly indispensable because, as has already been noted, the impression of the distance of things from us and the depth between them remains when we close one eye. (Many a person blind in one eye has excellent depth perception.)

Why does binocular disparity lead to depth perception? Horace Barlow, Colin Blakemore, and John Pettigrew recently discovered neurons in the brain that seem to have the function of "detecting" disparity. These neurons discharge rapidly when a contour stimulates a certain magnitude of disparity between corresponding retinal regions. Such a neural mechanism may explain how the perceptual system "knows" that disparity exists between the two retinal images, signaling that there is more or less of such disparity. But it does not tell us how the perceptual system interprets the disparity thus signaled. As will be seen, such an interpretation is subject to learning. Moreover, the disparity-detector mechanism does not tell us anything about how the perceptual system decides which retinal points of stimulation in noncorresponding regions of the retina match with one another—that is, which derive from the same contour in the outer world. In simple displays in everyday life, and in stereograms such as the one illustrated on the right, the problem does not seem to arise. For example, it is obvious that, when the observer fixates line A so that its images a and a' fall in corresponding places on both retinas (on the central region of vision, the fovea), line B yields images b and b' in noncorresponding places. Images b and b' must therefore represent the same outer thing. There is no other possibility.

But suppose, as is perhaps more typical, *something* stimulates each eye in corresponding places. Let us say the left eye received the stimulus XXAXXBXX and the right eye received the stimulus XXAXXXBX. If the observer fixates A, there is the possibility of fusing the left eye's B with the right eye's X and the left eye's X with the right eye's B, since these fall on corresponding points. But that will not happen: The left eye's A and B will be fused with the right eye's A and B, because of the similarity between them. Apparently, the perceptual system scans the two images and decides, on the basis of similarity, which units in each most probably correspond, the implication being that those that correspond are produced by the same contours in the outer world. Once this scanning takes place, the perceptual system can evaluate the disparity in terms of depth. If B is relatively near to A in the left eye's image but is farther from A in the right eye's image, then it follows that B is an object behind the plane of A. A process similar to reasoning must occur in arriving at the depth interpretation. If some agency of mind has available to it the sensory information reaching the two eyes, and if it "knows" in which

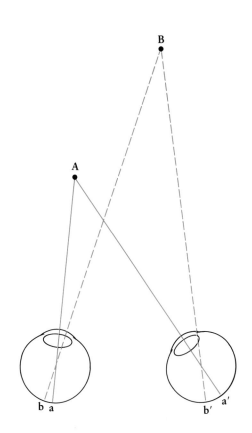

A simple display of two lines located at differing distances, shown in cross-section. The line that is not fixated by the two eyes, B, will fall on noncorresponding retinal loci. The perceptual system has no difficulty "deciding" that images b and b' correspond and represent the same object in the world.

eye each retinal stimulus originates, it can compute depth. A process of this kind would render understandable stereoscopic depth constancy. For example, if the perceptual system "knows" about diminished disparity as a function of distance, it can take distance into account in inferring the magnitude of depth.

Oculomotor Cues

In principle, it should be easy to determine if accommodation alone is a cue to the perception of depth. If you close one eye and view a solitary, unfamiliar, luminous object in a dark room with your head held still, the shape of the lens will automatically adjust itself for maximum sharpness of the image, based on the object's distance. Such a method would test the use of lens accommodation as a cue to *absolute* distance; the information about distance would have to derive ultimately from the altered state of the ciliary muscles in the eye that governs the shape of the lens. To test the value of lens accommodation in gauging *relative* distance or depth, we need only add several more objects, at varying distances, in the same dark room. As the eye accommodates for one object's distance, the images of the other objects will be blurred; the blurriness would presumably serve as a cue that those objects are not in the same plane as the one fixated. In this case, the information would come from the differential sharpness or blur of several simultaneously registered retinal images.

Accommodation of the lens turns out to be quite effective—as far as it goes. But experiments show that it seems to be effective for only a short distance, up to a few feet. Beyond that, observers simply cannot discriminate between one distance and another by means of this factor. Whether an object is 5 feet away or 50 feet away, a person in a dark room looking through one eye is as likely to judge it to be 8 feet away as to judge it correctly. With several objects visible, provided the nearest is beyond a few feet, observers will typically report that all of them are equidistant. These results are not surprising when one considers that, beyond several feet, objects at differing distances will all be in relatively sharp focus. Therefore, accommodation changes are not so necessary at these far distances.

Although the dark-room experiment seems to be a pure test of the accommodation cue alone, it is not. There is a strong link between accommodation and convergence (the two eyes working together) that even this experiment cannot eliminate. When one eye is focusing on an object, the other eye "wants" to work with it by aiming at the same object. Experiments have shown that, when one eye changes accommodation from near to far or from far to near, the other eye, when occluded, will change its direction appropriately so that both eyes are converged on the same point in the scene. To test the efficacy of both oculomotor cues together, observers can be asked to view a single object in a dark room with both eyes. Under these conditions, when all the information about distance seems to derive only from convergence and accommodation, observers can judge distance with a reasonable degree of accuracy up to about 10 feet. That the oculomotor cues, operating together, are indeed effective is borne out by the fact that constancy of size is maintained within this distance under the same conditions.

What effect does convergence alone have in the perception of distance and depth? The best method of isolating this cue is to hold accommodation constant by using a mirror stereoscope and then to vary the degree of convergence. As the illustration at right shows, the researcher can vary the angle of convergence merely by changing the lateral position of the cards on which the "stereograms" appear. (In this case, the "stereograms" are identical pictures of a single object or figure presented to each eye, since we are not interested in retinal disparity.) Because only the angle—not the distance—at which the cards are viewed changes, the lenses remain the same shape—that is, accommodation remains unchanged. If the figure is luminous and is viewed in the dark, we would then seem to have isolated convergence as the only varying factor.

When observers have only the cue of convergence to go on, their reports about distance are quite inaccurate and inconsistent. If the convergence movement of their eyes is inward, which ought to create the impression that the figure is approaching, subjects are just as likely to say the figure is receding or is not changing distance at all as they are to say that it is approaching. However, reported changes in the figure's *size* vary quite predictably; with increased convergence, for example, the figure will always be seen to diminish in size.

These findings about size and distance may seem counterintuitive, but there is a logic to each of them. The findings for size are precisely what we should predict on the basis of Emmert's law, that the perceived size of an object of constant visual angle varies directly with perceived distance. If we assume for the moment that convergence is a cue to distance and the eyes converge more sharply, the object viewed will be interpreted as coming nearer. Since the visual angle is constant in this case (because the figure remains at one distance), and since distance is perceived to decrease, then, according to Emmert's law, perceived size must decrease. The opposite result obtains when the eyes diverge.

How can we possibly explain the inaccuracy of observers' reports about distance if, as I have just argued, the results for size are based on the assumption that the distance change *is* perceived appropriately? The answer, I believe, is similar to the one advanced in Chapter 2 to explain a paradox about the moon illusion: Observers perceive the horizon moon

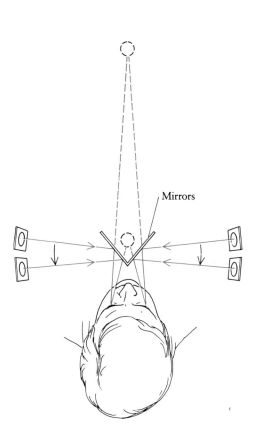

Method for varying convergence in order to study its effectiveness as a cue to distance.

to be larger because they perceive it to be *farther away*, yet precisely because they do perceive it to be larger, they conclude that it must appear *closer*, since they have learned that size varies with distance. In the convergence experiment, observers are also faced with two conflicting sources of information to which they must respond, and they also make a deduction about distance based not on a genuine perceptual cue but on apparent size. With an increase in convergence, the figure appears to shrink in size; observers are thus inclined to think, in response to the experimenter's question about distance change, "It is getting smaller, so it must be moving farther away." But if they use convergence as a direct cue to distance, they are inclined to give the opposite response. Information is available that the convergence of the eyes is increasing. Therefore, the perceptual system can infer that the eyes must be focusing on something that is coming closer. Observers thus face a conflict when it comes to responding about distance, but not when it comes to responding about size. That is why reports about size can sometimes be a more accurate, less-contaminated measure of the effectiveness of distance cues than are distance reports themselves. It is also why, in the convergence experiment, reports about size are more consistent than reports about distance.

Motion Cues

If oculomotor cues are only of limited value in perceiving distance, and if we can perceive depth fairly accurately with only one eye (thus ruling out retinal disparity as a necessary factor), where do we get our information about distance? Helmholtz in the nineteenth century and, primarily, Gibson in the twentieth argued that information derived from movement is the most important source.

The logic of motion parallax, the depth cue of movement discussed by Helmholtz, is simple enough. Whenever we move we can easily detect the shifting of objects' projections to the eye relative to one another. Each object in the field of view is seen in a particular direction. When we move, its direction changes. If the object is near, its direction changes considerably; if it is far, its direction changes very little, as the illustration on page 57 shows. If the object is to all intents and purposes infinitely far, such as a star in the sky, its direction does not change at all. Thus, the amount of change in the direction of a thing during our motion could be telling us how far away it is. Furthermore, when several things at differing distances are viewed, such as when we are speeding down a highway, the *difference* between their rates of change could inform us of their relative separations.

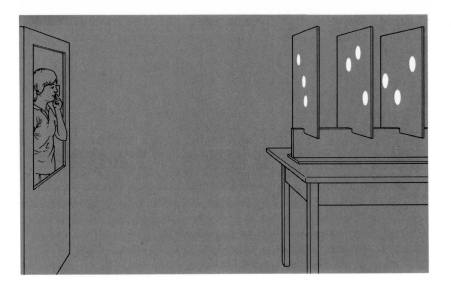

Arrangement for experiment on motion parallax. Subjects viewing the luminous circles with only one eye had no impression of depth, even when they moved their heads from side to side.

That motion parallax *could* be a valuable source of distance information does not mean that our perceptual apparatus actually makes use of it. Consider, for example, an experiment that Deborah Wheeler and I recently conducted. In a dark room, the observer viewed an array of luminous circles pasted on glass panes that were placed at differing distances, as shown above. To eliminate the pictorial cue of size, all the circles were drawn so that they would project images to the eye of equal size. To eliminate another pictorial cue, that of interposition, the circles were situated so that the observer could not see them overlap.

When subjects viewed the array with one eye and their heads held still, they reported what we should predict: that all the circles were in the same plane and of equal size. But even when the subjects moved their heads from side to side and could gather parallax information, by and large they still saw the circles as being in the same plane. The movement merely created the impression that circles in the same plane were shifting around in relation to one another. Only when the same observers were asked to view the array with their heads stationary but with both eyes open were they able to perceive correctly both the depth of the circles and their different sizes. Under these conditions, of course, retinal disparity and the oculomotor cues were at work, but motion parallax was not.

The results of this experiment, and those of some experiments by other investigators, including Gibson, suggest the radical conclusion that, while the perceptual system may "know" the rates of parallax change, motion parallax does not by itself seem to be a cue to distance or depth. This conclusion is at odds with a still commonly held belief, as the inclusion of motion parallax as an important cue in some textbooks. But, I hasten to add that motion parallax is defined here as simply the differing rate of change in the direction of objects at differing distances from the observer as a function of the observer's motion (or of the display's motion). Thus, even two points at different distances but at eye level would qualify as a motion-parallax paradigm when the observer moves sideways.

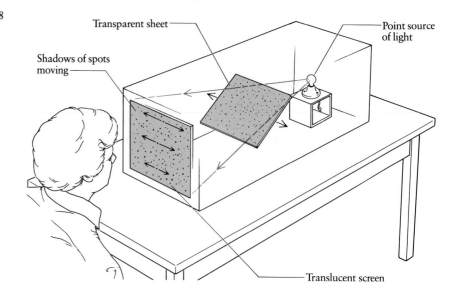

Arrangement for motion-perspective experiment. Observers viewing the moving shadows of the paint droplets on the screen were able to perceive that the plane was slanted.

In some situations, however, our motion or that of objects does seem to lead to the perception of depth. In contrast to viewing luminous circles that appear suspended in space, suppose, for example, that we see the elements in a plane change direction as we move. If we are watching the landscape pass by from a rapidly moving car, for instance, we see the elements of the texture of the ground, be they stalks of wheat or pebbles on a beach, change their direction as a function of their distance. Our motion creates a gradient of change in the direction of objects, with nearby elements changing rapidly and distant ones changing hardly at all. Gibson called the information we gather from such moving perception of elements in a plane *motion perspective*, because it is analogous to perspective information in stationary scenes, and he argued that it is a central factor in our perception of depth.

Eleanor and James Gibson and their associates performed experiments that at least partially bear out his contention. In one experiment, they spattered paint on a transparent sheet and, as can be seen in the illustration above, slanted the sheet away from the vertical plane. A small light was used to cast shadows of the paint droplets on a translucent vertical screen in front of the transparent sheet. When the sheet was moved back and forth, the shadows of the droplets moved back and forth over the screen. Because of the slant of the sheet, a gradient of motion velocity was created from the bottom to the top of the screen, with the shadows at the top of the screen moving more rapidly than those at the bottom. The investigators reasoned that, since the screen was actually vertical and flat, subjects looking at the moving shadows of the droplets on the screen would be able to perceive the slant of the sheet correctly only if motion perspective is a source of depth information.

In the experiment, subjects did perceive a slanted plane (although the slant they perceived was not as great as the actual slant), and they perceived the depth much more accurately when the sheet moved than when it was stationary. Notice that in this experiment it is the display that

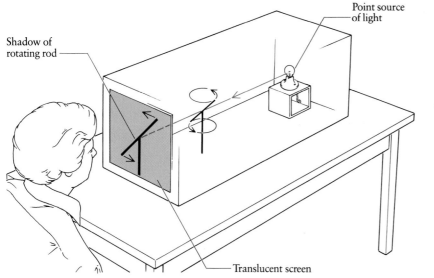

Shadow of
rotating rod

Point source
of light

69

Translucent screen

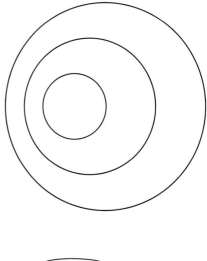

Arrangement for experiment on the kinetic depth effect. The subject views the shadow cast on the screen by the tilted rod rotating about its vertical axis. An alternate procedure is to have the subject view with one eye the rotating object itself.

moves, not the observer. It was presumed, though, that the exact same kind of information would be available were the display to be stationary and the observer to move, as is more typically the case in daily life.

Motion can create the impression of depth in other ways as well. For example, the shadow cast on a screen by the thin, tilted rod attached to a wire stem that is shown in the illustration above will appear to observers to be in a frontal plane, but, if the object is rotated, observers will perceive the pattern of cast shadows as an object rotating in the third dimension. When it is rotated, observers perceive veridically that the object is a rigid thing tilted in the third dimension rather than a thing changing in length and tilt in a frontal plane. Hans Wallach and his associates, who first conducted experiments along these lines, termed this phenomenon the *kinetic depth effect*. Again, we would expect the same outcome were the observer to circle the wire object from a distance of several feet, viewing its changing projection with one eye closed. Were the observer to remain stationary, the object would probably appear to be in a frontal plane because all other cues would be eliminated.

Perhaps the most striking example of depth achieved through motion, however, is the *stereokinetic effect*, first described in 1924 by C. L. Musatti. If the pattern on the disk shown at right is rotated about its center, the rotation soon leads to a powerful illusion of depth. If you trace the pattern and place it on a turntable, you will see either a truncated cone sticking out or a tunnel-like structure receding inward. Although the method of generating this effect (namely, rotating a patterned disk) differs from that of generating the kinetic depth effect (namely, casting shadows of rotating wire figures), both may be examples of the same phenomenon. What they have in common is the production of perceptual depth from rotating displays that yield a transformation in the retinal image of the component parts of the object.

Why do these motion-perspective, kinetic, and stereokinetic depth effects occur when it seems that motion parallax is not a useful depth cue?

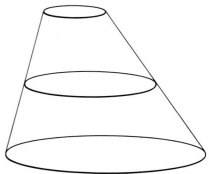

(Top) A pattern used in creating the stereokinetic effect. (Bottom) Side view of the perceived three-dimensional object when the pattern is rotated about its center.

Aren't these effects examples of motion parallax, the different rates at which objects or regions of an object change direction as a function of their differing distances from the observer?

The answers to these questions are still in dispute. Gibson argued that the texture of a plane that yields motion perspective provides richer, more naturalistic information than do laboratory environments that consist of such artificial elements as one or more spots floating in space. Wallach argued that in kinetic depth displays, in contrast to simple examples of motion parallax, not only do points within the object shift in direction as the object moves but the contours of the object simultaneously change in orientation and length. He believes it is this coupling of length change and orientation change that is crucial to the perception of depth generated by motion.

My own speculation is somewhat different. The transforming retinal image created by motion is ambiguous and thus poses a problem for the perceptual system: What outer arrangement of things or events can be inferred to have produced it? In the motion-parallax experiment, for example, the stimulus change when subjects moved their heads *could* be accounted for by, among other possibilities, circles in the same plane, moving at different rates of speed.

When, prior to motion, observers are able to organize the display into a unified structure, however, they can easily recognize the transforming pattern as a perspective change. The tendency to relate elements that are at differing distances from the observer to one another is, I believe, the key to understanding motion as a cue to depth. The moment a pattern is conceived of as the differing projections over time of some external structure, the solution that it is three-dimensional or oriented in the third dimension becomes likely. Thus, for example, the stereokinetic effect occurs because we organize the eccentric circles with the outer circle as parts of a unified whole, and this enables us to regard the transformation as successively different projections of the whole to the eye. Motion perspective is effective in producing a depth effect when we recognize that the texture elements are related to one another as part of one plane, even before motion is introduced. By contrast, simple parallax by itself is not effective in producing an impression of depth because the perceptual system treats the array as a mere collection of unrelated elements. Moreover, the circles in the experiment described that are in the same plane tend to be grouped together because they will seem to move at the same speed. This grouping may actually interfere with achieving the depth solution.

From this point of view, depth perception is not an inevitable solution to the problem posed by the transforming stimulus, but it is the preferred one. Why it is preferred we do not know. Although progress has been made in isolating the cues that govern our perception of the third dimension, little is known about what happens inside the head once the stimulus information that constitutes a cue is registered on the retina. Experiments designed to investigate this issue suggest that the answer may lie in some preference of the mind for solutions that are analogous to the principle of parsimony in science. Consider further the example given of the kinetic depth effect. Why does the transforming image yield an impression of a rod rotating in depth rather than simply an object simultaneously changing length and orientation? The answer could be that, for a perceptual system that faces a situation of ambiguity and "knows" about perspective foreshortening, the solution of a rigid object rotating in the third dimension is the one that most elegantly accounts for the facts. Later in this chapter, we will see a similar issue arise with regard to the pictorial cues.

The Pictorial Cues

For hundreds (in some instances, thousands) of years, artists have been able to create vivid impressions of depth on two-dimensional surfaces by using perspective, shading, and other methods. If the pictorial cues were only important in looking at paintings or photographs, they would of course be of only limited importance in understanding depth perception in daily life. But the pictorial cues do yield significant information about the relative, if not the absolute, distances among things that allows us to perceive depth in the real world. In fact, pictures can be so realistic precisely because artists have used the tricks of pictorial cues in creating images nearly identical to those yielded by the actual scene. Just how important these factors must be was evident in the thought experiment described earlier. If we view a scene with one eye and head held stationary, it will often appear almost as vividly three-dimensional as when we view it binocularly and move about. Yet, as can now be appreciated, in such an experiment all *but* the pictorial cues have been more or less eliminated.

What, then, are these pictorial cues that Leonardo and many others before and since have routinely used so effectively in drawings and paintings, and how do they contribute to depth perception in daily life? The cues fall into several groupings—interposition, shadow, perspective, and familiar size.

INTERPOSITION   In the painting shown on the following page, the child in the foreground partially covers, or occludes, the woman behind her, and she in turn partially occludes the man behind her, and so forth.

Gabriele Münter's Boating *(1910) illustrates the
effectiveness of interposition in creating an
impression of depth.*

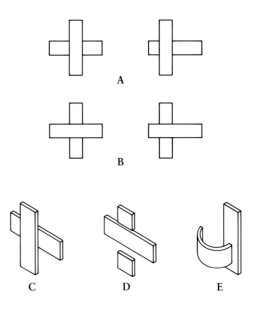

The partial covering of one object by another, or interposition, in pictures leads to a definite impression that one object is farther away than another, as artists have known for centuries. A moment's reflection makes clear that it will also do so in a real scene.

The depth implied by interposition is logically only the thickness of the occluding object. Yet interposition is a powerful cue to depth, experiments show. In stereogram *A* shown at right, retinal disparity leads to the perception of a vertical bar in front of a horizontal bar, as does the interposition pattern. But suppose instead the overlap pattern leads to the impression that the horizontal bar is closer, even though disparity alone would lead to the opposite effect. In such situations, interposition, a mere pictorial cue, usually dominates stereopsis, considered by many to be *the* physiological cue par excellence, probably innately determined and present in many animal species. (Of course there are individual differences in the way such cue-conflict experiments are resolved, so that some observers may see an incomplete, broken vertical bar in front in the figure.)

As a relation of objects in the world, interposition is simple enough to grasp, but, as a perceptual phenomenon, it is difficult to explain. The central problem can be seen by trying the following experiment. Cut out two cardboard objects, a circle and a rectangle. Cut a small notch in the circle into which the corner of the rectangle can fit, as shown in the illustration below. Then align the two objects as shown, with the rectangle

A. Stereogram in which retinal disparity and interposition both indicate that the vertical bar is in front of the horizontal bar (solution C). B. Stereogram in which disparity indicates that the vertical bar is in front whereas interposition indicates that the horizontal bar is in front. Interposition usually dominates, but other perceptual solutions are possible, such as seeing two unconnected vertical segments floating in front of the horizontal bar (D) or seeing the horizontal bar curved around in depth (E).

The cue of interposition leads to the illusion that the rectangle is in front of and partially occluding the circle when the objects are viewed from a particular position.

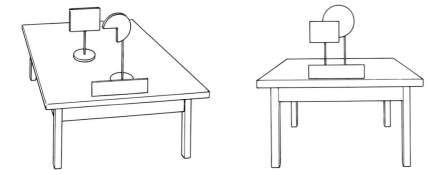

(Top) Mt. Rushmore with shadows visible. Shadow, particularly attached shadow, would seem to be the major determinant of perceived depth for distant objects.
(Bottom) When the shadow contrast is diminished, the faces appear relatively flat and indistinct.

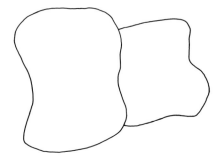

Unfamiliar shapes. We tend to see one of these shapes in front of the other even when familiarity offers no clue that one object is incomplete. It is believed that the nature of the junction of the contours of the two closed regions is the critical factor in seeing the objects interposed.

behind the circle. When you view the objects with one eye from the appropriate vantage point, it will seem that the rectangle is occluding the circle and you will receive the impression that the rectangle is *nearer*. But note that the stimulus your eye receives is ambiguous. You could just as easily perceive the arrangement veridically (as it is) as perceive it as two objects in the same plane fitted together like a jigsaw puzzle. The conclusion that the interposition depth interpretation is preferred therefore seems warranted.

How does the mind "know" that one object is occluded by the other rather than that both objects are in the same plane? The obvious answer is that we are familiar with the shapes of things and thus we can tell when they are incomplete. There is undoubtedly some truth in this answer. But even when viewing unfamiliar shapes, such as those that appear at left, we tend to see one shape in front of another. How can we know that such objects are incomplete? The answer to this question is in dispute, although, as we shall see in Chapter 5, some light can be shed on it by an understanding of how we perceive form.

SHADOW   The pictorial cue based on shading and shadow is also a critical factor in depth perception, both in pictures and in everyday life. Some of the most striking trompe l'oeil illusions are based on it, such as the impression we often have that the curtains on a stage are real when they are only paintings.

Consider a sculpture of uniform color, such as the one cut into Mt. Rushmore. The faces of the presidents appear three-dimensional even at distances at which all other cues must surely be ineffectual. Clearly it is the play of light and shadow that creates the veridical perception here. Primarily responsible is the shading that results from the depth within the object itself, referred to as *attached shadows*, or *chiaroscuro*, although *cast shadows*—the shadows that fall on surrounding surfaces—may also play a role.

Of the two types of shadow, attached shadow is the more important in creating an impression of depth. Although we often notice cast shadows, there is as yet little experimental evidence of their effectiveness as a depth cue. What evidence there is suggests that cast shadow is a cue to depth only in that it helps us to mentally construct a plane that might not otherwise be perceived.

The ubiquity and importance of shadow in depth perception can be gathered by simply looking around the room in which you are now sitting or by considering the effect of shade and shadow in the photographs and paintings in this book. There is a curious ambiguity about the meaning of shading, however. A depression and an elevation in a surface will both be shaded on one side, since the light comes predominantly from a particular direction. How, then, can we tell the difference? If we are aware of the direction from which the illumination comes as we look at the shaded region, we could, in principle, infer whether the region was elevated (e.g., a mound, bump, or bas relief) or depressed (e.g., a concave hollow, hole, or intaglio). If it were a mound, the shading would be on the side opposite to the source of light, whereas, if it were a hollow, the shading would be on the same side.

But what do we perceive when we do not know the direction of the source of light, as often we do not, particularly when viewing pictures? Although the stimulus is ambiguous, we tend to perceive a region immediately as elevated or depressed. In the left-hand photograph that appears at the top of the next page, we tend to see recessed regions, whereas in the right-hand photograph we tend to see mounds, even though the second photograph is simply the first one turned upside down. (This is another example in which perception is not affected by conscious knowledge.) Apparently, then, the perceptual system, in the absence of contradictory information, makes the assumption that the light is coming from above.

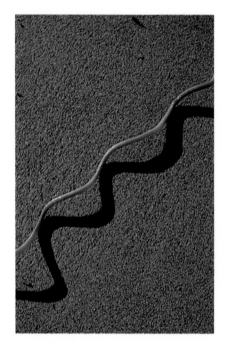

The shadow cast by a strand of kelp on the surface beneath it.

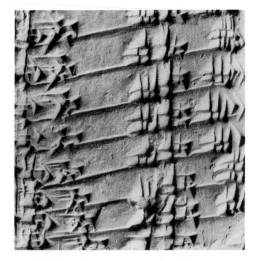 

The location of shadow determines whether the regions producing it are perceived as elevations or as indentations. The picture of the Babylonian cuneiform tablet on the right is simply the picture on the left inverted.

Thus we perceive elevated regions when the shadow is at the bottom and depressed regions when the shadow is at the top. Because light in the natural environment in which *Homo sapiens* evolved does come from above (from the sun or moon), it is plausible to believe that such an "assumption" has come to be innately built into our perceptual functioning. But, by the same token, because we live in a world in which light almost always comes from above, including artificial light in the environments we build, it is also possible that we have learned how the location of shadows signifies depressions or elevations. Later in the chapter, I will describe an experiment that was aimed at deciding between these two alternatives.

PERSPECTIVE   Of all the pictorial cues, perspective—the characteristics of the projection of a scene onto the retina (or onto a two-dimensional plane) as a function of the depth of the scene—is best known. Perspective includes more than linear perspective, the aspect of perspective that is perhaps most familiar. *Linear perspective* refers simply to the fact that parallel lines that recede into the third dimension project to the eye as converging lines. Another aspect of perspective is *size perspective*, which refers to the fact that objects of equal size at varying distances project images whose visual angles are inversely proportional to their distance. Gibson was referring to a special case of size perspective when he introduced the term *texture-density gradient*. Still another aspect of

In Canaletto's Campo San Zanipolo, Venice *(c. 1740), linear perspective, size perspective, foreshortening, shadow, and interposition are all cues to the scene's depth.*

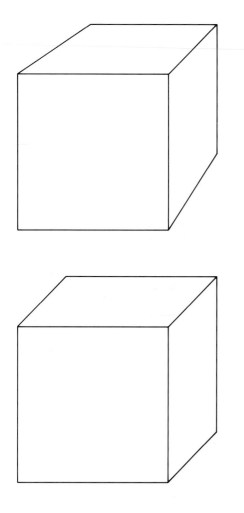

The cubes appear to be three-dimensional, whether they are drawn with or without linear perspective.

perspective is *foreshortening*—the difference in the projection of equal distances in the third dimension, such as the separations between the *ties* of a railroad track viewed head-on.

Leonardo and other Renaissance painters also made use of two other aspects of perspective: *detail perspective*—the loss of visible detail of very distant objects because of limitations of visual acuity—and *aerial perspective*—the tendency of distant objects to become tinged with blue because of impurities in the atmosphere. Although paintings may gain in realism by taking these factors into account, no one to my knowledge has ever shown experimentally that detail perspective and aerial perspective, in isolation, affect distance perception.

Perspective is a powerful force in creating the impression of depth, even when other cues work against it. A luminous trapezoid viewed in a frontal plane, for example, when seen with one eye in a dark room will look like a rectangle at a slant. Even when such a figure is viewed with both eyes, which provides information from stereopsis, perspective strongly affects what is perceived, as Barbara Gillam, then at the Australian National University, and William Epstein and his associates at the University of Wisconsin have shown. Moreover, Epstein has demonstrated that continued viewing of the trapezoid with both eyes in such a conflict-of-cues experiment will result in an adaptive recalibration of retinal disparity. Ordinarily, retinal disparity and perspective yield congruent information, such as, for example, that a rectangle is slanted back from the frontal plane by 30 degrees. In the experiment, however, the two eyes are made to provide discrepant information. Apparently, the subjects learn to associate unconsciously a given disparity with some new depth, not the depth the disparity signified before, because, in a subsequent test for depth based on disparity using a simple line figure, the subjects saw depth under conditions of zero disparity and, conversely, no depth when some actual disparity was present. Thus, in only minutes, the pictorial cue of linear perspective was sufficiently potent to reeducate the mind about stereopsis.

Despite the great influence of perspective, it does not always appear to be necessary to create a sense of pictorial depth. For example, the drawing of a cube looks three-dimensional even when linear perspective is eliminated. The edges of the receding sides of the lower cube shown at left are drawn parallel, not converging.

Some theorists, notably Gibson, have argued that at the core of our perception of the third dimension is our impression of plane surfaces such as the ground rather than our impression of objects separated from one another in empty space. Of all the cues we know about, only perspective, it seems, could provide direct information about planes and their

When this picture goes unrecognized, it is not perceived as a receding ground plane. As a result, if equally sized objects were placed at the extreme left and the extreme right of the picture, they would tend to look equal in size. When the picture is tilted 90 degrees clockwise and recognized, a receding plane is perceived, and the upper object would look larger than the lower one.

orientation with respect to us. Since we achieve quite veridical impressions of such planes as the ground without ourselves being in motion, we can assume that, whatever the contribution of motion perspective, it is not a *necessary* factor. Linear perspective and foreshortening can hardly be necessary factors because they are only present in the case of certain regular configurations, such as railroad tracks, roads, buildings, and the like. Of course, the image projected to the eye by every surface receding in depth—for example, from the ground or from a wall—will be foreshortened. But that in itself can hardly be a cue. This leaves size perspective and, in particular, texture gradients that contain objects or texture the average size of which is about the same throughout.

Should we assume then that a texture gradient, such as the ground,

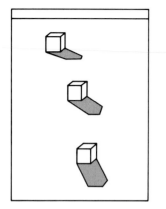

Arrangement without texture that suffices to create an impression of a receding surface with cubes resting on it. As a consequence of this impression, subjects perceive the cube farthest in the background as larger than the one in the foreground.

A seascape, painted without perspective or any other known pictorial cue, still looks like a body of water receding into the third dimension.

leads directly to the perception of a receding plane? There is reason to question such an assumption. Recognition of what we are looking at is often important in perception of a receding plane. For example, the photograph on the preceding page may look to many viewers more like a two-dimensional abstraction than the grassy field that it is, tilted 90 degrees counterclockwise. My associates and I have shown in an experiment that ignorance of the fact that the picture is disoriented seems to prevent recognition, which, in turn, seems to prevent the appropriate depth perception. Yet, if a gradient of texture density is a *direct* cue to depth, why should recognition matter?

Nor does the absence of a texture gradient eliminate the perception of receding planes. No texture or size gradient is present in some scenes we encounter, such as a field covered with snow or ice and, possibly, a desert vista in which the texture is too fine to be detected and where few objects are on the ground. We nonetheless perceive the ground plane correctly in these instances. We have tested this experimentally by presenting subjects with a plane *without* texture. This was achieved by a display such as the one illustrated at left, above, in which the only depth information available consisted of a few cubes of equal visual angle and the shadows they cast on a surface plus the presence of a horizon line. This stimulus display sufficed to create the impression of a receding table-top surface and, as a result, to yield an impression that the most distant cube was larger than the nearest one. Similarly, texture may be present, but even if it is uniform, as in the picture of the seascape at left below—in other words, a zero gradient—it is still compatible with an impression of a receding plane, in this case a body of water.

All of these facts suggest that perceived depth, including that of plane surfaces, is not so much the direct result of certain specifiable stimulus cues as it is a mental construction. Cast shadows or objects such as trees and roads suggest to the mind a plane on which objects are resting. The plane is thus constructed to encompass these objects. Cues such as size and linear perspective enhance the construction or make it more vivid.

FAMILIAR SIZE   If we are familiar with an object's typical size, our memory of its visual angle at varying distances could allow us to estimate its distance because visual angle and distance are directly related. A classic experiment by William Ittelson at Princeton University demonstrated the possible efficacy of size cues in depth perception. Subjects were seated in a dark room and were asked to look at playing cards with one eye. When a card twice the size of a normal playing card was presented, observers tended to say it was half its actual distance away. When they viewed a card one-half the size of a normal playing card, they tended to judge its distance to be twice as great as its distance actually was. In a variation of this experiment, subjects are shown a more ambiguous object, such as a white sphere. If they are told it is a Ping-Pong ball, they judge it to be nearer than if they are told it is a tennis ball. These effects depend upon the observer's stored knowledge of the visual angle subtended by various objective sizes at different distances—for example, that a 3-inch object subtends a particular visual angle at a particular distance.

Despite these results, the familiar-size cue may be more an intellectual judgment than a genuine perceptual cue to distance. One can figure out that a playing card that looms so large in one's field of view must be rather near. But that does not necessarily mean that it is *perceived* as near. Furthermore, it is unlikely that familiar size is a distance cue of much importance in daily life, when other cues are available. Experiments on this question are inconclusive. If we view an object of abnormal size under natural conditions, such as a dollhouse among a row of suburban homes, for example, we immediately detect its abnormality rather than reevaluate its distance or that of nearby homes.

Many textbooks also mention "height in the field" as a pictorial cue, but the argument used to support it is circular. Ordinarily, the farther away an object is, the higher will be its image in a picture or its projection to the eye. But this is true only for objects that rest on the ground, so that "height" could be a cue to depth only if the observer already perceived a ground plane, which, by definition, recedes into the distance. Even if the argument were not circular, "height in the field" would be an ambiguous cue to depth because the *lower* the location of an object is in a plane overhead, such as a cloudy sky or ceiling, the farther away it is.

All Cues Combined

Now that we have considered each possible cue to depth separately, we can ask the question of how the cues might work collectively in order to yield perception of the third dimension in daily life. We do not know the answer to this question. We can only surmise on the basis of logical considerations and general observations. For example, it is plausible to infer that the availability of several cues would lead to more reliable and accurate perception than just the availability of a single cue. Thus it is probable that the joint action of the oculomotor cues and stereopsis is quite effective at relatively near distances and more so than any one of these in isolation from the others. It is probable that when *all* known pictorial cues are present in a scene (or picture) the depth effect is stronger than when only one such cue is present. Stereograms based on photographs containing pictorial cues are more effective than those

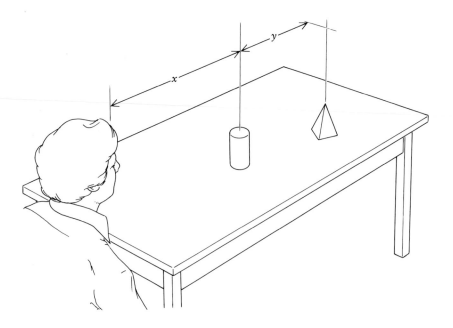

Interaction of cues. The perceptual system may infer the distance to the pyramid from convergence information about the cylinder's distance and retinal disparity information about the depth between the cylinder and the pyramid.

based only on geometrical line drawings. Moving pictures add depth to "frozen" static displays undoubtedly by virtue of the kinetic depth effect and motion-perspective effects they produce. Stereo movies approach the depth achieved under natural conditions in daily life.

But more interesting is the likelihood of *interaction* among cues. Interaction in science means that a combination of two factors produces an outcome (positive or negative) that neither alone nor the mere sum of the two would yield. As noted earlier, some kinds of information are absolute, referring to the distance of an object from us; other kinds of information are relative, referring to the depth between objects. One serious problem not yet considered is that few cues are suitable for giving us absolute distance information. Only convergence, accommodation, and familiar size qualify. For one reason or another already discussed, the second and third of these are questionable, thus leaving only convergence. But it seems unlikely that the angle at which the eyes converge on one object—which is potential information only about *its* distance and only for limited distances at that—could be the source of the simultaneous impression we typically seem to have of the distances from us of all things in the scene. But convergence in interaction with stereopsis or with pictorial cues could yield such an impression. The logic is this: If, in the figure above, the cylinder appears to be X distance from us because of the cue of convergence, and if the pyramid appears to be Y distance behind the cylinder because of the cue of stereopsis, it follows that the pyramid is $X + Y$ distance from us. Similar interactions may occur between convergence and pictorial information. Thus, if pictorial information leads to a perceptual scene that is vividly three-dimensional and convergence anchors any single point in it to a definite distance from us, then, ipso facto, the whole scene takes on the appropriate set of absolute distances. But without such absolute distance, the display lacks realism.

The Origin of Depth Perception

Let us assume that the combination or joint utilization of all the factors considered in this chapter accounts for our perception of the third dimension. Shall we assume further that the cues are innately given indicators of distance and depth that have come down to us and other animals through evolution? Obviously, organisms must be able to detect distance with some degree of accuracy in order to survive; thus, the emergence of mechanisms or stimulus "signs" that would yield veridical depth perception would confer an evolutionary advantage.

Alternatively, we could learn to utilize the cues to distance and depth in infancy or early childhood, and it could be that, at birth, we do not perceive (or do not perceive very accurately) the distance of things from us or from each other. It is not crucial for survival that we are capable of veridical distance and depth perception at the outset, the argument goes, because, in species such as *Homo sapiens* (or, more generally, in such orders as Primates), the young are nurtured and protected for a considerable period of time. In fact it can be argued that the great capacity for learning in various species is one of nature's ways of enhancing the probability of survival.

Long before psychology became a science, philosophers debated this issue. As discussed in Chapter 1, Berkeley took the position that a two-dimensional retina was logically incapable of directly yielding depth perception because it could receive only a two-dimensional image. We must learn to gauge the distance of things by a process of association. Accommodation and convergence are cues that ultimately become reliable signs of distance because we reach for or move toward things and this teaches us how to interpret these signs. Others emphasized inborn characteristics of mind such as the predisposition to locate things in three-dimensional space. If we did not by nature tend to organize the perceptual world spatially, so the argument goes, how could we ever learn about depth localization?

In trying to resolve this issue by experimentation, modern psychologists encounter the same problems they do in attempting to discover the origins of constancy. Newborn animals, human or otherwise, can only "tell" us what they perceive through performance on behavioral tests of learning, of which very immature organisms are usually not capable, while rearing animals without vision until they are mature enough to test leads to severe deterioration of the visual nervous system and prevention of normal maturation.

Eleanor Gibson and Richard Walk at Cornell University invented an ingenious solution to these problems by making use of the innate fear of height. One might assume that even a newly born organism would show some fear of height, which is simply distance in a downward direction, if

The "visual cliff" used to test distance per-
ception in animals and infants.

it could perceive that height. The investigators placed the animal on an opaque strip in the middle of a large sheet of glass. This strip, seen in the photograph above, becomes a "visual cliff." On one side, there is a deep visual drop to the surface; on the other side, there is an opaque surface directly underneath, signifying no depth at all. The glass on both sides of the strip is from the same pane, equal in support and physical texture, but the view through the glass is quite different on the two sides. When placed on the center strip, is the subject equally likely to move off it to either side (implying no depth perception or no fear of height), or is it more likely to move off only to the "shallow" side?

A wide variety of species tested—chicks, infant rats, kittens, puppies, lambs, kids, pigs, snow leopard cubs, monkeys, and human infants— showed a strong preference for the shallow side. For the most part, these animals were very reluctant to go to the deep side of the "cliff." Moreover, three-day-old infant monkeys and very young human infants showed signs of distress when placed directly on the glass over the deep side. Thus, the experiment resolves the long-standing controversy: Distance perception is present from the very beginning of an organism's life.

Which cues enabled the animals tested to perceive distance? Subsequent experiments suggest, by a process of elimination, that motion parallax is the critical factor. Yet the study of motion parallax described earlier indicates that this factor is ineffectual among adult subjects. Therefore, until direct tests of the role of parallax on the visual cliff are made, it is best that this question remain open.

Motion of a different kind definitely does appear to be an important source of information about distance very early in an animal's life, many studies consistently show. The experiments on the alarm reactions of infants to the "looming effect" that were discussed in Chapter 2 suggest that there is an innate preference on the part of the perceptual system to interpret expanding and contracting retinal images of an object as changes in the object's distance rather than changes in its size.

Although these studies suggest that the capacity to perceive depth is innate, this does not mean that learning plays no role in the development of depth perception. We have already seen that the perceptual system is capable of a kind of learning: after a short period of exposure to conflicting cues (the trapezoid that looks like a rectangle at a slant vs. stereopsis), observers recalibrated the depth implied by a given degree of retinal disparity. Experiments in which observers view the world through prisms, such as one conducted by Arien Mack and Deanna Chitayat at the New School for Social Research, have yielded similar results. They had their subjects wear prisms over each eye that tilted the images slightly in opposite directions. As a consequence, a vertical rod appeared to be sloping slightly toward the observer. But after a period during which the observer walked around while wearing the prisms, this distorting effect wore off. When the prisms were removed, vertical lines in the scene for which there was no disparity now gave the impression that they were sloping away from the observer. Thus, even information provided by retinal disparity, for which there is an innate physiological basis, seems to be subject to learned modification.

Many students of perception believe that experience plays a major role in the genesis of depth perception in the case of the pictorial cues. Consider a factor such as linear perspective—the converging projection of parallel contours receding into the distance. This kind of pattern is far more prevalent in the constructed environment of modern society than it is in the more natural environment in which *Homo sapiens* evolved. Therefore it is not likely that linear perspective would have evolved as an innate sign of depth.

But how would we have learned to perceive depth on the basis of linear perspective? Simply by moving around in the world and discovering that what had appeared to be converging lines in a frontal plane are actually receding parallel lines? This would assume that knowledge about the world can affect our perceptions of it, which, as we have seen, is contrary to the nature of perception. A better explanation is the following. When, as children, we first view parallel lines in depth and receive the image of converging lines, we also have available other sensory information about depth from cues such as retinal disparity, convergence, and accommodation. These physiological cues produce veridical perception of the parallel lines. At this point, linear perspective is not functioning as a cue. But it is present. Therefore, we can associate the converging pattern with parallel lines in depth. Because of this association, later on, the converging pattern by itself can evoke the interpretation of parallel lines in depth. It thus would have become a learned cue.

Hans Wallach and his associates at Swarthmore College showed just such a learning process at work in depth perception, although not with respect to linear perspective. In one experiment, they used the simple wire object, the projection of which is shown at left, selected so as not to convey any impression of three-dimensionality at the outset. Subjects were first shown a shadow pattern of such a wire object cast on a screen, which they perceived as two-dimensional. Then the investigators set the wire object in motion, creating a kinetic depth effect in which the transforming shadow pattern yielded a three-dimensional impression. Finally, the subjects viewed the shadow pattern when it was again stationary. They now perceived it to be three-dimensional. Presumably, therefore, observers learned that this two-dimensional pattern signified a three-dimensional object and they perceived it accordingly.

Although most pictorial cues may be learned, responsiveness to the cue of cast shadow appears to be innate, at least in chickens. Wayne Hershberger at Northern Illinois University trained two groups of chicks, one group to peck at mounds rather than at depressions, and the other group the reverse, by rewarding them with food when they made the correct choice. The mounds and depressions were devoid of any shadows; thus, the correct perception of their depth depended entirely upon binocular or motion cues. Following this learning, the chicks were presented with pictures of mounds or depressions in which shadow was the only cue. If a chick had learned to peck at mounds, it should peck at the photograph it perceived as a mound—presumably the photograph with shadow at the bottom, which would look like a mound to us. If neither photograph looked more like a mound than the other, the chick should peck randomly or not peck at the pictures at all.

The shadow cast by this wire object will appear two-dimensional unless observers have previously been exposed to its stimulus pattern when other cues caused it to appear three-dimensional.

The chicks seemed to perceive the photographs exactly as we would. Those trained to peck at mounds pecked at the photograph with the shadow at the bottom. Those trained to peck at depressions pecked at the photograph with the shadow at the top. Thus, at least one pictorial cue is effective in an animal. Rarely do animals lower than primates react to pictures, probably because they respond directly to the picture as a two-dimensional surface rather than to what the contours on the surface represent symbolically. But what is most astounding about these results is that half of the chicks in each group were raised from the time of hatching in cages where the light always came from below. Thus, for these chicks, if any learning about the significance of shadow occurred, it would be the opposite of what would be learned under natural conditions. But whether the chicks were reared with light from above or from below, the result was the same. Shadow at the top cued depressions, and shadow at the bottom cued elevations. If there are no flaws to be found in this experiment and the findings can be confirmed, we must conclude that cast shadow as a cue to depth is innate, not learned.

If the belief that a pictorial cue is an innate stimulus sign of depth is one theory and that it is a learned sign of depth is another, there is a third alternative, initially suggested by the Gestalt psychologists. In this view, the preference for the depth "solution" over the two-dimensional "solution" of what a pictorial stimulus pattern represents in the world is based on a tendency of the mind to prefer simplicity.

Suppose, for example, that we are looking at the upper pattern shown at right, referred to as the Necker cube. We perceive it as three-dimensional. Why do we not perceive it as a two-dimensional arrangement of lines instead? The Gestalt answer is that the two-dimensional percept is a much more complex structure than the three-dimensional percept. A regular cube is quite simple: All the faces are equal, as are all the angles, opposite sides are parallel, and so forth. Now consider the pattern shown below the Necker cube. It tends to appear spontaneously as two-dimensional. Yet, if examined carefully, it can be seen to represent a regular cube tipped up on an edge, with the topmost point in the figure representing the top rear corner of the cube. For such a pattern, the two-dimensional percept is as "simple" as that of a cube: a hexagon with symmetrically placed straight lines inside it. Thus, the advantage of seeing it as a three-dimensional percept has disappeared.

This theory is a controversial one and may seem farfetched, but it has great predictive power. For example, the interposition cue can be interpreted along these lines. Seeing "two rectangles" in the illustration on the following page is simpler than seeing a rectangle nestled against an L-shaped figure because a rectangle is more regular than an L-shape and

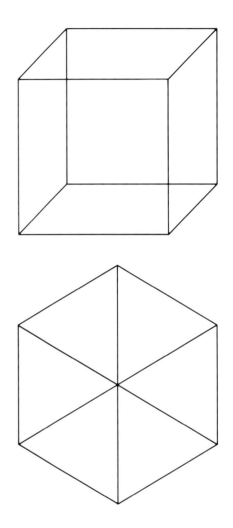

(Top) The Necker cube. (Bottom) The regular and symmetrical projection of the same cube when viewed from a particular vantage point.

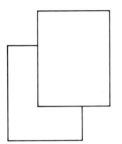

We tend to see these shapes as two rectangles, one behind the other, although we could just as well see a rectangle and an L in the same plane.

because both figures are then alike. In the cue of size perspective, the outcome is that the objects all become equal in size rather than different. In the case of the kinetic depth effect, one might say that a rigid object rotating in depth is a simpler outcome than an object transforming in length and orientation within a plane.

The simplicity-preference theory is not without its weaknesses, however. One weakness is that it offers no rigorous definition of what is simple in perception. "Two rectangles" is perhaps intuitively simpler than "a rectangle and an L," but, by the same token, the one plane entailed by the latter would seem simpler than the two planes entailed by the former. In response to this criticism, Julian Hochberg and others have attempted to define simplicity more objectively, in terms compatible with modern information theory. They argue that simplicity can be defined as the minimum information necessary to describe, or encode, a percept. Given an ambiguous pattern, for example, we tend to perceive the alternative that can be specified with the least information. Regular and symmetrical structures are redundant and thus can be encoded more efficiently. These investigators have shown that it is indeed possible to specify alternative percepts in objective terms.

A second weakness of the theory is that the preferred perception does not always seem to support the theory's predictions. In the case of interposition of unfamiliar, irregular shapes that appear on page 74, for example, the perception of depth seems no simpler than the perception of two shapes in the same plane, although we tend to perceive the former. Other examples of figures that seem to contradict the prediction of the simplicity-preference theory, recently published by Gaetano Kanizsa of the University of Trieste, are shown on the facing page.

The simplicity-preference theory of depth perception is of course one in which depth is achieved on the basis of a built-in predisposition of the nervous system rather than on past experience. Presumably, a brain that is so organized as to lead to simpler perceptual outcomes will have an evolutionary advantage. It is not clear, however, whether this is because of the economy of the encoding process or because whichever percept can be more efficiently encoded is more likely to represent what is actually there in the world. In any event, while this theory implies innate determination of perception, it is not the same as one that says that each particular pictorial cue is an innate sign of depth. In other words, what is innate according to this theory is the general tendency of mind to prefer perceptions that are simple rather than a tendency to interpret a specific pictorial cue as signifying depth.

What, then, can we conclude about the origins of depth perception? We appear to be born with the axiomatic "assumption" that we are localized within a three-dimensional spatial world. From the very outset,

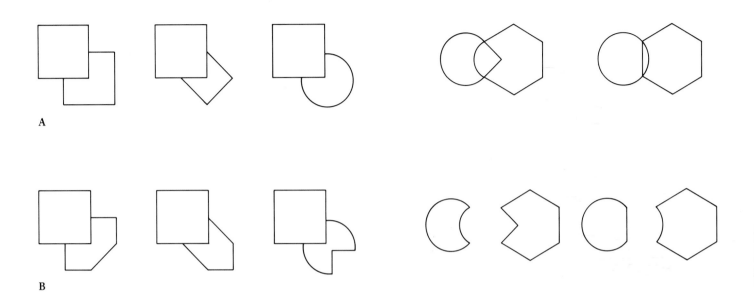

A

B

we perceive things as distant from ourselves, and from each other, their precise location in the third dimension being based on certain innately given cues. But we learn to use additional cues and learn to interpret given cues with greater precision after birth. This point of view, while it acknowledges the importance of learning, avoids the dilemma of explaining how depth perception could arise in the first place if it were *entirely* a matter of learning. Moreover, it explains how some cues to depth could be acquired: by a process of association with certain innate cues.

Students of perception, therefore, have advanced beyond the global, all-or-nothing Nativism-Empiricism controversy. Instead of asking whether space perception is learned or innate, they now approach the issue in more specific terms. Is this or that cue learned? It is plausible to assume that some cues have an innate significance while others come to indicate distance and depth because they happen to be present in the stimulus along with innate cues. This approach permits us to see that the perceptual system can be more easily modified than the Nativists recognized. On the other hand, the Empiricists had no way of explaining how learning could occur except by retreating to other sense modalities. This approach permits an alternative explanation.

The discussion of constancy in the previous chapter and of pictorial cues to depth in this one provides the necessary background for a discussion of the perception and creation of pictures. It is to these topics, considered as part of the broader problem of perception and art, that I turn in Chapter 4.

A. The dominant perceptions in these figures suggest a preference for the simpler organization. B. But the dominant perceptions in the corresponding figures suggest that the preferences in A were more likely based on other principles of grouping (to be discussed in Chapter 5).

4 PERCEPTION AND ART

If visitors to the Church of Sant' Ignazio in Rome stand at a place on the floor marked by a yellow marble disk and look up at the ceiling of the nave, they will see a three-dimensional panorama of arches supported by columns, windows, and sky, with human figures arranged in various positions throughout, some of them seemingly suspended in midair. The spectators will know that this scene is a painting, because the human figures appear lifeless, but it looks real, so real that it is virtually impossible to tell where the architecture of the church ends and the painting begins. The painting, shown on the facing page, was made by Fra Andrea Pozzo at the end of the seventeenth century. It is the best-known example of a trompe l'oeil production and is all the more remarkable for having been painted on a hemicylindrical rather than a flat surface.

That the eye can be fooled into perceiving a painting or photograph as real—as the things represented rather than as a pictorial representation of those things—is not that surprising given what we know about pictorial cues to depth. But the deception is effective only in certain circumstances. Spectators must view the picture from the same position from which the artist viewed it or the camera photographed it. This position is referred to as the center of projection, so called because it is the apex of all the straight lines that could be drawn or projected from each point in the scene. These lines all intersect the picture plane such that, with the eye at the apex, each line is the projection of both the point in the scene and the same point as represented in the picture. Only then will the rays of light from all points in the picture yield a retinal image exactly like the one that is yielded by the scene itself. If the spectator moves away from the designated point of observation in Sant' Ignazio, for instance, the painting will look distorted and thus somewhat unreal.

Other factors can also weaken or destroy the illusory effect. If the

Fra Andrea Pozzo, The Glorification of St. Ignatius, 1691–94. Trompe l'oeil painting on the ceiling of the Church of Sant' Ignazio, Rome.

Two views of the same portion of Pozzo's painting, one from the center of projection (top) and the other from a point distant from the center of projection (bottom).

texture of the photographic image or the surface of the painting is visible, it will lead to the perception of an ordinary picture on a surface. If the picture is nearby, oculomotor or retinal disparity cues may inform observers of the presence of a flat picture surface, or the frame of the picture may provide this information. Pozzo was able to circumvent all these problems because the ceiling was roughly 100 feet above the floor. Spectators do not perceive the surface of the ceiling as such, even viewing it binocularly.

Pictures of this kind, pictures that are not perceived as pictures, are remarkable achievements, tributes to the great skill and knowledge of their originators. They are also acid proof of the efficacy of pictorial cues. In such pictures, nonpictorial depth cues either are absent or contradict the pictorial cues; yet the scenes depicted appear vividly three-dimensional. Among works of art, however, trompe l'oeil productions are exceptional, and perception of them differs from the perception of other pictures. Even within the domain of aesthetics it can be argued that trompe l'oeil productions are not really examples of paintings *qua* art. For a painting is meant to be seen *as* a painting, as representing something else but at the same time as an object unto itself.

This last point brings us to the very essence of the perception of pictures: namely, a dual awareness that we have as we look at them. At least in the case of viewing *representational* art—that is, art intended to represent objects or scenes realistically—we perceive the scene or object that is depicted, generally three-dimensionally, *and* we perceive the lines, markings, or colors of the picture itself and the two-dimensional surface on which these appear. The philosopher Michael Polanyi referred to our consciousness of the characteristics of the surface of a picture as "subsidiary awareness," in contrast to our "focal awareness" of the objects represented. One can, of course, reverse this state of affairs by focusing on the brush strokes and markings as such. It is important to keep this dual awareness in mind if we are to understand the nature of picture perception. In this chapter, I will consider some of the questions that arise about perceiving and drawing representational pictures: Why do we see some representational pictures as distorted and others not? Why do we see representational pictures as likenesses of reality? Why is representational drawing so difficult for most of us? In exploring these questions, I will restrict the discussion to Western, representational art such as that which characterizes Renaissance and post-Renaissance realism.

The Problem of Distortion

That dual modes of awareness are important in perceiving pictures is brought out by one of the most striking facts about picture perception:

The brushstrokes in Vincent van Gogh's View of Arles (1890) are so noticeable that one is likely to have an awareness of the painting's surface simultaneous with an awareness of what is represented.

(Right) Henri Fantin-Latour, Still Life, *1866. (Left) How the ellipses that represent the cup and saucer in Fantin-Latour's painting would project to the eye if the painting were viewed from the side.*

Neither the appreciation of a picture's artistic merit nor a proper perception of what it represents depends upon any particular viewing position. If this were not true, we would have to maneuver ourselves into a special position in viewing a picture, much as one has to do in viewing the Pozzo ceiling. The picture's retinal image is distorted when we view it from the side, from below, or from above, but we correct for the distortion.

Suppose, for example, the artist has represented a sphere by a circle. If we view the canvas from the side, the circle projects as an ellipse. But because we have information that we are viewing the canvas from the side, we take that orientation into account in interpreting what the elliptical image represents—namely, a circle. Thus we implicitly assume that the correct position for viewing pictures is from directly in front. Such a process of achieving shape constancy must occur before we go on to interpret what the shapes on the canvas represent in the world. The perceived circle is then interpreted as representing a sphere.

The existence of these two stages of the perceptual processing of pictures is even more evident in a more complex example. Suppose the artist has represented a saucer resting on a table in proper perspective by painting an elliptical figure on the canvas, as shown in the illustration above.

If we view the picture from a position to the side, that elliptical figure on the canvas projects a circular image or, possibly, an elliptical image whose vertical axis is longer than its horizontal one (the opposite of what the artist has drawn). In order to know the shape that the figure is intended to represent, we first must achieve shape constancy for the drawn figure by perceiving it as an ellipse whose horizontal axis is longer than its vertical one. Only then can we process the perceived shape to recover what it represents in the scene depicted. The perceived elliptical shape is now perceived as a circular saucer. Of course, we will achieve constancy for the object represented only if the necessary information about depth is conveyed in the painting. Were just the saucer outline visible, it would simply look like an ellipse in a vertical plane. We are not aware of these stages of processing and thus experience the saucer as a circular object more or less immediately.

At this point the reader may quite legitimately be puzzled. Earlier I said that any departure from the correct position of observation, the so-called center of projection in the case of trompe l'oeil examples, leads to perceived distortion. Now I am saying that departures from head-on viewing of ordinary pictures does not lead to perceptual distortion but rather to a process of correction. Is there a contradiction here? Not at all. Whether or not we are aware that we are looking at a picture, the projection of a shape on the canvas to the eye will change as we move from in front of the picture to the side. But in the case of trompe l'oeil, we do not see the object as a painting but as the object itself; thus there is no reason for a constancy-like process of correction of the picture's image to be triggered. Hence the retinal-image distortion remains uncorrected.

To illustrate the point, suppose there is a sphere, represented by a circle, in the trompe l'oeil painting. Viewed from the side, it will project to the eye as an ellipse exactly as in the example of an ordinary painting discussed above. But, because it is not seen as a picture on a surface, shape constancy is not achieved: The shape looks like an ellipse and not a sphere. That is a perceptual distortion.

The importance of being aware of the orientation of the surface of the picture in relation to ourselves, so that we can make the necessary correction, is dramatically illustrated by a photograph of a photograph such as the one shown on the next page. The photograph of the poster was taken from the side, but we have no perceptual awareness of this in viewing the picture in this book. Thus, no constancy-like operation is initiated in us as we look at it. The image the poster projects to our eye is essentially the same as the one we would have received had we been standing next to the photographer at the Nixon gathering itself. In that event, however, we would not have experienced the distortion because we would have had a dual perceptual awareness in viewing the poster. The photograph of the

A photograph of a photograph taken from the side appears distorted.

poster thus illustrates what distortion we would experience whenever we looked at pictures from "incorrect positions" were no constancy-like correction achieved. We owe this particular demonstration to M. H. Pirenne, who has written extensively on vision in relation to painting and photography.

Understanding the nature of distortion or its absence in looking at pictures can help us explain some curious effects of picture perception. Perhaps the best known is the impression we have that the eyes in pictures of faces always seem to be looking at us no matter how far off to the side we stand. This is of course only true when the person in the picture has been painted or photographed as looking at the location of the painter's eye or the lens of the camera, such as in the painting shown on the facing page. In these instances, the pupil of the eye is centered with respect to the eye when it is looking at something, as, for example, at us. If,

Camille Pissarro, The Artist's Daughter, Jeanne, *1872. The eyes of the child appear to be looking at you whether you are in front or to the side of the picture.*

while the person (not the picture of the person) held that direction of gaze, we were to view his or her eye from the side, the location of the pupil in the eye would appear asymmetrical and the person would not seem to be looking at us. But when we view the *picture* of the eye from the side, the pupil's image remains more or less centered. In my opinion, this is the main reason for the curious effect. Of course, as we move to the side, the projection of the eye in the picture will become distorted and our perceptual system will correct for the distortion so that the shape of the eye will be perceived veridically. This step of correction is no doubt part of the explanation, but the effect will occur even without such correction. The central location of the pupil in the visible part of the eye is *not* altered very much even while other kinds of distortion occur from abnormal positions of viewing (e.g., the shape of the image of the entire eye changes).

The arms of the woman appear extended toward you no matter from what position you view the poster.

Other effects have a similar explanation. Consider, for example, the case of objects depicted as jutting out toward the observer, such as the arms in the poster reproduced above. Viewed from the side, the arms still seem to reach out toward us. If we viewed real arms outstretched in this way from the side, they would project quite differently. Where their projection, when viewed from straight ahead, is the one illustrated above, it would become increasingly horizontal as we moved around to the side. But when we view the *picture* from the side, the orientation of the arms in the picture remains more or less unchanged, and we continue to see the arms opening toward us.

Why Do We See Pictures As We Do?

Why do we perceive most pictures, at least those intended to be representational, as good likenesses of reality, with depth and the tendency toward constancy? Even if we correct for the distortions that arise by virtue of a mismatch between the center of projection for the picture and our location while looking at the picture, there is still a problem here. After all, a picture is simply a two-dimensional surface on which lines, markings, or color appear.

A plausible answer, and one to which I subscribe, is that there is a great deal of similarity between the retinal image from the picture and the image from the scene it represents. Of what does this similarity consist? Of many things, such as shape, size relations, depth information, lightness, and color. Artists who seek to achieve some degree of realistic representation draw or paint in perspective. That entails foreshortening extents that recede in depth, rendering distant objects that are equal in size to nearer ones as smaller on the canvas, depicting parallel contours in the scene as converging, and so forth. But these are precisely the features that obtain within the retinal image of the scene itself, as we saw in the preceding chapter. Therefore, in looking at such a picture we receive a stimulus that is highly similar to the one we receive from the world itself. Of course, to be perceived, that image must be processed by the perceptual system to achieve depth and constancy, just as the image from the scene itself must be.

Clearly it is the *relations* within the picture that are similar to those within the image of the scene, not absolute properties. The actual size of the picture and everything in it are immaterial as long as all the objects and distances are drawn to scale from the point of view of the artist and they are drawn in perspective. Although the use of color is important in achieving a realistic likeness to a scene rich in color, its absence, as drawings, woodcuts, and black-and-white photographs show, does not prevent recognition of the things depicted.

I must confess, however, that I have oversimplified the problem. Although a photograph of a scene will yield an image very similar to that directly yielded by the scene itself, paintings and drawings will not necessarily do so. Even photographs entail some important differences. The maximum reflectance difference between the lightest and darkest region in a photograph is no more than a factor of around 30, for example, whereas regions in the scene itself can differ by a factor of 100,000 or more. Drawings and paintings are limited in the same way, and these limitations present artists with a challenge when they want to represent very light or strongly illuminated regions.

Paintings and drawings differ in other important respects from the scenes they represent, even aside from the different ways in which two artists might render the same scene. Consider, for instance, the line drawing shown at right, selected from a book on picture perception by John M. Kennedy of the University of Toronto. We have no difficulty in perceiving this drawing appropriately, as representations of a house and some nearby hills, with water and sky in the background. Yet all these objects are represented only by lines. Much that is in the scene is left out. Here, then, is a major difference between the real world and many pictures. In the world, the internal and outer contours of objects generally

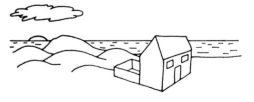

A line drawing of a scene without shading or color.

Master of the Life of Saint John the Baptist, Madonna and Child with Angels, *c. 1330/1340. The face of the baby Jesus looks more like an adult's face in miniature than an infant's.*

consist of edges. By an *edge* I mean the contour that separates one object surface of generally uniform solid color, lightness, or texture from another or from a background surface or region. In some pictures, however, such edges are often represented by lines—simply very narrow ribbons of uniform pigment or reflectance. A picture often does contain the same kind of information that edges do in the world, but, as is evident in the illustration under discussion, they need not. In the drawing, lines suffice to represent edges, and edges of different kinds at that. For example, a line can represent the visible edge or boundary of a hill that occludes objects beyond it, or it can represent the edge of the angle formed by the intersection of two walls of a house.

The use of lines in pictures raises a larger issue about perception, pictures, and art in general that has generated much controversy among art historians and psychologists. Is our perception of pictures simply based on convention, or is it, as I have been arguing, rooted in the similarity of pictures to the "picture" the eye receives from the real scene?

Convention and Picture Perception

According to the convention theory, the representation of edges or boundaries by lines is an artistic convention that we have learned to interpret correctly. Perhaps over the centuries the practice of using lines in drawings and paintings has become deeply ingrained and each new generation learns about it in childhood. That might explain why it has been claimed that animals, along with individuals in certain less "advanced" societies, do not perceive pictorial representations the way we do. Conventions must be learned. The convention theory would also explain the major differences in modes of pictorial representation over the centuries. The very fact that the use of perspective in art was so late in becoming prevalent might be taken to support this theory.

There has been much in artistic representation that is conventional. Spectators have tended either to be unaware of these conventions or not to realize that there might be other methods of representation. The ancient Egyptians perhaps did not realize that their mode of representing the human figure—part frontal view, part profile view—was a matter of convention and only one of many possible ways to represent it. The early Greeks (circa 600 B.C.) probably did not recognize their way of rendering the human figure in paintings and statues as a convention but thought of it as the only true way to do so. It is possible that pre-Renaissance painters and some later painters did not realize that their paintings of infant faces were simply smaller likenesses of adult faces and that this was a matter of convention. Yet one would also think that in such cases both artists and spectators would have realized that the painting differed from

From Land of Black Gold *(The Adventures of Tintin) by Herge. Art copyright by Casterman. Text copyright by Methuen/Little Brown.*

the object painted in certain respects and that this realization would have given rise to a vague feeling of dissatisfaction with the painting. In contemporary art, an example of convention is the use of streaks behind figures in cartoons to convey an impression of rapid motion, a convention that likely arose from looking at photographs of rapidly moving objects. Another example, found in some cartoons and drawings, is the use of lines to indicate color differences, such as the use of outline to indicate a giraffe's colored spots. Kennedy reports that members of New Guinea's Songe tribe do not understand this usage.

If some modes of representation can plausibly be explained as conventions, can the use of lines in pictures be explained in the same way? Perhaps the sharp outline of the cloud in Kennedy's picture is accepted, by convention, as representing a cloud, even though the boundaries of real clouds are typically much "softer" and gradual. Perhaps the streaks in the water are partially based on convention. Although these particular explanations may be correct, in general the convention theory can be faulted both on logical and on empirical grounds, as Kennedy has noted. On logical grounds, the fact is that, despite solidly colored and textured surfaces between edges in real scenes, it is the contours at such edges that are of primary importance in conveying information about object and depth relations in the scene. Contours at edges are very similar to lines as used in pictures. Thus the drawing of the house contains much the same information as does the eye's image of the house itself.

Furthermore, the phenomenon of figure-ground organization (as we shall see in the next chapter) suggests that there is a universal and probably unlearned tendency to perceive the region within certain contours as a solid two-dimensional object with a particular shape on a background region. For example, in the illustration on the following page, the circle

(Top) Some conventions in contemporary cartoons. (Bottom) Typical rendering of human figures in early Egyptian art.

The representation of colored spots by closed outlines.

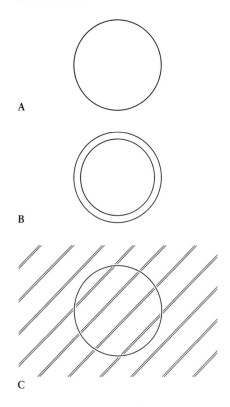

A

B

C

A circular outline tends to be seen as a solid disk rather than as a mere perimeter. For the outline to appear as a perimeter, other lines must be added, such as a second outline or lines that indicate a common background outside and inside the circle.

appears to us not as a mere outline—which, physically speaking, is all it is—but as a solid or "filled" disk. In fact, to produce an impression of a perimeter or outline object *only*, an artist would have to introduce additional lines or information—for example, by drawing a double outline or objects inside and outside the outline that are continuous with one another, as shown at left, below. If a region enclosed by a line is spontaneously perceived as a surface or a thing because that is how perceptual organization works, there is no need to invoke convention as an explanation of why we tend to perceive (and make) line drawings as representations of a world of objects.

A good case can be made for a more radical view of the relation between line drawings and the objects or scenes they represent. It has often been presumed that, because line pictures leave out surface texture, color, shading, and detail, they are impoverished representations. But simple line drawings or sparse paintings may actually be *better* representations than more complex renderings or photographs. Line figures are simple and uncluttered compared to photographs or other kinds of drawings. They tend to bring out the essence of the thing represented. In fact, caricature drawings that distort the object depicted can bring out the object's essence even better than more accurate line drawings. Experiments have shown that caricatures require less time for correct recognition than do more "realistic" pictures.

On empirical grounds, the convention explanation can be faulted in a number of respects. Consider, for instance, the result of a bold experiment done by Julian Hochberg and Virginia Brooks at Cornell University. They raised their son for the first two years without allowing him to see pictures, even advertisements on food containers or billboards. In situations where the child might have seen a picture inadvertently, they provided no interpretation of or label for it. When the boy was about 2 years old, he was asked to identify pictures of various kinds, including simple line drawings of shoes and other familiar objects. He had no difficulty identifying the pictures. If we assume that this finding can be generalized, therefore, it can hardly be argued that the perception and recognition of line drawings is a matter of learned convention.

How, then, are we to interpret the data accumulated by anthropologists and psychologists that are said to show that people in technologically backward societies, who have no experience viewing pictures, are incapable of, or extremely poor at, perceiving pictures as representations? The answer is that the data available simply do not justify that conclusion. It is undoubtedly true that, on being shown pictures or even photographs for the first time, individuals in certain societies express puzzlement and often *seem* not to recognize what is represented. But is this surprising? A picture is itself an object, a two-dimensional object at that, with certain markings on it. Observers must adopt the pictorial attitude, one in which they are prepared to perceive a picture in two different ways simultaneously. We are used to doing this, but the people tested were not. Only when observers understand that they must adopt this attitude can we ask whether or not they are capable of recognizing what is depicted. The evidence available is unequivocal on this question. They do recognize people, animals, and other familiar objects depicted in drawings and photographs. Their interpretation of what is happening in a picture may vary from our own—as, for example, whether a group of people are dancing or fighting—but this fact should hardly surprise us either. Interpretation on this level *ought* to be a function of cultural background.

But what about reports that some of the people tested did not perceive perspective representation appropriately—specifically, that they did not perceive depth in pictures as we do—even if they did recognize the objects represented. If they did not, the presumption is that they have not had the opportunity to learn the conventions of depth representation. The illustration below that William Hudson used in a study in South Africa has become well known in this regard. The subjects were asked whether the spear was aimed at the elephant or the antelope. To us, the answer is supposed to be obvious because we respond appropriately to the depth cues, which in this case would be interposition, perspective, and familiar size. But these cues are, at best, weak in the figure. Even for us, there is ambiguity here; thus it is hardly surprising that the subjects in the experiment often said that the spear was aimed at the elephant.

One should also be cautious about using size or shape perception as an indicator of depth perception in pictures. That is because there is only a tendency toward constancy (rather than perfect constancy) in viewing pictures, even pictures rich in effective depth cues (to say nothing of pictures, such as the one in the illustration below, in which the cues are so

A caricature line drawing may be a more easily identified representation than a more "realistic" photograph.

A figure Hudson used in his study of pictorial depth perception among various African groups.

In viewing pictures, the limited distance perception that can be achieved limits the achievement of veridical size perception for distant objects. (Left) Honoré Daumier, in O Lune! . . . inspire-moi ce soir *(1844), painted the moon much larger to compensate for this fact. (Right) Had he painted the moon in correct proportion to other objects in the scene, it would appear about the size shown in this altered copy.*

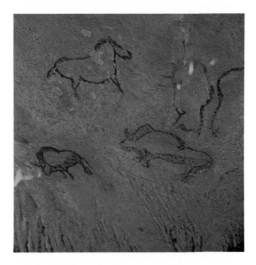

Prehistoric drawings discovered in the Santamanine cave in Sagna, Spain.

poor that the elephant looks as small as its relatively small visual angle would lead one to predict). Thus, if members of some African tribes report that an animal in the picture near the horizon looks much smaller than the one of the same species in the foreground of the picture, it should not be assumed that they are perceiving any differently than we do.

Still another kind of evidence against the convention theory derives from studies of individuals who have been blind from birth or from within a few months of birth. Kennedy and his associates have demonstrated that such individuals are generally able to recognize raised-line "picture" displays of objects that they explore with their fingers. Since these subjects had no experience whatever with pictures, with the visually seen objects they represent, or with raised-line tactual pictures, these results are quite impressive. They are further confirmation that outlined figures are perceived as things rather than mere outlines and that this perception occurs without benefit of a learned convention.

Finally, there is the fact that prehistoric cave paintings are often outline drawings. Many such pictures are very good indeed, even by modern standards of realistic representation. Kennedy and his associates have found that outline was used in much the same way in cave paintings from distant parts of the world, again suggesting that this mode of representation is not a convention passed from person to person.

Let us assume, then, that past experience with pictures is not necessary to perceive pictures as representations of objects or scenes. It is not mere convention that leads us to this capability but the detection of an intrinsic similarity between the picture and the object. Recognition therefore occurs. But along with recognition come certain aspects of perception that would not otherwise occur—notably, depth perception. An example is the perceptual change that occurs in viewing a fragmented figure of the kind illustrated at right, at the moment of recognition. At first, the illustration seems to be a rather meaningless array of fragments. Suddenly, it is recognized as a man sitting on a bench, and it then looks three-dimensional. This example suggests that, while prior experience with pictures may not directly govern picture perception, past experience with the objects represented may play an important role in picture perception. Thus, to us, as well as to the 2-year-old child reared without exposure to pictures, the picture of the house, hills, and water or a picture of a shoe might be perceived differently from the way in which it appears were it not for our accumulated experience in daily life with structures of these kinds.

Having explored some of the major problems about perception of pictorial art, I turn now to consider some problems about the process of creating such art, the drawing or painting of pictures. On the face of it, one might think that drawing and painting, being motor acts or behaviors, are far afield from the topic of perception. But, on further reflection, it is evident that what and how one draws must be intimately connected with what and how one perceives. In that respect, artistic performance is not very different from other motor performance. Motor acts are triggered and guided by what we perceive, even in so simple an act as picking up an object from a table. Of course, other cognitive processes, such as those that underlie memory and the utilization of knowledge, also govern overt behavior, and, as I will suggest, the same is true for the special type of behavior we call drawing and painting.

Drawing

Psychologists have often thought that what one draws can be taken to be a good index of what one perceives. For example, children at a certain age will often copy letters backward. Does that mean they perceive an S as an ℥? If they did, they should draw the S correctly because, once drawn, it too should be perceived backward. Otherwise the drawing and the letter copied ought to look different. A similar problem arises with the interpretation that some art historians make of El Greco's elongated paintings of people—namely, that he suffered from astigmatism, a defect in the lens that can stretch the image. There is an error in reasoning here that has been called the El Greco fallacy. If El Greco misperceived the shape of people, he should also have misperceived his paintings of them; only by painting them correctly would he have misperceived both in the same way. Otherwise, his paintings would have looked different to him than did the object painted.

There are other cases in which drawings do not necessarily reflect what is perceived. Clinical psychologists and psychiatrists make use of a diagnostic tool known as the Bender-Gestalt test. Many psychologists

The figure represented in these fragments generally is not immediately perceived. Recognition is accompanied by altered form and depth perception.

El Greco (Domeniko Theotokopoulos), St. Andrew and St. Francis, *about 1608, showing the artist's tendency to paint elongated figures.*

have interpreted the errors individuals make in copying various geometrical patterns on this test as perceptual in origin. For reasons similar to those given above, it seems to me to be highly unlikely that this is the case. Rather, for unknown reasons, individuals do not draw what they perceive. Similar errors of reasoning were made in the history of psychology with respect to memory and drawing. To study how a figure was remembered, subjects were asked to draw it from memory. Later it was realized that there were better ways to probe the accuracy of memory than by a drawing task.

Given these confusions, it is important to discuss the relevance of perception to drawing or painting. As will become evident, I believe that, in certain cases, what we draw *does* reflect how we perceive. But from the examples above it is clear that what we draw is governed by many factors other than perceptual ones.

Why is drawing so difficult for most of us? Why do children draw the way they do? Why did good representational perspective art flower so late historically? We cannot answer these questions with any finality, but I believe that the psychology of perception can shed some light on them.

The problems most people have in drawing are not primarily ones of motor skill. After all, most of us can do a reasonably good job of copying a triangle, a rectangle, or even a simple, irregular two-dimensional shape. The problems, I believe, are instead mainly perceptual or cognitive in nature. Their origins lie in how we perceive, how we copy things, how and what we know about things, and how we remember things.

DRAWING AND PERCEPTUAL CONSTANCY   To make a representational drawing of a three-dimensional object or scene, we must draw a picture that will give the observer a retinal image similar to the one obtained in viewing the object or scene itself. But we do not directly perceive our retinal images. Instead, we spontaneously perceive a world of objects and planes that departs considerably from the size and shape relations given within the image. Thus, if we draw what we perceive, we will not draw in perspective.

The major difficulty in drawing—at least in drawing by copying from the scene—is that we are foiled by the achievements of our perceptions, which accord so well with the actual characteristics of objects instead of with the characteristics of the stimulation reaching the eye. This is particularly noticeable in the art of children. If children are asked to copy a table while standing at one end of it, they tend frequently to draw what they perceive: a rectangular surface the far end of which is equal to the near end, with nonconverging sides and length not foreshortened. Plates on the table are likely to be drawn as circles, not ellipses.

How then does anybody ever manage to draw properly? One answer is that we are taught or teach ourselves. There is of course much truth in this. Leonardo taught the principles of perspective and methods for their utilization to his disciples, and art teachers have been doing the same ever since. We also pick up a good deal of information about the geometry of perspective informally, through trial and error and by looking at pictures.

But another answer may be more important. There is a way in which we do perceive in accord with the two-dimensional characteristics of the retinal image, which I referred to earlier as perception in the proximal mode. We do perceive railroad tracks and roads as converging, for instance, even while we perceive them as parallel, and we do perceive plates on a table as "elliptical," even while perceiving them as circular. Although constancy is our dominant mode of perception, the presence of the proximal mode, or the potential to focus on it, may play a major role in drawing. When faced with the task of drawing a road, for example, the presence of the proximal mode allows us to copy the percept in which the sides of the road converge rather than the usually dominant percept in which they are parallel.

Some conditions make it easier to abstract the proximal-mode relations than others do. For example, when the images of two objects in the scene are adjacent and parallel—as with the wooden ties of the railroad track—it is relatively easy to see that one is "shorter" than the other. When, however, the objects are widely separated and must be viewed successively, it is difficult to abstract these features. That may be why artists use their thumb or a pencil to try to ascertain the proper visual angle of one thing in relation to another.

Some people may also be better than others at capturing the proximal-mode character of their perception. In the scientific literature on perception, theorists have sometimes speculated about differences among people in this regard, referring to such perceptual or cognitive "styles" as analytical versus integrative or as field-independent versus field-dependent. Those individuals who are more easily able to attend to their proximal-mode perceptions may be the ones we say are endowed with artistic ability, although such a capacity would be but one component of overall talent in art. Whether this capacity is innate or learned is a further question. The question of whether artists are made or born is still controversial in psychology.

The same analysis can be extended to the late development of perspective representation in the history of art. Not only did pre-Renaissance artists have the same problem of escaping from their own perceptual constancy, as it were, but they had few earlier examples of perspective art and no photographs to educate them. The dominance of some artistic conventions may have also been a contributing factor. Pre-Renaissance

A child's drawing of a table is unlikely to be in correct perspective because constancy of size and shape is achieved in perceiving the real table.

artists may have thought about the possibility of perspective representation but did little about it. One does find many early paintings, perhaps most, in which objects are rendered with correct foreshortening and many paintings in which distant objects are appropriately rendered as smaller than near ones of the same objective size. Although it is beyond my knowledge and competence and beyond the scope of this chapter to deal with this historical problem adequately, I do think that the constancy explanation must play a role in it.

DRAWING SUBTLE SHAPES   A second difficulty in drawing accurately even when copying from actual objects or other pictures concerns the subtle spatial relations that constitute certain shapes. For example, suppose we attempt to sketch a horse or a picture of one. For most of us, this is difficult to do well, even if we take great pains with it. We realize when we look at our first attempt that it is not right, but, curiously, we do not necessarily know why it is misshapen. If we continue to revise the sketch, we can recognize when it is improved. By converting the task into one of correction through recognition, we may eventually achieve a satisfactory drawing, but few take the trouble to do so.

Why we have trouble drawing subtle shapes is not understood, nor, to my knowledge, has it been discussed before. In my view, the difficulty we have in rendering subtle shapes can be traced to the fact that we are not consciously aware of the internal processes that underlie form perception. In order to copy a figure we first need to encode an accurate description of it and then use that encoding to instruct ourselves as to how to reproduce it. If the figure is simple, we can describe it to ourselves consciously—for example, "a rectangle, twice as long as it is high." But if it is subtle and complex, such as the shape of a horse is, we cannot easily generate an accurate description of the shape that we could then use to guide us in copying it.

We have roughly the same difficulty in attempting to copy a completely *unfamiliar*, novel shape that is not easily described, such as the one in the illustration at left. If this analysis of the problem is correct, again we would still have the problem of understanding why some people—artists in particular—manage to overcome the difficulty. To simply say "practice" begs the question. It presupposes that artistic ability is entirely learned and thus fails to account for the fact that some children are good at artistic representation very early in their lives.

The argument here is not that we have difficulty *perceiving* shapes, a process that I suggest in the next chapter is based on unconscious description. Rather it is that we have difficulty extracting or making such description conscious in order to guide us in copying certain shapes whose spatial relations are subtle.

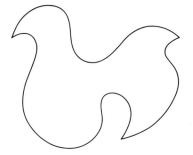

An unfamiliar shape whose subtle spatial relations make it difficult to copy.

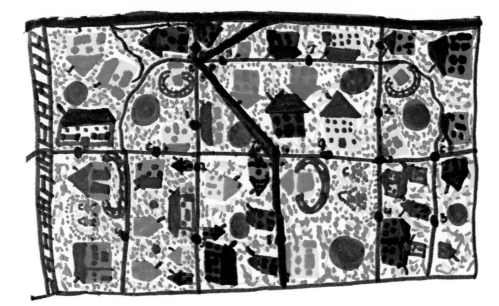

DRAWING FROM MEMORY   Drawing or painting from memory is even more difficult than copying figures. The constancy problem is probably a major reason again, all the more so because in drawing from memory it is not possible to make use of proximal-mode perception of the scene. Thus if we are trying to draw an object or scene and we remember it or imagine it on the basis of how things look, it is likely to be difficult indeed to draw in terms of the laws of perspective projection.

It is probably true, as has been suggested by the art historian E. H. Gombrich and others, that we tend to draw what we know. This is all the more likely to occur in children. Therefore, if a young child makes a drawing of the street in which he or she lives, a typical example might look like the illustration above. Rather than a picture in perspective, the objects depicted are laid out so as to show them in their most representational view, which might be regarded more as a rather intelligent solution than as an error. To some extent, children may depict objects in this way even when asked to copy something.

This idea of drawing what we know is similiar to the one I have advocated—that we tend to draw on the basis of what we perceive, as in the case of constancy. Some students of art unfamiliar with the concept of constancy in perception may believe that failure to draw properly in perspective is based on knowledge of the true sizes and shapes of things since, aside from perception, we generally do have such knowledge about these properties of the things at which we are looking. My argument would be that it is unnecessary to invoke "knowledge" as explanation when perception itself can explain the errors children and adults make in drawing a scene. However, there are cases in which knowledge and not perception may explain artistic distortions, particularly in the case of children drawing from memory. The illustration of the street scene is a

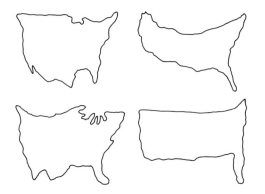

Typical drawings by adults from memory of the outline of the continental United States.

A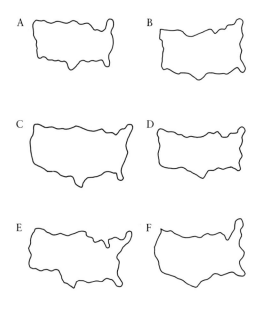

A recognition test of the outline of the continental United States. Most people correctly choose "C" as the right answer.

case in point, as would be the drawing by a young child of a room with four walls. It is impossible to see all four walls at any one moment, but the child knows that a room has four walls. Or a child may draw a top view of an animal with four legs visible and extending outward although this tendency can hardly be based on the memory of any perception.

Apart from the difficulty of escaping from constancy perception and the tendency to draw what we know, drawing from memory presents a further problem. To draw from memory, we must have a reasonably clear image in mind from which we can "copy." Try, for example, to draw from memory an outline map of the United States. Generally, we are poor at this kind of task, typical drawings from a sample of adults being of the kind shown in the top figure at left. That this difficulty is not simply a function of failure to have ever established the memory adequately is shown by the excellent performance of which we are capable when given a recognition-choice test. As shown in the illustration at the lower left, most observers can pick out the correct answer, though even the poorest of the alternatives given is probably better than most people can draw from memory. Thus, we must have a reasonably faithful memory of the shape of the United States, but apparently we cannot adequately call it up without the help of a recognition stimulus. If we cannot adequately evoke our memory of a thing, we cannot draw a very good picture of it.

We might call this an imagery problem without necessarily implying anything about the nature of imagery. Most people are very poor at evoking images, at least images clear enough to permit a good representational drawing to be made from them. Often, even those who can make faithful copies of models, still-lifes, or landscapes cannot render the same subjects faithfully from memory. Why some artists have this additional gift is still a mystery.

Given this difficulty, it is probable that certain internalized schemas—representations of objects, events, or processes—that we possess guide us in drawing and lead to certain errors. An interesting example is the case of the human face. The reader is invited to make a quick sketch of a face without looking at one. A very common error is to draw the eyes much too high in the head. In fact, the eyes are much closer to the middle of the head. Since the error is widespread among those untrained in drawing, it is plausible to suppose that it is based on a mental schema of faces that is simply incorrect—for example, "eyes are near the top of the face, right below the forehead."

Whether or not we have an incorrect memory schema of an object in most cases, there can be no doubt that we have difficulty in achieving imagery from memory that is good enough to allow us to draw many objects adequately. The kind of object to which this difficulty applies is, I believe, precisely the kind that was discussed above in the case of copying—namely, one in which the shape is qualitatively subtle, such as the human body, a dog or other animal, a geographical shape, a bicycle, or an automobile. The kind to which it would not apply is one in which the shape is relatively simple or unsubtle—a book, a simple wooden chair, the outline of a house, a staircase, a lamp, or the like. It is true that our own drawing becomes an object for recognition, and this is all the more important in the case of drawing from memory than it is in copying. Since the memory schema may well be a rather faithful representation of the object, even if it is not easily evoked without the help of a stimulus figure, we can compare the drawing to the schema. The mismatch tells us the drawing is not right, but not necessarily in what respect. In theory, if we continued revising the drawing, we should be able to achieve an excellent likeness. However, as was noted with respect to copying pictures, few if any people ever proceed in this way.

In this discussion, I have suggested several reasons why drawing or painting is difficult and why the productions of children and of artists of antiquity contain certain kinds of "errors." However, I must add an important disclaimer. Drawings or paintings that are poor representations of objects and scenes by our standards and expectations of realism need not be the result of the perceptual or cognitive limitations I have suggested; rather, they may be the result of an intention or convention to draw in a particular way. Perhaps the Egyptians drew pictures of people the way they did because they believed that side views of faces and feet and frontal views of torsos were the most informative about the human body. The lack of perspective in painting does not necessarily mean the absence of the ability to use it. The realistic aim is not the only aim in art, and it only appears here and there in different cultures and at different times in history. Similarly, children are not always concerned with making realistic drawings but instead may be motivated to express themselves in form and color. It would be absurd to infer from Picasso's more abstract paintings that he could not draw realistically when some of his other work shows how great a master of realistic portrayal he was when he chose to be. If one did not know about the realistic paintings, however, one might make just that wrong inference from the abstract ones.

In this and the preceding chapters, I have necessarily referred often to object and shape (or form) perception. From this one might draw the conclusion that such perception is based solely on the reception of the shape of the object's image on the retina as given by its contours. As will be seen in the next chapter, nothing could be farther from the truth. Even so simple a perception as that of a single two-dimensional shape poses many difficult problems.

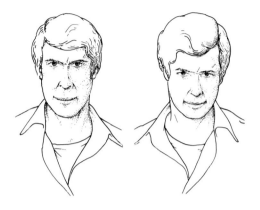

(Left) Typical drawing of the human face in which the eyes are placed high in the head when in fact they are close to the middle, as shown at right.

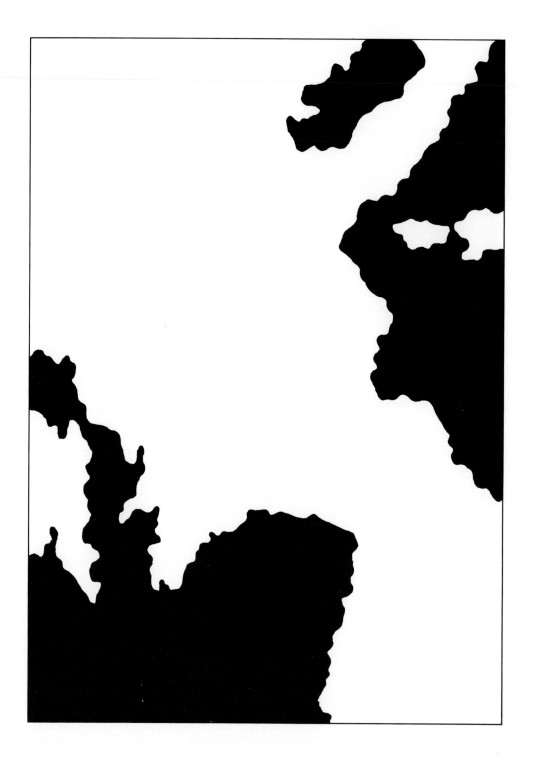

5 FORM AND ORGANIZATION

When we look at the illustration on the facing page, we initially tend to see a pattern of unfamiliar dark fragments. At most, the detail in the outlines may suggest a map of an unrecognizable region. In fact, the outline of much of Europe is present in the illustration, although even with that hint it may not be detected. To see Europe's outline, the illustration must be rotated 90 degrees clockwise and the central white region rather than the black fragments must become the primary object of awareness.

Although it may be intuitively understandable that disorientation and black-white reversal interfere with spontaneous recognition in this example, it is by no means easy to explain why they should do so. After all, because we are viewing a two-dimensional object in the frontal plane, the correct outline of Europe is present on the retina. Nevertheless, the correct shape is not initially perceived, and for this reason it is not recognized.

The image that appears on the retina is simply an optical matter, merely the beginning of a chain of events that leads to a percept and, generally, to recognition of the thing perceived. In order for us to perceive a world of differentiated shapes, some internal process must construct them from the neural energy that emanates from the millions of rods and cones in the retina and that is transmitted along the hundreds of thousands of fibers in the optic nerve. In this chapter, I will explore what principles the mind uses to impose an organization on the mosaic of visual stimuli and what role experience plays in the perception of shape.

Because the object represented in this pattern is shown in white and rotated 90 degrees counterclockwise, it is unlikely to be spontaneously perceived and recognized.

Figure-Ground Differentiation

In initially viewing the map of Europe, our attention is drawn to the black regions because they are smaller than and more or less surrounded

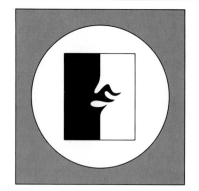

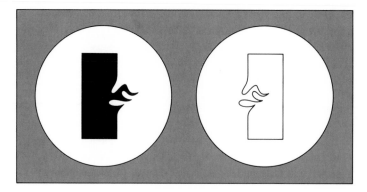

The configuration on the left can be perceived in either one of the two ways shown on the right, but not in both ways simultaneously.

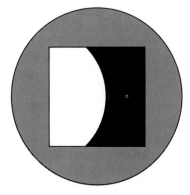

When the central curved contour is organized as belonging to the region at the left, we perceive a convex shape; when it is organized as belonging to the region on the right, we perceive a concave shape.

by the white regions, because they contrast more sharply with the white page than do the white regions, and because the convention in our society is to color or outline things in black on a white background. For these reasons, we tend unconsciously to regard the black regions as the "things" and the white regions as the background. In so doing, we assign the outline between black and white to the black regions. The black regions thus take on a certain shape.

The mind, then, *organizes* the pattern in a particular way, into a particular *figure-ground differentiation*. This mental process, which was described in 1921 by the Danish psychologist Edgar Rubin, is fundamental in all perception. The terms "figure" and "ground" have filtered into the common lexicon, but they are often simply understood to differentiate the object that stands out (figure) from the object or objects that recede into the background (ground). But that is only part of their meaning.

Left out in this description of figure-ground is any mention of borders, the assignment of which is central to shape perception. At any given time, we assign the common border between regions to one region or the other, with the consequence that the region to which the border is assigned takes on a particular perceptual shape. When the assignment is reversed, the shape perceived is dramatically different. For example, when the central curved contour in the illustration at left is assigned to the region on the left in the figure, that region appears convex on one side; when it is assigned to the region on the right, that region appears concave on one side. Note that the contour itself, thought of as just a line, is neither convex nor concave.

In the illustration at the top of this page, it is evident that two entirely different shapes emerge; which one does so depends only upon the organization of one region or the other as figure. The black "figure" consists of a protruding sharp claw, whereas the white "figure" has two soft

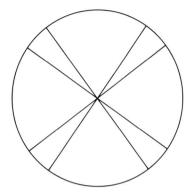  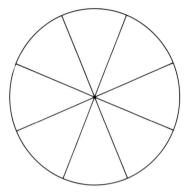

protruding parts. The two figural percepts are so different from one another as shapes, despite their dependence on an identical contour, that we may predict that if observers organize the pattern one way at one time, the pattern as a whole will not be recognized if it is organized the opposite way at a later time. Rubin did this experiment with just this result.

In the pattern just illustrated, which region any given observer will first perceive as figure may be largely a matter of chance, particularly if the surrounding region is made gray, as it is here. The black region is then not strongly favored because it contrasts more with the white of the page than does the white region. But in patterns such as those shown above, there are characteristics that influence our perception of a particular region as figure. We tend to perceive as figure those regions that are surrounded or smaller, symmetrical, and vertical or horizontal. It can now be understood why, in viewing the map of Europe, we at first organize the pattern into black figural regions and why, given the fact that these regions are novel shapes and given the lack of perception of a shape corresponding to the continent of Europe, we initially do not recognize anything.

In ambiguous patterns, smaller regions (as in the pattern on the left), symmetrical regions (as in the pattern in the middle), and vertically or horizontally oriented regions (as in the pattern on the right) tend to be perceived as figures.

Grouping

Figure-ground differentiation is only one kind of organization imposed by the mind on stimulus patterns, although it may well be the most pervasive and fundamental in daily life. The Gestalt psychologists uncovered various other principles that our minds use to achieve spontaneous groupings of elements or stimulus components. To appreciate fully the contribution a process of internal organization makes to what we perceive, it must first be grasped that, logically, no one region of a stimulus pattern falling upon the retina belongs to or is part of any other region.

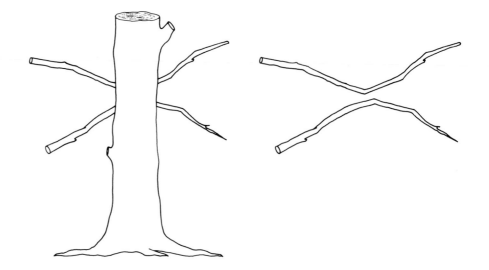

Grouping according to the principle of good continuation may lead to a nonveridical percept.

Because of the principle of good continuation, in this particular figure we tend to group together the parts of the curved line, excluding the straight line.

Thus, even though one region of the image—for example, one emanating from a surface of an object—is adjacent to another region that emanates from an adjacent region of the same object surface, these two regions of the image have no particular physical kinship to one another. If they are perceived as belonging to the same object surface, it must be because we impose that organization. In doing so, we recover the kinship that obtains in the object.

In imposing an organization, the mind can also easily achieve a false, nonveridical kinship (or, conversely, miss a kinship that in fact does exist in the world). In the left-hand figure above, two thin objects are seen to be crossing one another behind a tree. Logically speaking, that immediate, spontaneous, and compelling perception is not a required outcome. One could just as well perceive four independent objects, each of which is partially hidden. (Here we see that the pictorial depth cue of interposition itself represents the achievement of a particular perceptual organization.) Alternatively, one could perceive two noncrossing objects, the view of which is occluded by the tree. This last percept in fact could represent the actual state of affairs. But this percept is difficult to achieve and unlikely to occur. Of all the percepts, the first—that of two crossing objects—is much the most likely to occur, even though it may be incorrect.

This preferred outcome can be explained on the basis of "good continuation," a principle of grouping Max Wertheimer uncovered in 1923. *Good continuation* refers to our tendency to group together in a single structure those parts or units that appear to be aligned with, or smooth directional continuations of, one another, other things being equal. As a glance at the figure at left will indicate, contours that constitute abrupt discontinuities of direction tend not to be regarded as parts of the same overall structure. Because we tend to perceive in accordance with this

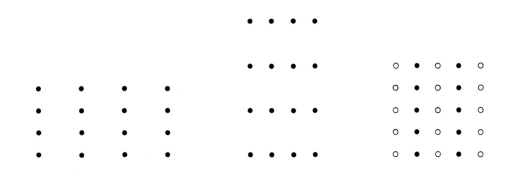

principle, it seems plausible to conclude that we generally recover in our perceptions the same structures and groupings that exist in the world. That is because such smooth continuations ordinarily are inherent in parts of the same object. It would be coincidental for these continuations to exist within the retinal image when they result from objects or parts that have no connection whatsoever with one another. If we assume that the illustration at the top of page 116 represents just such a coincidence, it would result in a false percept. In that case, the operation of the principle of good continuation would result in a camouflage of the actual state of affairs. In fact, camouflage, both as it occurs in nature and as it is produced by humans, makes use of the principles of organization to yield perceptual objects different from the actual objects present, either by obscuring actual objects or by creating perceptual objects not actually present.

Two other important principles of organization, illustrated in the figures above, are proximity and similarity. Other things being equal, we tend to organize units that are closest together as parts of an overall whole. *Proximity* is, of course, relative. Thus, the separations that are the greater in one array of units, and therefore do not lead to groupings, may become the lesser in another array and thus lead to groupings.

Other things being equal, we also tend to group together units that are similar to one another. *Similarity* can be of color, of lightness, or of size. The similarity of the shapes of the units to one another is more problematic. A method for determining the effectiveness of different kinds of similarity for grouping is shown in the illustration on the following page, top left. If similar units are grouped, these units will appear to be segregated from the remainder of the units, which also tend to be grouped. Thus, we will perceive one quadrant as segregated from the remainder of

The laws of proximity and similarity. We tend to group the spots in the pattern on the left into columns, and those in the pattern in the middle into rows, because of their relative nearness to one another. In the pattern on the right, we tend to group together the spots that are similar to one another. In this pattern, the separations between rows are the same as those between columns, thus neutralizing the law of proximity.

 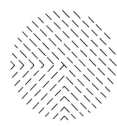  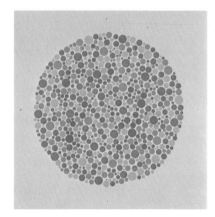

(Left) Grouping by similarity of line orientation results in the spontaneous segregation of one region in the left and center arrays, but grouping by similarity of form in the array at right does not.

(Right) The pseudoisochromatic test for color vision is based on the principle of grouping by similarity of color.

the array. A well-known test for color vision is based on segregation as a function of color similarity. If one is colorblind, a grouping by color similarity will not occur. In experiments using this technique, it has been found that similarity of line orientation of the units or of parts of the units will lead to segregation, but that, generally, similarity of form where line orientation remains the same will not lead to segregation.

Similarity is a principle that is clearly important in camouflage, such as in countershading in fish. A fish is typically dark on its dorsal surface so that, when viewed from above, it blends with the dark appearance of water below; when viewed from below, its light ventral surface blends with the light color of the water's surface and the sky above.

Among the other principles of grouping that Wertheimer singled out were common fate and closure. *Common fate* refers to the tendency to group those units that move together in the same direction and at the same speed. Where grouping would not otherwise occur in stationary displays, as in a well-camouflaged animal standing still, it will occur as soon as the display moves. When the animal moves, its various visible parts move together, and it is suddenly perceived. Similarly, clouds that do not appear to be separate when stationary are perceived as separate the moment they are seen to move relative to one another.

Closure is the tendency, other things being equal, to group into unified structures those components that together constitute a closed entity rather than an open one. However, closure is better known not as a principle of grouping but as a tendency, noted by the Gestaltists, to complete otherwise incomplete units. One might regard the perception of the unit that appears behind another in an interposition pattern as a manifestation of closure. (See the illustration on page 88 for an example.)

These are the principles that the Gestalt psychologists have advanced

Camouflage in fish.

The array of fragments in the left-hand figure does not reveal the organization and consequent recognition that occurs in the right-hand one, although the same fragments are present in both figures. Information is available in the right-hand figure that something is occluding those fragments, and this permits a different grouping, completion, or closure to occur.

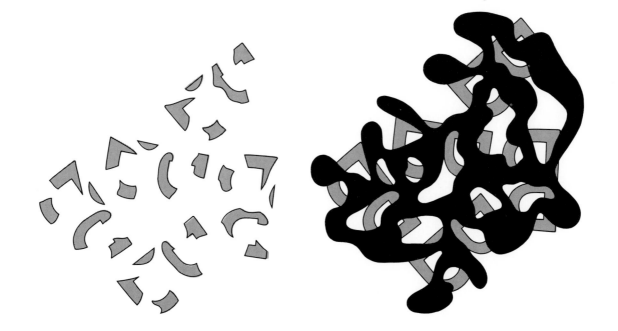

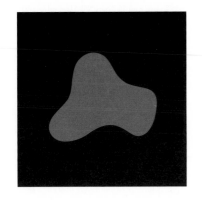

Either the green or the black region can be organized as a figure, but the latter organization does not occur spontaneously.

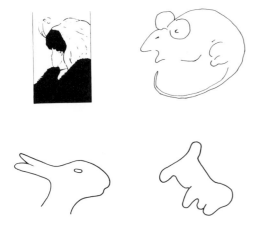

Four reversible figures.

and that students of perception have generally accepted ever since to account for the fact of organization of the perceptual world. A few investigators, however, have failed to grasp the fact that some such explanation is needed to account for perception. The difficulty in grasping it is this: Since we perceive the world as we do, as made up of segregated and distinct objects each of which is a figure on a ground, there is a tendency to think that such organization is simply given to us by the stimulus input that establishes the retinal image. However, it takes a mind viewing such a picture to achieve the groupings and figure-ground differentiations that characterize our perception.

Perceptual Reversal

In some of the examples just discussed, I have noted that two (or more) organizations are possible. This fact brings out a most important point: The stimulus input is, logically speaking, ambiguous. We considered another instance of ambiguity in discussing size and shape constancy. An image of a given visual angle can represent objects of all possible sizes; only by taking account of distance can the perceptual system infer what sized object is producing that image.

In the case of organization, however, the various percepts that the same stimulus can represent are *qualitatively* distinct. Which one is selected (or preferred) by the perceptual system depends upon the principles of organization and grouping. In most instances, the selection is decisive, and only one perception occurs. Although the pattern in the top illustration at left logically can represent either an inner green figure or a hole in a surrounding black figure, the former will be spontaneously "preferred." In this instance, there is no conflict between organizing principles: We tend to see the green area as figure because it is a surrounded region, although we can reverse this outcome by an intentional effort to perceive the green area as a hole.

In some cases, however, one outcome is not overwhelmingly favored by any organizational principle. Several of the illustrations already discussed are of this kind. The perception changes from time to time even as we continue to look at the stimulus figure. Such cases are referred to as *reversible* (or *ambiguous*) *figures*. In addition to figure-ground reversibility, another kind of reversibility concerns the meaningful content of what is seen (in the illustrations at left, a young or old woman, a rat or a man's face, a duck or a rabbit, a chef or a dog). In these cases it is not as easy to state what principle of organization is at work. Pictures in which the impression of perspective can be reversed represent still another kind of reversible figure. The Necker cube and the Albers steps shown at the top of the facing page are two examples among many of this kind.

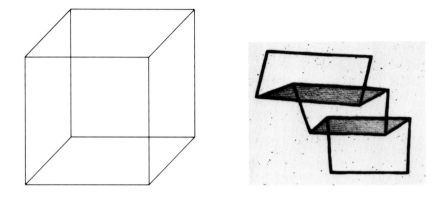

Both the Necker cube and the portion of Steps by Josef Albers (1939) are reversible perspective figures.

Does such reversibility require special explanation or does it suffice to say (as I already have) that, because the stimulus can (more or less) equally represent these different objects, it is perfectly understandable that perception will shift from time to time? Most psychologists would say that reversal requires explanation because a "decision" has been made by the perceptual system as to what the stimulus represents; thus some event must have occurred to change the perception at a particular moment. The only explanation of reversal that has been given any currency in the psychological literature for the last half century is the satiation theory, or fatigue theory. According to this theory, advanced most forcefully and explicitly by the Gestalt psychologist Wolfgang Köhler, each perceptual organization is determined by a separate neural event in the brain. If one ongoing neural event becomes satiated or fatigued (much the way neural discharge is known to become fatigued and resistant to further discharge in other realms, such as in color vision), we can assume that the brain resists its further occurrence. When the resistance reaches the point of completely blocking that neural event, the stage is set for a switch to the other neural event, the one to which the stimulus can equally well lead. When that switch occurs, it is experienced consciously as a change in the percept.

Some evidence supports this theory. The strongest comes from experiments performed first by Julian Hochberg, then at the University of California, and later, with even more convincing results, by Virgil R. Carlson of the National Institute of Mental Health. In these experiments, the subject was first shown an unambiguous figure, such as the one in the illustration at right. After viewing it for 15 seconds—during which period the neural event determining the percept was presumably satiated— the subject was shown an ambiguous composite that could be perceived in either of two ways. If one organization had been satiated, the other

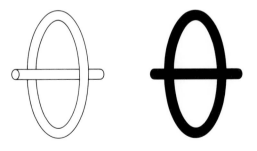

In the experiment on satiation, subjects were first shown the unambiguous figure on the left and then the ambiguous composite test figure on the right.

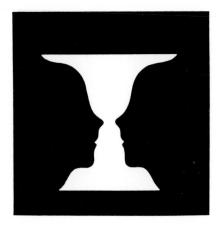

Rubin's vase-and-faces pattern.

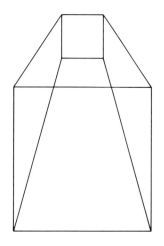

Ambiguous perspective figure. The pattern can be seen either as a hallway (or box) or as a truncated pyramid.

should then be perceived in the composite—as indeed it was, according to the results of these experiments.

Other evidence is less direct. If fatigue is cumulative rather than quickly dissipated, a given subject shown an ambiguous figure *A–B* that can be perceived as either *A* or *B* should, after a number of previous reversals, be expected to switch between *A* and *B* with increasing rapidity. Such acceleration of the rate of reversal has been reported by many investigators.

There are several reasons to be skeptical of the satiation theory, however. Among them is a finding from our own laboratory at Rutgers that reversal often fails to occur if the subject does not realize that the figure is ambiguous. Ordinarily, in experiments on reversal, the subject is first shown the figure and told (or shown) the two different ways in which it can be seen. Then the ambiguous figure is presented continuously, and the subject is instructed to respond every time it is perceived to reverse. Since the investigators want to study perceptual reversal, it is natural enough that they first make sure that the subject knows what the alternatives are. But giving subjects such instructions and information not only establishes the alternatives in the memory of the subject. It may also create what psychologists call a "demand character" in the experiment—the subject assumes that reversal is what is expected.

In our experiments, therefore, we say nothing about the potential reversibility of the figure. We present either Rubin's well-known figure of the vase and faces or the figure shown below it, which can be seen either as a hallway (or box) *or* as a truncated pyramid. Then we ascertain how the figure is perceived, either by occasional samplings or by a careful interview after the period of presentation is over. By conducting experiments in this way, we have found that high-school students often do not reverse at all. More than half of them continue to see whatever they perceive at the outset for up to a minute or so. The remainder may reverse once or, at most, a few times in the period—a far cry from reversal every 5 or 10 seconds, the typical outcome using the traditional method. In fact, these same subjects will reverse frequently when later given the traditional instructions.

These findings suggest that the satiation theory is incorrect. Satiation is presumably a process that is automatic and inexorable, given the stimulus presentation. Whether or not the subject knows that the figure can be reversed and what the specific alternatives are should have no influence on the process.

These findings also suggest that reversal can be explained in an entirely different way. When one does not know that a figure can be seen in more than one way, one tends to organize it on the basis of certain principles—for instance, in favor of the central region of Rubin's vase and faces as figure rather than ground or, in the case of the Necker cube, in favor of the depth organization in which the cube appears to be horizontal rather than tipped on an edge. These preferences were in fact manifested in our experiment. Of course, if no such lawful factors are operating (as in the top left illustration on page 114), the initial organization might be based on chance factors, such as where in the figure the observer happens to be fixating. Once that organization occurs, the naive observer may stick with it, there being no particular reason to alter it. After a long period of inspection, which is only likely to occur in experiments, the observer may become bored (satiated, in the psychological meaning of the word). Or the observer may begin to wonder why he or she is supposed to continue looking at it and begin to look for alternatives, which of course would change the equation. Another possibility is that the observer's attention may wander, thus interfering with the maintenance of the initial organization. Obviously, naive observers sometimes do achieve a reversal, or reversible figures would never have been discovered.

Once the alternative is achieved—or what amounts to the same thing, when subjects are initially told about the alternatives—the situation is entirely different psychologically. Now the observer knows that the figure is reversible. Moreover, the alternative perceptions are represented in memory. Therefore, merely thinking about the alternative not being perceived at any given moment may suffice to lead to a perceptual reorganization in which it *is* perceived. In short, the explanation of reversal in the case of informed observers may have more to do with a shifting memory reference than with neural fatigue.

Recognition and Identification

Earlier, I spoke of the *recognition* of the map of Europe and said it was based upon the proper *perception* of the pattern in the illustration. One can distinguish between a process that leads only to a perception of shape (or of depth, or of size, or of any object property) and a process that leads beyond perception of shape to its recognition and identification. Once we organize the pattern properly and perceive the white region as figure (and rotate it mentally to its upright position), we can recognize this shape as familiar and identify it as representing the continent of Europe. Ordinarily then, for familiar objects at least, recognition occurs after shape has been perceived. To be sure, in our subjective experience, recognition seems to be simultaneous with our perception of shape. But logically we must presume that the process underlying the perception of shape precedes by some finite interval of time, however brief, the process underlying recognition. Of course for unfamiliar, novel shapes, the perception of

Rearrangement of the parts of the letter E creates a shape with little similarity to the original.

Changes in the constituent parts of the letter do not much affect our perception of similarity if the organizational relations are preserved.

shape will not lead to any such recognition. Recognition and identification necessarily imply some contribution from past experience to the present experience, but perception does not.

If recognition implies a contribution from past experience, some enduring repository of such experience must exist in the brain at the time of the present perception. Psychologists refer to such a representation of past experience as a *memory trace* (or, simply, a *trace*). Presumably every prior perception (as well as every thought, feeling, or other conscious mental event) has left behind a memory trace. Psychologists agree, and indeed logic dictates, that access to the appropriate memory trace following perception of a particular shape is based upon the similarity of the trace to that percept. Once a perception occurs, it is as if a search is conducted, obviously at an incredibly rapid rate, through all the traces stored in memory, or perhaps through all the traces classified in some particular category. The search ends when a trace is found that is similar to the present perception. Recognition is based on the unconscious acceptance of the match between trace and percept.

Whether pattern recognition is based upon parallel processing or upon serial processing is still in dispute. In serial processing, one item is processed at a time. In parallel processing, all items are processed simultaneously. There are difficulties with each possibility. Serial processing would take too long, even if each comparison of the percept with a different trace required only a few milliseconds. After all, there are almost an infinite number of memories, while recognition takes only a fraction of a second. Yet the results of an experiment conducted by Saul Sternberg of Bell Laboratories favors serial comparison. Subjects were first given a list of items to memorize. Shortly thereafter they were shown an "old" or a "new" item and were asked to indicate whether or not it had been on the list. Sternberg discovered that observers' reaction time increased by a constant amount for each additional item on the memorized list. This suggests that the list had been "searched" serially. On the other hand, parallel processing would take little time, but then what mechanism would permit matching a percept to all possible traces at once?

What properties of an object's shape make it seem more or less similar to other shapes? The answer to this question is of direct relevance to our understanding of recognition as well as form perception. In the case of recognition, such properties would provide the basis for the search of one's memories. If we wanted to build a machine that could "recognize" figures—for example, one that could "read"—we must know what properties of the object now detected govern the search for similar memories, or prototypes, stored in the machine's memory.

The most obvious answer to the question of what makes one figure look like another is that it is the number of parts, or "features," they have in common. Some letters of the alphabet, for instance, have common features: both *O* and *Q* contain an oval, both *M* and *W* have four vertical or near vertical lines, an *E* is an *F* with an extra line, and so on.

However, the geometry of a figure—its shape—can hardly be reduced to a sum of its parts. Consider the two figures on the facing page. If the parts of an *E* are rearranged, there may be little similarity between it and an *E*. Clearly it is the position of the parts relative to one another that matters. If the relations between the parts are preserved, the whole shape will remain unchanged, despite rather extreme changes in the parts themselves. This was a point the Gestaltists emphasized: Visual and auditory patterns depend upon stimulus relations; if such relations are preserved, a pattern can be transposed without any effect on the perceived similarity of the whole. In music, one can transpose a melody in key or octave and preserve the recognizability of the melody. All or many of the parts, the individual tones, are now different from those in the original melody, but the tonal "steps" and rhythmical relations are preserved. By the same token, a visual pattern can be transposed in size, in the make-up of the contour, and in the location of the image on the retina without altering its appearance very much, if at all.

Another answer that has been proposed to explain what makes one figure look like another is that similarity is based on a neural matching process. However, a figure's image will rarely fall upon the retina in exactly the same place as before. A simple experiment shows that such correspondence is not essential for the perception of similarity and the consequent recognition to occur. First, look at the left portion of the illustration at right by fixating X_1; then, fixate X_2. From what is known about the anatomy of the visual pathways, these two images stimulate different retinal loci and are transmitted to entirely different terminal loci in the visual cortex. Therefore, unless there is some still higher center to which the pattern of neural transmission is projected, where somehow these images *do* correspond point for point—which seems highly unlikely—perception of similarity and the resulting recognition are not based upon identity of locus of the underlying neural event. Such a neural matching process, were it to occur, has been referred to as *template matching* in the experimental literature. Template matching has been considered to be a possible basis for a machine to "recognize" patterns and is indeed actually used in some cases (for example, in the recognition of checks by the numbers imprinted on them). However, for template matching to occur despite the continual changes in the position, size, and orientation of figures, the pattern would first have to be normalized, or transformed into the correct position, size, and orientation. In order to know precisely how to normalize a figure, however, the figure would first have to be recognized by the machine!

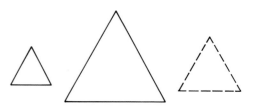

Transpositions of size, type of contour, or locus of a figure's projection on the retina have little, if any, adverse effect on perceived similarity.

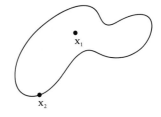

If point X_1 is fixated and then point X_2, the loci of the retinal and cortical patterns of excitation are different. Yet form perception is little affected, if at all.

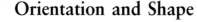

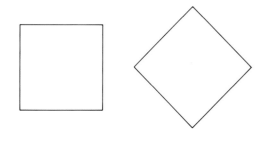

A square and a diamond, although identical except for their orientation, look very different as shapes.

Orientation and Shape

These considerations suggest that the most important determinant of shape perception that allows us to recognize one figure as similar to another and different from a third is its internal geometry. They also suggest that such internal geometry is a function of the spatial relation of a figure's parts to one another. There is a fact about form perception that seems to contradict this principle, however. Consider the difference in appearance of the square and the diamond in the illustration at left. As the great physicist Ernst Mach pointed out around the turn of the century, these two figures are geometrically identical and differ only in orientation. If perceived shape were only a function of internal geometry, orientation should not affect the way they look, but obviously it does. Further proof that it does is given in the illustration of the map of Europe. Even if we organize this pattern appropriately when first viewing it and see the white region as figure, we are not likely to recognize it unless we realize that it has been tilted 90 degrees.

Why should orientation affect perceived shape? Some investigators have argued that the explanation has something to do with the changed orientation of the image on the retina, which would lead to a change in the orientation of the pattern projected onto the visual cortex of the brain. One can do a very simple experiment to test this idea: Prop up this book so that the page is vertical. Then tilt your head by 45 degrees and look again at the square and diamond. The square will probably continue to look like a square and the diamond like a diamond. Yet because of the head tilt, which carries the eyes along with it, the square now leads to a retinal image of a diamond and the diamond to a retinal image of a square. Therefore, if it were the altered orientation of the image of an object that causes it to look different, the square should now look like a diamond and the diamond like a square.

Why don't they? Because we continue to perceive the orientation of these figures in the same way with the head (and eyes) tilted as with the head upright. Orientation constancy is achieved. Thus, the sides of the square appear to be horizontal and vertical no matter what the orientation of their retinal images. Similarly, the sides of the diamond appear to be oblique even with the head tilted. Only a change in *perceived* orientation affects perceived shape. In the case of the map of Europe, because the naive observer does not know it is disoriented, entirely different regions appear to be at the top, bottom, and sides than those that constitute the north, south, east, and west of the continent. Of course, once we know about disorientation, as with the map or the square and diamond, we can rotate a figure in imagination and thus overcome any effect of disorientation. For that reason, it is generally important in experiments

Yields "diamond"
image

Yields square
image

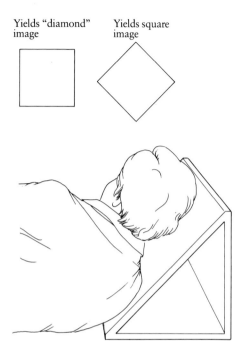

This experiment demonstrates that the perception of square and diamond shapes is not based on their differing retinal orientations.

on this issue to be sure that the observer does not know about the change of orientation.

Why should a change in a figure's perceived orientation affect its perceived shape? Although the answer to this question is still in dispute, I believe that it has far-reaching implications for the entire problem of form perception. In my view, the answer lies in a process of form description in which our perceptual system engages. Compare, for example, the two figures at the right. The one on the left initially looks like an irregular quadrilateral resting solidly on one of its sides; the one on the right resembles a symmetrical diamondlike figure balanced precariously on its tip. Yet the two figures differ only in orientation.

The different appearances of this pattern suggest that they are based on a process of mental description of which we are unaware. The pattern looks different because its unconscious (and nonverbal) descriptions differ drastically in these two cases, one entailing irregularity and the other symmetry. In other words, the figure on the left is unconsciously described as "an irregular four-sided figure resting stably on a horizontal base" and the one on the right as "a symmetrical diamondlike figure balanced on a point." However, the description is not expressed in natural language such as is written here but in the same kind of language upon which thought is based and which may be used by animals and infants in their thinking as well as their perception. That symmetry should be part of the description in one case but not in the other may seem odd, since of course both figures are symmetrical about the long

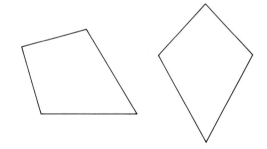

These figures, identical except for their orientation, look very different unless one of them is mentally rotated. It is proposed that they look different because their unconscious descriptions differ.

axis, but experiments indicate that we are most likely to detect symmetry when the axis is vertical and less likely to do so (or we do not do so at all) when it is horizontal or oblique.

The theory I am suggesting for all of form perception, not merely for the aspect of it affected by orientation, then, is that perceived shape is determined by the content of an unconscious description we make of objects. That description is a joint function of the object's geometry and its perceived orientation, although other factors enter in as well.

There is a seeming flaw in the entire argument presented here about orientation and form. If one uses certain kinds of material other than simple geometrical forms, such as pictures of faces or printed or written words, and conducts the experiment on head tilt described on page 126 but for head tilts of 90 degrees or more, and particularly for tilts of 180 degrees, the outcome is the opposite of what I have maintained. The cartoon at left makes the point succinctly. To read print or to recognize faces, it is better to maintain the image's retinal orientation than to maintain the figure's orientation in the environment.

How can these seemingly contradictory examples be explained? After all, in these cases there is no real change in perceived orientation when the figure is tilted along with the head because we remain perfectly aware of which region is the top of the face or of the word. But, if these figures remain upright and are not tilted along with the head, a difficulty does arise. For simple material it is easy enough to achieve the proper description despite the retinal abnormality of orientation of the image. In viewing a square with the head tilted 45 degrees, for example, it is easy enough to recover the fact that its sides are horizontal and vertical, which is the essence of perceptual "squareness." But this process of correction is far more difficult to achieve when the stimulus consists of multiple parts, as is the case with the letters making up words or the features making up a face. If we cannot correct all these parts and the relation among them in one operation, many will remain uncorrected and thus will be seen as if their tops and bottoms were governed by retinal orientation. That leads to the wrong description. Our initial lack of awareness of the extreme distortion of the face in the left-hand photograph on the facing page is testimony to the inadequacy of our perception when the image is inverted on the retina. Similarly, when printed words are viewed upside down, various letters are incorrectly "described" on the basis of their retinal orientation—a *u* becomes an *n*, or a *d* a *p*, and so forth.

Effects of Past Experience

In order to recognize and identify an object, we must first perceive it. The process underlying the perception of form itself must occur before con-

"*. . . and now a few words for our prone viewers . . .*"

To recognize faces, it is best to maintain the normal orientation of the retinal image.

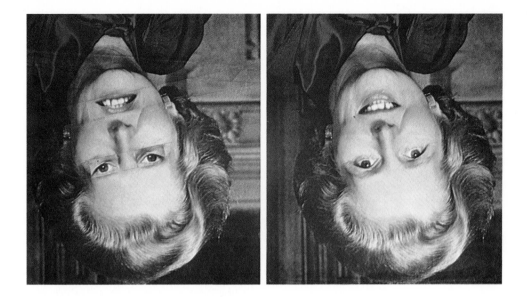

tact with memory traces. Thus, memory content (or past experience) ought not to determine form perception. As noted, this argument gains in plausibility when we realize that the very basis of accessing memories is the similarity between the perception and the (relevant) memories that are stored. The process leading to perception must thus occur first in order for the specific similarity that is to govern memory-search to be established. In more contemporary jargon, psychologists would say that perception is a bottom-up process, not a top-down process. *Bottom up* means that the process proceeds from lower levels of sensory processing toward higher cognitive events; *top down* means that higher cognitive mental activity somehow affects lower levels of processing, such as the detection or encoding of contours or sounds.

Logic thus seems to rule out the possibility that past experience can affect perception of properties such as form or depth. However, consider what happens when we view the illustrations on the following page. At first these fragmented figures are not identifiable, but with continued inspection or a hint, the fragments suddenly are perceptually reorganized and recognized. In one, a Dalmatian can be seen where before it was well camouflaged in the array of spots; in another, a bearded face like that of Jesus emerges where it had no perceptual reality before. And consider what happens in viewing the two figures at the top of page 131 in which recognition requires not overcoming a false grouping with elements outside the object but rather grouping the same elements differently. In all these cases, an impression of depth emerges where before only two dimensions were seen.

Arriving at these impressions of form and depth is not *merely* a matter of going from perception to identification in a bottom-up direction because along with such identification comes a perceptual change. Whereas normally recognition of an object does not alter our perception of its form or depth, these patterns *look* different in several ways when they are

The distortion of Margaret Thatcher's face in one of these pictures may go unnoticed unless the book is turned upside down.

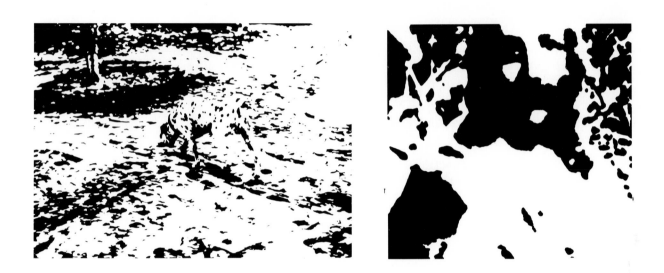

Past experience enables a change in perceptual organization and description at the moment that recognition of these patterns occurs.

recognized. Grouping is different, as is most clearly seen in the picture of the Dalmatian; depth generally emerges that was not present before; and, perhaps most importantly, the figures now look like the objects they represent—they have the shapes and depth relations of those objects. If these fragmented-figure effects were not perceptual in character, it would be mysterious indeed why viewing them would not lead immediately to recognition. Thus we can assume that some mental process that precedes or accompanies the moment of recognition entails a perceptual reorganization.

The examples of fragmented figures indicate that past experience with the objects represented affects our perception of the figures—otherwise, we would be unlikely to hit upon the reorganization that allows us to see a Dalmatian or a bearded face. Past experience also affects our perception of these figures in another way. Robert Leeper, then at Cornell University, has shown that, if observers are presented with these fragmented figures again some time after they first succeed in identifying them, they can always perceive them correctly, even when shown them very briefly.

When these figures are recognized, an impression of depth is created.

This greater ease in reorganizing such figures is based on experience with the fragmented figures themselves rather than on experience with the objects they represent.

The effects of past experience on perception of form are evident in other instances as well. When we first look at the illustration at right, we are likely to see the black regions as figure. If the white spaces were not representations of something familiar, they would remain as ground. However, once we realize what is potentially present in the white space, we can reverse the figure-ground organization. It is then difficult *not* to perceive the white spaces as figure. This difficulty reveals an important principle: Preferred organizations tend to be irresistible and irreversible. In the present example, one might say that the presence of a memory trace for the shape of the white region but not the black region leads to a stabilizing effect such that the white region remains as figure.

A similar effect is shown in the illustration on the following page. A shape is seen for which much of the contour is not present. To perceive this shape, one must reverse figure and ground since at the outset the

When the white region is organized as figure, a familiar pattern is seen. Once that happens, the white figure tends to remain dominant.

black regions, being surrounded by white, are favored as figure. This effect is referred to as that of *illusory contours*. While it was first reported years ago, the current interest was ignited by striking figures such as the one at left below created by Gaetano Kanizsa. Not only does one see contours that are not present, but the figure thus defined acquires a lightness different from that of the surrounding page, which has the same physical reflectance. In the illustration, the white figure looks whiter than the white page.

The explanation of this effect is in dispute. Based on research I conducted with Richard Anson, my own view is that perceiving the figure with its illusory contour is an elegant solution to the problem of what such a retinal image might represent. That stimulus after all is ambiguous, and at first one may tend to perceive the isolated black fragments. But the illusory figure percept integrates all fragments into one coherent solution and accounts both for alignment of some of the contours with one another and for the incompleteness of various fragments. Thus, in the figure at left, instead of perceiving three black pies with sectors missing and three angles, various elements of which are inexplicably aligned with one another, one perceives a solid white triangle covering three black disks and an entire inverted triangle.

Is past experience a factor here? In some cases, it undoubtedly is. Where incomplete fragments of familiar shapes are present, they serve to suggest the complete object occluded by an interposed object. But this factor is not a necessary one. In any event, once the interposed region is perceived as figure with its illusory contours, it is irreversibly preferred.

More generally, many line drawings would probably not look the way they do were it not for experience with the kind of object they represent. We saw an example of this in Chapter 3. Prior experience with real cubes or boxlike structures is quite probably necessary in order to perceive the drawing of the lower cube that appears on page 78 as three-dimensional since there are no known depth cues in the illustration.

A very important principle is implicit in the foregoing discussion. When experience affects perception, it does not do so by molding the stimulus to conform to how things were seen in the past. It is not entirely a top-down process. Rather, in the cases we considered, such as the perception of fragmented figures, *something* was first perceived bottom-up, on the basis of certain principles of organization and without recourse to experience. Once that initial perception occurred, if what was seen was similar in some respect to objects seen in the past, those memories were accessed and they played a role in the further processing of the stimulus input. A useful term to characterize effects of this kind is *enrichment*. The perception is enriched by, though not entirely determined by, memories of earlier perceptual experience. Another way of describing these effects

A figure containing illusory contours. The subjectively constructed figure appears to be whiter than the page itself.

is to divide up the processing of the stimulus into stages. In the first stage, the stimulus is organized in accordance with various principles such as the Gestalt psychologists uncovered. In a further stage, the shape of units that are segregated and organized as the figure is described. In many cases, the process ends there, because the observer does not know that an alternative exists and is not searching for one. But if a search does take place, or if the organized stimulus is sufficiently similar to certain stored memories, then a final stage occurs. In this stage, the memory content is accessed and is woven into the final percept so as to enrich it.

Discriminating Among Similar Objects

Past experience also affects our perception of differences among members of a class of objects. For the casual visitor to a zoo, all monkeys tend to look alike, but they look quite different to their keepers. At first, twins look identical to us, but the differences emerge quite clearly on further contact. To children, printed words look very similar to one another. The initial difficulty in distinguishing between very similar "objects" can be seen in the photographs of twins at right and on the overleaf.

These examples raise two questions: Why are the members of a class indistinguishable at the outset? What happens with continued experience to change perception? The answer to the first question seems to be fairly obvious: The members of a class are very similar to one another. Therefore, whether we encounter one or another member of it, the perception is much the same and thus is likely to lead to the same memory trace. But since the pictures of, say, the twins *are* different in subtle respects from one another, why don't we detect these differences in the first place? No doubt we would do so if the pictures were placed side by side and if we were looking for the differences because we knew that they were there. That we generally do not do this seems to be telling us something important about perception, something that concerns *attention*.

ATTENTION   When we first encounter a member of a class with which we are relatively unfamiliar, I believe that we attend to those global properties that distinguish it from other classes of objects: for the infant, a face as against all other things; for the adult, one twin face as against all other faces; and so forth. We "describe" only those characteristics to which we attend. That, in turn, means that the memory trace left behind contains no more specificity than did the global percept.

In our laboratory, my colleagues and I have done an experiment on form perception that demonstrates this hypothesized failure to perceive all the subtle nuances in a complex figure. The subjects saw a figure, such as figure A at the top of the next page, for a brief period. Shortly thereaf-

The girl pictured on the following page initially looks identical to her twin pictured here. With experience, however, we would readily be able to distinguish between them.

Experiment on the nuances of form perception. After briefly viewing A, subjects had great difficulty identifying it when shown A and B together. However, they had little difficulty selecting the correct one when shown C and D together.

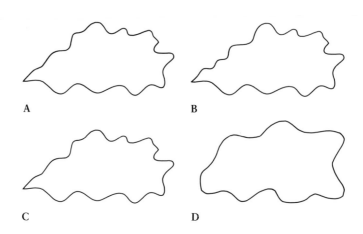

A   B

C   D

ter they took a test consisting of two or more figures, one of which was the same as the one just seen. The others were similar globally but differed in specifics. Our subjects did no better than chance in selecting the correct alternative among the shapes illustrated. Yet, when they were given an easier test in which none of the wrong alternatives was of the same overall shape as the original, the subjects had no difficulty in selecting the right one. Thus, it is clear that the global character of the shape was perceived and encoded into memory, but the details of it were not.

In daily life, however, we are usually required to discriminate among similar members of a class. The infant must learn its parents' faces, the child must learn to read, the zookeeper must learn to differentiate the monkeys, and so on. By dint of necessity, then, whether or not we are consciously aware of doing so, we begin to attend to the subtle nuances or details. Naturally, when we do so, the perception changes in the direction of greater specificity and precision. Once that happens, we acquire a family of slightly different memories rather than merely the one undifferentiated memory we had at the outset. We can then make separate associations to each of these—for example, a name. If at this point, when looking at twins, we notice that one has a wide nose and high cheekbones whereas the other has a narrower nose and lower cheekbones, we can say that we perceive the twins differently.

If this reasoning is correct, attention is a very important factor in perception. The claim is not merely that we can bring this or that object, all of which are perceived, into the center stage of awareness. The claim is that such a manipulation of attention affects perception itself.

In a now classic study initiated by E. Colin Cherry at the University of London and MIT, two verbal messages were simultaneously "fed" to a subject, each through a separate earphone. The analogy was to the situation in a cocktail party where we are confronted by several simultaneous streams of conversation but can only attend to one. In the experiment, the subject had to do so by repeating one message aloud as it was heard. The subject was then tested for recall of *both* messages. The message the subject repeated aloud was well recalled, but little of the unattended one was recalled. Subsequent research using this method established that very little of the unattended message is perceived.

Analogous experiments have been done in vision. In an experiment that Dan Gutman and I did, overlapping visual figures of novel shapes in differing colors were presented to subjects at a fairly rapid rate. The subject was to rate all red (or for other subjects, green) figures on a scale of aesthetic preference—a slight deception intended to focus attention on one figure only in each overlapping pair. When all pairs in the series had been shown, the subject was given a recognition test to determine whether the unattended figures as well as the attended ones could be recognized. The results indicated significant recognition of the attended figures but performance no better than chance for the unattended ones. Follow-up experiments showed that even directly after a given slide had been seen there was no evidence for any memory of the unattended figure, even if it was the outline of a very familiar shape.

Why does the perception of shape require attention? This is a matter about which investigators can disagree, but I believe it can be explained in terms of the description process that I suggested is the basis of form perception. Such description occurs for the attended figure in each pair in the foregoing experiment but not for the unattended figure. Here we have a more drastic consequence of the absence of attention than was suggested in the cases of initial failure to discriminate among members of a class of objects. In these cases, attention is given to each member when it is seen, but it is focused on its global properties and not on its details.

What has been said thus far about the role of past experience in visual perception can be summarized by the following statements:

1. Past experience is not generally necessary for the perception of form because form perception is based upon bottom-up organization of the stimulus, along the lines suggested by the Gestalt psychologists, and upon a process of description of the organized units.

2. Past experience does lead to the recognition and identification of familiar objects based on the similarity of the perceived form of such objects to the appropriate memory.

3. Under certain conditions, past experience can lead to an alteration (enrichment) in the appearance of a pattern.

4. Under certain conditions, past experience can also lead to stabilization in the way a stimulus pattern is organized.

5. For similar members of certain classes of objects, past experience can lead to perceptual discriminations that otherwise would not occur.

Overlapping figures used in the experiment on attention. In attending to one of these figures, the other is not processed adequately and thus is not recognized in a subsequent test.

These effects occur as a second stage of perception, by way of supplementing perceptions that would presumably occur in a bottom-up direction even without any past experience; in fact, they presuppose that the first stage of perception is not based on such experience. Implicit here is the further assumption that the past experience that can yield these effects is *visual* and that it does so by virtue of *visual* memories.

The argument, then, is not that perception is a function of past experience but only that there are certain perceptual effects of such experience. However, in the history of the study of perception, the claim about past experience has been much more extreme and far-reaching. As we have seen, one of the most influential theories about visual perception was Berkeley's theory that visual perception is learned on the basis of information available from the sense of touch.

VISION AND TOUCH   Berkeley argued that touch educates vision so that eventually we seem to experience visual distance directly. He made the same argument with respect to other visual properties, such as size, orientation, and even shape (which he referred to as "figure"). Some might say that Berkeley could hardly have argued that touch educates vision if his central thesis was that the two senses were totally distinct, separate, and incommensurate. However, because vision and touch occur together, Berkeley was able to maintain that, despite their distinctness, associations could be formed between the two, just as is possible between words and things, despite *their* distinctness. "Visible figures are the marks of tangible figures and . . . it is plain, that in themselves they are little regarded, or upon any other score than for their connection with tangible figures, which by nature they are ordained to signify."

What Berkeley meant was that, while a square and a circle might in some sense look different from one another (because, he hints, the square has "parts" and the circle doesn't), their particular shapes do not arise in perception until we have learned to identify each image with the way each object feels when it is grasped.

Berkeley's argument presupposes that there are no problems to be explained about tactual, or haptic, perception. It implies that the world of touch is organized, although it too is based upon incoming sensory data upon which, in fact, organization must be imposed. And it implies that touch perception is sufficiently precise to be able to educate vision to perform with such exquisite precision with respect to shape, size, and distance. In fact, however, touch (or proprioception based on manual or bodily motion) undoubtedly permits far less in the way of precision.

Although the Berkeleyan thesis was very influential, it faded into the background in the first half of this century. But more recently it has come under scrutiny again because of experiments that have been performed in which a conflict was created between visual and tactually based information. One of the first observations of this kind was made by James Gibson in the early 1930s. In the course of conducting an experiment on the effect of continued exposure to a visually curved line, Gibson required the observers to look at a perfectly straight rod through a wedge prism, which rendered its image curved. He reported that, when subjects were allowed to run their hands along the rod, which should have provided haptic information that the rod was straight, it neither looked straight nor felt straight. In fact, it felt curved, just the way it looked. For Gibson, this observation was tangential to the purpose of the experiment, and he did not follow it up.

In Gibson's experiment, visual perception and touch perception are in direct conflict. If touch information is the ultimate source of how things appear visually, as Berkeley argued, one would think that touch would be dominant. However, when psychologists began to test this thesis directly a few decades later, the result was always the same as in Gibson's observation. Not only did vision *dominate*, so that observers judged the object more in terms of the visual than the tactual information, but the tactual "feel" of the object conformed to the visual "look" of it. Vision captured touch.

In one experiment, for example, Jack Victor and I created a conflict of *size* between the two senses. The subject looked through a lens (without realizing it was a lens) at a square of a certain size. Using vision alone, subjects judged the square to be about one-half its true size (exactly what one would predict knowing the minification value of the lens). Using touch alone—grasping the square without looking at it—subjects judged the size more or less correctly, as they should have, since there was no distortion with respect to touch. But when looking and grasping *simultaneously*, subjects experienced the square to be half its size, corresponding more or less exactly to how they experienced it by vision alone. Moreover, the square *felt* to them as if it were half size. We did a similar experiment on *shape*. The cylindrical lens we used altered size along one axis, so that a square looked like a rectangle. The result was the same. The shape percept was dominated by vision and visual capture of touch occurred.

One might argue, however, that these experiments are not decisive with respect to Berkeley's thesis because vision may not innately signify particular shapes at the outset of life but may nevertheless become dominant later on. Thus, after a lifetime of associated tactual experience, a straight visual image might become a strong cue to the presence of a straight object. The proper experiment would either be one with infants or one with adults in which they would be exposed to the sensory conflict long enough for a possible process of reeducation to occur.

Arrangement for the study of perception when there is conflicting sensory information about the shape of an object. Vision both dominates and captures touch.

Some research has been launched in the study of this problem in infants, but not enough has been done to draw final conclusions. However, experiments of the kind described have been conducted with adults. For example, subjects looking through a distorting optical device were given a task that required them to continuously look at objects while grasping them. Thus the possibility existed for an adaptive change in vision to occur, because haptic information could serve to indicate that the visual image signified an object of a size, shape, or orientation that was different from what the visual image had indicated at the outset. In other words, in this kind of experiment, unlike the one simply testing the immediate impact of the sensory conflict, the possibility exists for touch to recalibrate visual sensations. The result, however, was just the opposite. Touch perception was altered or recalibrated. At the end of the adaptation period, when tested by vision alone, subjects judged the properties of an object in much the same way as they did at the outset; when tested by touch alone, however, they judged the properties of the object differently. For example, a 1-inch square, when grasped (but not seen), was interpreted as smaller than an inch if the subjects had viewed the square through a minifying lens during the adaptation phase. The reason for this change is not hard to understand. By virtue of continued visual capture, the squares all looked smaller and felt smaller than they were. Thus the "feel" normally associated with a visual square of a given size became associated with a smaller square. This new association endured, at least through the experiment until the time of the test. In one experiment of this kind conducted by Charles S. and Judith R. Harris, then at the University of Pennsylvania, subjects who drew pictures and doodled while looking through left-right reversing prisms made many errors afterward when asked to write letters and numbers without seeing them. They either drew many letters or numbers backward or felt that they had done so when they had not. This occurred after only 30 to 60 minutes of exposure to the prisms. Apparently, the subjects had learned to feel a left-to-right movement of the hand as right-to-left, and vice versa.

A somewhat different question concerns the plasticity or malleability of visual perception. Is it possible that, if by optical distortion a straight contour happened to yield a curved image instead of a straight one, such an image could come, by means of the appropriate experience, to signify a straight contour? The method employed to answer this question has been to require subjects to view the world through wedge prisms placed in goggles.

We have seen that, given contradictory information from touch, visual capture occurs rather than any change of visual shape based on tactual information. But suppose that the observer is encouraged to move around actively in the environment. There may then be other kinds of

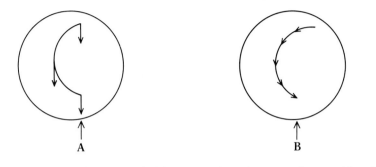

When an observer walks by a curved line, the image of the line will flow across the retina as shown in A. When the observer walks by a straight line while wearing prisms, the image of the line will flow as shown in B.

information than that provided by manual exploration that could indicate that the curved images in reality emanate from straight contours. For example, when an observer wearing prisms moves along a straight line or edge, the flow of its curved image over the retina conforms to the behavior of the image of a straight line viewed by a moving observer without prisms, as shown in figure B above. It does not conform to the "flow" of the image of a curved line seen without prisms, as shown in figure A above. Or, to give another example, if one were to walk around to the opposite side of a curved rod, the sign of its curvature would ordinarily change. Through the prism, a straight vertical rod appears curved, but it does not change the sign of its curvature when one walks to the opposite side because the prism always displaces the rays of light to one particular side. As a result, a straight vertical rod will always produce an image that is curved in one particular direction.

Therefore, a process of perceptual learning might occur, leading to a change in the way things look. The critical test of whether or not visual perception has changed is to ask how things look on removing the optical device. In a dark room, for example, the observer is asked to indicate when a luminous line whose curvature is variable appears straight. Suppose adaptation has occurred during the wearing of the prism goggles such that a straight line, seen through a prism that is, let us say, of 20 diopters strength and that renders the image of the line convex to the left, appears less curved than it did at the outset, or appears entirely straight. If such image curvature now signifies straightness, a straight line viewed in the dark should appear quite curved, as if convex to the right. To counteract such an adaptive effect, the observer would have to select a line that was convex to the left. The magnitude of curvature that appears straight, measured in prism diopters, would be a measure of the degree of adaptation.

How much (if any) adaptation occurs? Disappointingly little. In an experiment done by John Hay and Herbert Pick, Jr., then at Cornell University, subjects wore 20-diopter prisms for 42 days. The illustration on the following page shows how a straight line looks through a prism of

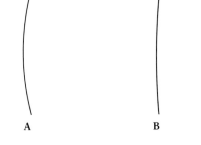

A. *How a vertical straight line looks when viewed at reading distance through a 20-diopter wedge prism.* B. *How the same line looks through a 6-diopter prism.*

this strength. The degree of adaptation obtained averaged 6 diopters. The illustration shows that this degree of curvature is just noticeably different from a straight line. Moreover, only some of the effect after 42 days can be attributed to perceptual learning. There is an adaptative effect in viewing curved lines that is of an entirely different kind (more like color adaptation). This effect occurs within a matter of minutes, and it is of the order of around 3 diopters. One might conclude, therefore, that the experiment is more of a demonstration of *lack* of perceptual learning as regards shape than it is of an adaptive change. Thus, straightness and curvature, as shape properties, may be determined more by innate factors than by past experience. More generally, the results of these experiments, and of other experiments on the dominance of vision as compared to touch, suggest that the visual perception of shape is innate and occurs in a bottom-up direction.

Form Perception Without Past Experience

What evidence is there that form perception is, in fact, innate? The most direct way to discover the answer to this question would be to study individuals who were born blind and later gained their sight. The philosopher William Molyneux asked precisely this question in a famous letter to his friend John Locke, published in 1706:

> Suppose a man *born* blind, and now adult, and taught by his *touch* to distinguish between a cube and a sphere of the same metal, and nighly of the same bigness, so as to tell, when he felt one and the other, which is the cube, which the sphere. Suppose then the cube and sphere be placed on a table, and the blind man be made to see: *query*, whether *by his sight, before he touched them* he could now distinguish and tell which is the globe, which the cube?

The matter is not that simple, however. The experiment Molyneux proposed could not resolve the question of the innateness of visual form perception because it presupposes immediate transfer from touch to vision. What we want to know is whether or not a person, on first regaining sight, could discriminate visually between two figures such as a sphere and a cube—that is, whether or not they would look different from one another and, if so, whether or not the person would perceive each shape the way we do. We need not expect that by sight alone the sphere would also suggest to the observer the tactual feel with which it was associated before sight was restored. The data we have on this question derive from medical reports over a few centuries, gathered together in a book by M. von Senden in 1932. Unfortunately, the attending physicians generally did not know precisely what questions to ask or what experiments to do (assuming they were even interested in the scientific issue under discussion here). To be valid and useful cases, the patients had to be totally blind in both eyes from birth, to recover vision in at least one eye through the removal of the lens containing an opacity (cataract), to be old enough to be able to answer questions, to be successfully fitted with a new lens capable of yielding an adequately focused image, and to have recovered from the physical and emotional trauma of the surgery. The written records of the case must also be adequate and intelligible. Few of the recorded cases fulfill these necessary requirements; those that do are ambiguous as to their implications. Nowadays, few such cases are recorded in the scientific literature because, among populations in which the issue is likely to be studied, surgery is performed early in infancy if it can be performed at all.

EVIDENCE FROM ANIMALS DEPRIVED OF NORMAL VISION The next best kind of data, it might be thought, would come from animals reared in the dark and tested when they achieve maturity. Such experiments have been performed, but, as we have seen in previous chapters, rearing in the dark prevents the normal maturation of the visual nervous system.

Even animals reared under conditions in which they are exposed to homogeneous but unpatterned light stimulation during part or all of each day do not mature normally. This finding grows out of research following up David Hubel's and Torsten Wiesel's discoveries at Harvard University in the early 1960s of detector mechanisms in the brain that were most responsive to contours stimulating a given region of the retina in one particular orientation. These detector mechanisms were assumed to be present at birth, but later research revealed that the nature of the detector mechanisms found depended on the kind of environment in which the animal was reared in its earliest days. For example, if only vertical contours are present in the early environment, then only detectors for that orientation of a retinal contour can later be found. If few or no contours are present in the early environment, then few detectors for any contour orientation can later be found.

Although it is not yet clear what role such detector mechanisms play in visual form perception, the evidence supports the hypothesis that rearing animals in deprived visual environments will lead to impairment of vision. In fact, it would seem that the requirement for normal maturation of the visual nervous system (which may include special kinds of growth of neurons in the brain) rules out all experiments in which animals are deprived of normal vision as a source of definitive evidence about the innateness of form perception. The same reasoning applies to the study of individuals born blind who gain their sight; it is likely that these people have suffered some degree of impairment of their visual system.

Various species will transfer the learned discrimination between the pair of shapes on the left to the similar pairs of shapes shown in the center and on the right.

EVIDENCE FROM NEWLY BORN ORGANISMS   Mature members of such species as chimpanzees, monkeys, elephants, cats, rats, chickens, pigeons, and fish can discriminate differing visual forms from one another. That these animals are indeed perceiving shape rather than merely responding to the specific size of a form or specific details, such as the vertex of a triangle at the top of a figure, is indicated by the transfer of a learned discrimination to another pair of figures. For example, having learned to discriminate between a triangle and a cross, primates and some other species will typically transfer that learning to a test pair of such shapes of a larger or smaller size or in a different orientation. A particularly interesting finding is that discrimination transfers from black on white to white on black or from solidly colored figures to outline figures. Thus, although form perception undoubtedly differs across species, particularly between some animals and humans with respect to acuity, to attributes, to locations that receive attention, and to the range of transferability or generalizability, it also is similar in certain important respects. Figure-ground differentiation and perceptual organization are undoubtedly common factors for most if not all species.

Is such form perception as is typical in adult animals present at birth in such animals? We have some data suggesting an affirmative answer to this question. One experiment is based on an entirely different method from the traditional one of requiring discrimination learning, which, as we have seen in previous chapters, poses inherent problems because newborns may not have the behavioral repertoires or cognitive capacities to respond to discrimination tests in ways that reveal much about what they perceive. Suppose a certain behavior is "instinctual" (now referred to in the field as "species specific" behavior) and occurs shortly after birth or hatching. If that behavior is triggered by a particular perception, we would know that that perception would have to be innately determined. (The thinking here parallels the utilization of the visual cliff to study the possible innate presence of distance perception in animals, as discussed in Chapter 3.)

So reasoned Robert Fantz at the University of Chicago 25 years ago in wondering about the vision of newly hatched chicks. Chicks tend to peck at small particles or small spots that stand out from the rest of the ground. Because grain, the chicken's source of food, is oval in shape, there would be an evolutionary advantage if they preferred to peck at small particles of a roundish shape rather than at those of other shapes. Evidence of such a preference would therefore implicate form perception as the necessary basis of it. To test this hypothesis, Fantz placed one- to three-day-old chicks (kept in the dark until the experiment began) in a box with variously shaped small objects arranged around the walls. The objects were set into transparent plastic covers behind which were sensitive microswitches that could record each peck. The number of pecks of all chicks recorded at each figure could thus be used as a measure of their preference. The results of one experiment using 100 chicks were as follows: spherical object, 24,346; ellipsoidal object, 28,122; pyramidal object, 2492; star-shaped object, 2076. There were thus roughly ten times as many pecks to rounded shapes—a clear preference. It would seem safe to conclude that chicks perceive form from birth and not on the basis of past experience.

Form appears to be a property capable of eliciting or "releasing" instinctual reactions in other species as well. For example, herring-gull chicks, on the day after hatching, will "beg" far more frequently at a model whose shape resembles the bill of the parent than at models of other shapes. No such preference could be manifested unless the capability of form perception itself was present from birth.

Human infants also show preferences with respect to what shapes they will look at during extended periods of observation. To discover such preferences, psychologists monitor the direction of the infant's gaze. A common technique for doing so is illustrated at right. The object at which the infant looks is reflected off the cornea over the pupil of the eye. The experimenter can simply clock the amount of time spent looking at one thing or another or, better yet, can record the session on film or videotape and analyze it later. In recent research, the infant's eye movements are accurately determined by an apparatus that tracks the eyes.

In the earliest experiments using techniques of this kind, psychologists found that infants preferred to look at some colors more than others, from which it was inferred, reasonably enough, that infants can perceive colors. But Robert Fantz realized that the same technique could be used to study form perception in infants. If infants could indeed discriminate among forms, and if they preferred to look at one pattern more than at another, then they would spend more time gazing at that pattern. The results of this kind of research on human infants can be summarized as follows: In the first month of life, infants show no preference for one simple geometrical shape, such as a circle or a cross, over another. But they do spend more time looking at a complex pattern (such as a checkerboard) than at a simple one (such as an outline square). They prefer to look at drawings of the human face rather than at drawings of the same overall shape and size, but they show the same preference for face configurations in which the features are so thoroughly scrambled that one must wonder if the figures have any quality at all that makes them facelike.

Infants' form preference is studied by observing their preferences for gazing at different patterns.

After the first month, and increasingly so with advancing age, infants show a preference for a normal as opposed to a scrambled face and for some simple shapes over others.

To ascertain with greater precision exactly what region within a figure an infant is looking at, more sophisticated devices for recording eye movement and position have been used. With one such apparatus, Philip Salapatek and his associates at Yale University were able to show that newborn infants, in looking at a triangle, tended to direct their gaze at its vertices. Further research suggests that infants tend to seek out areas of the greatest change or discontinuity.

What this research based on direction of gaze means is not yet clear because preference and perception are both determinants of the behavior under study. A clear preference to look at a certain object tells us that the requisite perception must be occurring, but the absence of such a preference can mean either the absence of the necessary perceptual ability or the absence of a preference. Infants under a month of age may have no strong liking for a square as compared to a circle, yet they may perceive the difference. That would help explain why they gaze more at a checkerboard than at an outline square. Here they *do* show a preference, perhaps because degree of complexity is a difference that makes a difference to an infant. In other words, a mere shape difference without a complexity difference may not affect a two-week-old infant's interest.

Another experiment that strongly supports the inference that form perception is present in the young infant, at least in the monkey infant, was conducted by Robert Zimmerman and Charles Torrey at Cornell University. They used the traditional technique of discrimination learning. They attempted to teach rhesus monkeys as young as 11 days of age to discriminate between a triangle and a circle. The monkeys were given 25 trials a day and were scored as having solved the problem only if they were correct on 21 of these trials for two consecutive days. On the average, it took them 10 days to succeed. To evaluate this performance, one needs to know that it took a comparable group of monkeys roughly the same number of days to learn to distinguish between two gray rectangles of differing lightnesses and even longer for another group to learn a size discrimination. Since neither lightness nor size perception of objects at the same distance would be thought to require past experience, it is plausible to conclude that the performance on shape discrimination did not entail any additional period during which the capability for form perception per se was learned. Rather, the learning period for all three problems can best be understood as the time necessary for the monkey to solve the problem of which object will consistently be rewarded. But the animals start out *perceiving* the shape, lightness, and size difference from the very first trial.

These results are supported by a remarkable finding by Gene Sackett at the University of Wisconsin on the perception of pictures of monkey faces by six-week-old infant monkeys. The infants reacted strongly to pictures of monkeys that were threatening and to pictures of other infant monkeys. This preference or aversion is proof that rather subtle form characteristics of the pictures were discriminated at this very early age. What makes the findings all the more remarkable, however, are the fact that they presuppose adequate *picture perception* among the monkeys and the fact that these monkeys were raised in isolated cages from birth. Therefore, the results would seem to be evidence that monkey faces can serve as "innate releasing mechanisms," meaning that the stimulus of a threatening face of a monkey can be thought of in the same way as other stimuli that trigger instinctual responses in various species. Whether or not this view is correct, the fact remains that we have strong evidence that form perception is innately determined in Primates, the same order of mammals to which we belong.

The Effect of Motives and Emotions on Perception

From all the evidence considered in this chapter, one can reasonably conclude that form and object perception proceeds in a bottom-up direction on the basis of innately given processing capabilities of the visual nervous system. We have also seen, however, that past experience may enrich or otherwise affect what we perceive. One final question to be considered is the possible effect of motives and emotions on what we perceive. One might think that it would be very useful to the organism to be sensitive to (or more inclined to perceive) objects that have the potential of satisfying a need.

Coincident with a drastic change in the length of women's dresses following World War II, referred to as the "new look," was a movement in psychology, also dubbed the "new look," to change drastically the narrowly conceived approach in laboratory experimentation. The aim of this movement was to do justice to human needs, emotions, and values and to each person's unique personality when studying his or her cognitive functioning. Insights that came out of psychoanalysis and the psychology clinic had not previously made their way into the corpus of knowledge based on research in the laboratory.

For perception, the aim was to demonstrate how such neglected factors as motivation, conscious or unconscious, affected what we perceive or, conversely, what we avoid perceiving. After all, clinicians had for years been using projective tests. The idea behind these tests was that

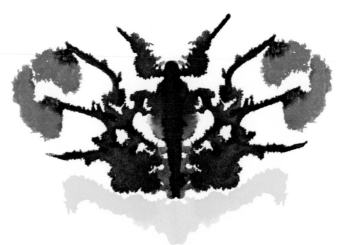

A figure similar to those used in the Rorschach test.

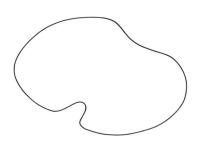

A novel figure will elicit many different interpretations of what it represents although it retains the same perceptual shape for all viewers.

individuals would project onto the ambiguous stimuli of the test their own personalities. In the test Hermann Rorschach devised, for example, what the individual perceives in the inkblots can hardly be determined entirely by the stimulus because it is both unfamiliar and amorphous. How the individual interprets what is happening between the people pictured on the cards of the Thematic Apperception Test devised by Henry Murray can hardly be determined entirely by the ambiguous scene.

But *are* the responses to these tests actually reflecting individual differences in *perception*? Suppose the test consisted of a simple figure, such as the one shown at left, and observers were asked to report what they perceived. There is no reason to think that individuals would differ in their perception of it as a *shape*. The difference comes in the *interpretation* of the figure. The novel shape might be said to look like any number of things, from an artist's palette to an amoeba. That observers would interpret the figure differently is not surprising. That such differences would stem from differences in recent or long-range past experience is also not surprising. Nor perhaps is it surprising that such differences might reflect differences in present need states; for example, hungry people might interpret the figure as an item of food because food would be on their minds.

But such effects are not perceptual in the way I have been using the term. The stimulus figure's perceptual shape, size, depth, lightness, and the like are essentially the same for everyone. Of course, the figure is an oversimplified analogue of an inkblot, and I have not done justice to the subtleties of interpretation of patients' responses that clinicians make. These include not merely the *content* of what is identified but the *way* in which the patient responds to the test figure: Is the whole pattern described, or only a part of it? Is color or texture incorporated into the

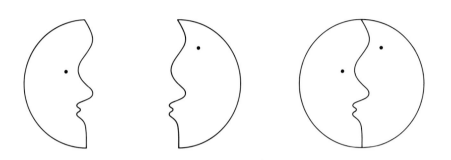

response, or is it ignored? How many responses to a test card are given? There is at least one clear case in which perception *is* implicated— namely, when the patient perceives an object in the white background of a Rorschach card rather than in the dark regions of the pattern, a figure-ground reversal. Even when this occurs, however, we are not in a position to attribute its cause to unique personality traits. Such reversals can occur for many different reasons.

In order to make such an attribution, experiments are necessary in which motivational factors are deliberately introduced. One of the experiments that launched the "new look" was performed by Roy Schafer and Gardner Murphy, then at the City College of New York. They used the ambiguous figure (shown above) of two faces whose profiles mesh at the center contour. Presumably, one perceives this composite figure as one face or the other at any given moment. Subjects were first exposed to a training procedure in which they were shown each half of the composite at a time, one face at a time. When one of these faces was shown, the subject was given money; when the other was shown, money was taken from them. Thus each face was presumably associated either with reward or with punishment. Two composite figures were used, each with its corresponding half views, so that in the training phase each subject saw four unambiguous faces, two of which were rewarded and two of which were punished. Following that, the two composites were shown, each for one-third of a second.

The investigators predicted that subjects would tend to organize the composite in favor of prior reward—that is, to see the face that had been rewarded (or equally, to avoid seeing the face that had been punished). If this happened, it would be an example of need or emotional state influencing perception, in this case figure-ground organization. The data

In one of the first experiments on the effect of needs on perception, subjects were rewarded when they saw either of the figures on the left and punished when they saw the other. When subjects were shown the composite figure on the right, they tended to perceive the previously rewarded face.

consist of the subjects' reports of what they perceived when each of the composites was presented in the final test. The subjects had not seen the composites before and did not know that they potentially contained two faces rather than one. The investigators found a statistically significant tendency to report the "rewarded" face in the composite, the actual ratio for "rewarded" to "punished" face responses being slightly more than 4 to 1. However, other investigators, including myself, have not always been able to obtain this result. Therefore, if such a tendency exists, it is not a very strong one.

There is a good reason for *not* expecting this effect to occur. In order for it to occur, the perceptual system must first "know" that the composite contains the rewarded and punished face figures. Otherwise, why would it bring to bear the motives and emotions relevant to those figures? Stated differently, there must be something detected about the composite that is similar to one or both of the previously seen faces; otherwise, why should memories of those faces, each with their associated emotion, be accessed at the time the composite is shown? Thus, if there is something detected, perception must first proceed in a bottom-up direction, perhaps as far as figure-ground organization, on an unconscious level. Only then can we understand the step of accessing the appropriate memories. At that moment, the perceptual system, knowing what perceptual alternatives are potentially present in the figure, can select the one that has positive rather than negative emotional connotations associated with it. If this analysis is correct, if bottom-up processing first proceeds to figure-ground organization before any effect of needs or of past experience in general can become manifest, then one can see why the conscious perception of one of the faces as figure rather than the other might have no connection whatever with the previous reward and punishment. Of course, once a face is seen and reported, the subject might be pleased or feel good if it was the one that had been rewarded and be displeased or feel bad if it was the one that had been punished. But that is a different hypothesis from the one that predicts which face will be perceived.

The question here, of a possible influence of motivational state on perception, then, is very similar to the one considered throughout this chapter of the role of past experience in perception. In the experiment under discussion, what is being tested is whether or not the organization of the composite face will favor one previously experienced region over another previously experienced region because one is a more positive memory than the other. That being the case, the same kinds of logical difficulties hold for effects of motivational state as for effects of experience. How can the need or desire to perceive or not perceive something control the bottom-up processing that must occur before such need states can be activated or accessed?

Quite a few experiments have attempted to demonstrate that we will *recognize* pictures or words more readily if they represent objects toward which we feel positive or, conversely, less readily if they represent objects that are threatening to us. For example, it was argued that the recognition of words presented for a fraction of a second would be more difficult if such words were threatening or embarrassing. The technique consists of flashing words for such a brief duration that they cannot be recognized and then, in subsequent presentations, gradually increasing the duration. The duration at which they are recognized is the threshold. In an early experiment of this kind, done in 1949 at the University of Alabama, Elliott McGinnies found that the threshold for the identification of taboo or "dirty" words was indeed higher than that for more neutral comparison words, supposedly because they were felt to be threatening. But other psychologists were quick to point out that subjects would be reluctant to say such words because of embarrassment or unwillingness to believe that these words would be presented at a university laboratory until it was unavoidably clear that they were indeed the words on the screen. (After all, the year was 1949.) Another criticism was that, while such words might often be *used* by the subjects (college students), they were not often seen *in print*. Therefore, the elevated threshold could be attributed to less past experience with such words as visual stimuli rather than to unconscious avoidance of recognition. This last criticism is one that can be made of all such experiments. Recognition responses under such conditions in large measure reflect a tendency to guess what is represented on the basis of some partial information that has been definitely picked up (for example *some* letters of a word) *and* on the basis of items in memory that are highly available and thus readily come to mind. Therefore, past experience will surely be one determinant of the recognition threshold.

Implicit in this kind of research is the assumption that the stimulus item is perceived and recognized unconsciously before it is recognized consciously. The perceptual system must know that something is present if it is to take steps to avoid conscious identification of it. Therefore, this kind of effect has been referred to as *perceptual defense* (as in the defense mechanisms postulated by psychoanalysts) and the unconscious perception has been referred to as *subception* or *subliminal perception*.

In a widely cited experiment of this kind that Richard Lazarus and Robert McLeary performed in 1951 at Johns Hopkins University, subjects were given a mild electric shock when certain nonsense words were shown in a training phase. Would the threshold be elevated for these words as compared to otherwise comparable nonsense words that were shown in the training phase with which no such shock was associated? Not only was such an elevated threshold effect obtained, it was further shown that there was a significant change in the electrical resistance of the skin—the so-called galvanic skin response (GSR) often used in lie-detector tests—when these words were presented in the test prior to their conscious recognitions. The GSR is considered to be a sign of reactivity of the autonomic nervous system. Presumably, then, words are "perceived" at an unconscious level and some mechanism brings it about that we avoid identifying them consciously as long as possible.

Despite the ingenuity and the results of this experiment and others like it, the community of scientific psychology has been skeptical and critical of the findings. Some of the experimental results have been difficult to confirm, and alternative hypotheses have been suggested. For example, in the just-described experiment on perceptual defense, psychologists have argued that, prior to reaching the recognition threshold for the word as a whole, some letters are consciously identified. Although the extent of such identification is not enough to lead to the word response, it may be enough to lead to the GSR since these letters are associated with the previously shocked words. If, moreover, these letters suggest the shocked words to the subject, they may lead to a strategy to avoid these word responses precisely because they invoke fear of shock.

The most radical claim to grow out of experiments on the effect of emotion on perception is that an item such as a word or picture could be presented at so brief an interval that no awareness whatsoever of the item occurs but that it would nonetheless be perceived on an unconscious level. If true, then a brand name could be flashed on the television screen while the observer was viewing a scene. For advertising purposes, the further assumption was implicit that this so-called subliminal perception would have "consequences" for behavior, probably more so than would conscious perception: People would be motivated to buy the product. Besides the question of the validity of this claim (something very much in doubt), there are other considerations that would seem to rule against it. Stimulus input must be processed if it is to achieve the status of a percept and, subsequently, a memory. We know from a now famous experiment conducted by George Sperling at Harvard in 1960 that, when an array of letters is flashed, any given letter is stored if and only if that letter is processed in some further way when it is presented or shortly thereafter. Although discharging of receptors occurs during the presence of a stimulus and although neurons may continue discharging for a brief duration after the stimulus disappears, such a sensory event will have no further psychological consequences unless some further processing of it occurs. In other words, a percept must be *constructed* from a stimulus. Because it seems unlikely that a perception would be constructed from a stimulus flashed so briefly and weakly that it is not visible at all, there is good reason for psychologists to be skeptical of this particular claim of subliminal perception.

In conclusion, one might ask whether or not, apart from laboratory demonstrations, there is any evidence from daily life that motives and emotions affect the perception of object properties such as form, size, or depth. (To be sure, there are many cases in which we *interpret* a situation in accordance with our needs and wishes, as for example when we mistakenly believe that someone approaching in the distance is the person for whom we have been waiting.) In fact, one might ask whether or not it really would be adaptive to perceive in accordance with one's needs. It is more plausible to believe that it is important for survival and successful adaptation to the environment that we continue to perceive veridically despite the vicissitudes of our motivational and emotional states. To perceive food where there is none when we are very hungry is to hallucinate. Thus, it is perhaps very fortunate that, by and large, perception is insulated from our internal states.

For the most part, we have been concerned in this chapter with veridical perception, how innate processes of organization and form description (with the help of past experience, under some conditions) enable us to reconstruct a perceptual world that adequately corresponds to the objects in the real world. Only occasionally did we encounter examples of nonveridical perception, as in the case of camouflage—and, interestingly enough, camouflage reflects the working of the same perceptual processes of organization that ordinarily lead to veridicality. In the next chapter, the emphasis is reversed, with the focus on illusions in patterns of one kind or another. The question will be whether or not we can explain these illusions in terms of the very same principles that, under other circumstances, lead to correct perception.

6 GEOMETRICAL ILLUSIONS

In the photograph on the facing page the upper horizontal bar that is superimposed on the road looks longer than the lower one. Both lines are actually equal in length, however. Although the illusion is a striking one, it raises a question sometimes asked about geometrical illusions: Why expend an enormous effort studying an apparently esoteric phenomenon, one that seems to have little to do with explaining how we perceive the world?

True, the illusion on the facing page is an illusion in a picture, but looking at pictures is an important part of perception in everyday life. In this scene and those depicted at the top of the following two pages, the extents that look different in length *are* different in length in the world—as, for example, the heights of the buildings between each pair of dots. We would not want to describe *that* perception as illusory, even though the retinal images between each of the pairs of dots are equal in length. Illusions must be defined as a discrepancy between what is perceived and what is objectively present in the world, not as a discrepancy between what is in the retinal image and what is present in the world. However, as we have already seen and will see in subsequent chapters, perception in daily life is shot through with illusions, including those of the geometrical kind to be addressed in this chapter. Sometimes we are aware of them, but more often we are not—for the simple reason that we do not go around measuring the objects we perceive. To give just one example of an illusion that we frequently experience, a vertical extent will look some-what longer than a horizontal one of equal length. This is referred to as the horizontal-vertical illusion. Thus, a square will look more like a rectangle, as can be seen in the illustration to the left on the following page, and a rectangle of just the right proportions will look like a square.

The Ponzo illusion in a realistic setting. The superimposed horizontal line in the background looks longer than the one in the foreground, but they are both equal in extent.

The vertical separations between each pair of white dots in the photograph are equal.

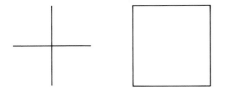

The horizontal-vertical illusion. The vertical line in the cross looks longer than the horizontal one, while the perfect square looks like a rectangle because its height appears to be slightly greater than its width.

Illusions *are* among our daily perceptions, but a more general answer to the question is the one given in the first chapter: Both illusions and veridical percepts must be manifestations of the same lawful processes of perceptual functioning. Therefore, we stand to gain as much knowledge by studying the one as by studying the other, and ultimately our theories must be able to explain both. Research on geometrical illusions has been active for over a century, but—and this is an embarrassment to investigators in perception—they remain, for the most part, unexplained. Of course, progress has been made and theories have been advanced, but, as we shall see, no one theory does justice to them all.

Rather than attempt to catalogue all the known illusions, I will restrict the discussion to just a few of them. They are among the better known and can serve the purpose of illustrating the major theories.

The Ponzo Illusion

The illusion shown at the far right, which is the same as that shown in a more realistic setting on the preceding page, is named after the Italian psychologist Mario Ponzo. The illusion, of course, depends on the presence of the two oblique lines within each illustration. To distinguish among the elements of an illusion figure, psychologists term the features that undergo distortion the *test components*, and the remaining features, which create the illusory effect, the *inducing components*.

How can we explain the effect the two oblique lines have on our perception of the relative lengths of the horizontal lines? According to the currently favored theory, the Ponzo illusion results from the same percep-

All of the major illusions discussed in this chapter are contained in this scene. One dog looks longer than the other (the Ponzo illusion), the line of molding on the right is a continuation of the line of the baseboard on the left (the Poggendorff illusion), and the front end of the carpet looks shorter than the bottom edge of the back wall (a variation of the Müller-Lyer illusion and an example of the corridor illusion).

tual process that leads to constancy of size. Because the inducing lines appear to converge, they create the impression, on a two-dimensional surface, of parallel lines receding in depth, such as the sides of a road or railroad tracks. Thus we perceive the figure as if it had depth. Because the top line appears to be farther away than the bottom line, it must look longer. Like the moon illusion discussed in Chapter 2, the Ponzo illusion can thus be regarded as an example of Emmert's law, according to which objects yielding retinal images of the same size will look different in size if they appear to be located at different distances.

This type of explanation, first proposed in the nineteenth century by Armand Thiéry, is not only plausible but follows directly from what is known about perception of size and its dependence on distance in daily life. If we did not know about this illusion, we would still be able to predict it. The *depth-processing theory*, as this explanation is sometimes called, also receives empirical support from experiments such as one done by Herschel Leibowitz and his associates at Pennsylvania State University. They portrayed the converging contours and horizontal lines of the Ponzo illusion with varying degrees of realism. At one extreme was a photograph of a scene with two parallel objects on the ground; at the other extreme was the two-dimensional drawing shown at right, which is typically used to study the Ponzo illusion. The investigators found that the more realistic and three-dimensional the display, the greater the illusion. Thus one might conclude that the effect shown in the photograph on page 152 can be attributed to depth processing. It is but a small step from this conclusion to the inference that the effect of the original illusion figure is based on the same perceptual process.

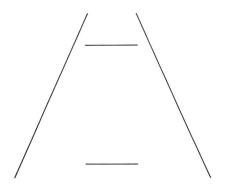

The Ponzo illusion in its original form.

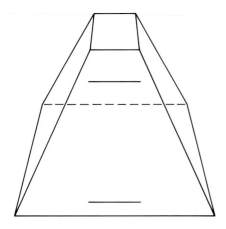

The upper horizontal line on the face of the truncated pyramid appears to be nearer than the lower one, but it still tends to look longer than the lower line, which appears farther away.

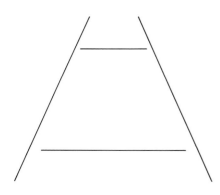

According to the depth-processing theory, the unequal horizontal lines ought to look more nearly equal in length than they actually do.

The assumption of the depth-processing theory is that we experience the illusion because the figure gives the impression of depth. Yet some evidence suggests that we experience the illusion even when we do not see the figure three-dimensionally. For example, we do not necessarily perceive the converging lines as receding in depth, at least we may not do so unless the depth effect is pointed out. Nonetheless, the illusion occurs. Invert the figure or tilt it by 90 degrees (by rotating the book): The impression of depth diminishes or disappears, but the magnitude of the illusion remains unchanged. Even if the pattern is so altered that perceived depth is reversed, some illusion persists, as can be seen in the illustration directly to the left.

There are several other problems with the depth-processing explanation of the Ponzo illusion. Suppose, for example, that the test lines are made *unequal* in length, as shown in the lower illustration at left. The test lines in the figure should now represent two objects of equal length, with one being farther from the observer than the other. If the two horizontal lines are placed within converging lines that create an impression of depth, one would expect the observer to perceive the two horizontal lines as more nearly equal in length. When Arien Mack of the New School for Social Research and I tested this prediction, however, we found only a small effect. Observers perceived the horizontal lines more or less veridically—that is, they perceived them to be as unequal as their size ratio would warrant. Finally, the test lines that are oriented vertically in the illustration at the far right ought to create as much of an illusion as the test lines in the original illusion, if depth processing were the whole story. As can be seen, however, the illusion is diminished or nonexistent here.

Although it often suffices, in proving a point about a possible explanation of an illusion, to make up a particular modification of the figure and simply look at it—a demonstration, as it were—in fact, psychologists generally do formal experiments with the modified figure. In these experiments, the observer is asked to match one test line to the other until they look equal. In experiments with the Ponzo illusion, for example, on some trials the lower test line is the standard and observers match the upper one (called the *comparison stimulus*) to it, in this case by making it shorter. On other trials, the upper test line is the standard and subjects match the lower one to it by making it longer. The average amount by which the observers must change the comparison line in order to match the standard line, for all trials and for many subjects, is a measure of the illusion. In the case of the illustrated example of the Ponzo illusion on page 155, the illusory length effect would be of the order of around 10 to 15%. (In this chapter, I will generally not give such quantitative data or describe details of experiments. However, the statements I make about

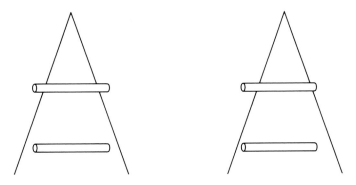

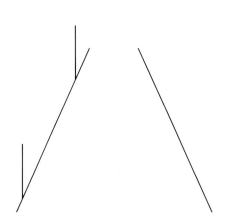

A stereogram used to test the depth-processing theory of a version of the Ponzo illusion. When the two views are fused, so that the test and the inducing components appear in differing planes, the horizontal cylinders tend to look equal in length.

how an illusion figure or a variation of it is perceived are typically based on such formal experiments.)

Some of the criticism above of the depth-processing theory centers either on the fact that depth is not experienced in the Ponzo figure or on the fact that the depth that is experienced can be experimentally contrived to contradict what is required by the theory. Yet the illusion persists more or less undiminished. The contemporary proponents of this theory, notably Richard Gregory at the University of Bristol and Barbara Gillam at the College of Optometry of the State University of New York, however, have argued that it is not necessary that depth be consciously experienced in order for it to influence perception. One argument is that, because the page on which the illusory pattern is drawn is flat, there are several depth cues that interfere with seeing the pattern as three-dimensional. Gregory has shown that we will often perceive many of these patterns as three-dimensional when they are made of luminous lines and viewed in a dark room with one eye. This procedure is said to eliminate the flatness information in a picture. But this argument about the flatness of the page seems to miss the point. The theory only requires that the illusion pattern look like a *drawing* or a *picture* of a three-dimensional scene or object. In that sense, all pictures are seen to be flat but nonetheless can represent scenes in depth. Therefore, if an illusory pattern doesn't even look like a *picture* of something in three dimensions, something is wrong with applying the theory to that pattern. A different argument that advocates of the theory have made is that it suffices that the relevant depth or perspective information is present in the pattern and is registered by the perceptual system since, if it is, it may directly affect perceived size, shape, or direction. The pattern need not lead to the conscious experience of depth. Stated in this way, the theory becomes difficult to test.

According to the depth-processing theory, the two equal vertical lines ought to look as unequal as do the equal horizontal lines in the Ponzo illusion, but they do not.

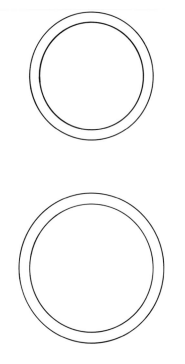

The Delboeuf illusion. The outer circle in the top figure assimilates to the smaller circle it surrounds and the inner circle in the bottom figure assimilates to the larger circle around it so that the two circles to be compared appear unequal in size.

A test of the contrast and assimilation theory of the Ponzo illusion. The horizontal test lines are surrounded by frames of reference, the vertical contours of which have the same separation from the ends of the test lines as do the converging lines at that height in the original Ponzo illusion. Only a slight illusion occurs.

If the depth-processing theory is incorrect or inadequate to explain the Ponzo illusion, what other explanation might be offered? Another general theory of geometrical illusions draws upon the opposing concepts of contrast and assimilation. *Contrast* is the tendency to perceive an object's properties by comparing them with the properties of the object's background or context and exaggerating these differences. We have encountered some examples of this in earlier chapters. The effect of a white or black background on the appearance of a gray region is a case in point: White makes the gray appear darker and black makes it appear lighter. Frame of reference affects the perception of size in a similar way. The contrast between an object and a large frame of reference seems to decrease the object's size. In the Ponzo illusion, the lower line looks small in contrast with the large empty space at either end of it. The upper line looks large in contrast to the small space at either end of it. Therefore, the lower line should appear smaller than the upper line.

Assimilation implies the opposite process—that is, a tendency to perceive an object as including or incorporating the properties of certain background elements. A good example is the Delboeuf illusion, shown in the illustration at left, above. In that illustration, the inner circle below looks larger than the outer circle above although both are the same size. One might say that this occurs because the inner circle on the bottom assimilates to its larger surrounding circle, while the outer circle on the top assimilates to the smaller circle it surrounds. In the case of the Ponzo illusion, the upper line can be said to assimilate to the inducing lines so that it tends to "stretch," to appear as wide as the distance between the converging lines at the same height in the field. Thus, the effect of contrast is to diminish the perceived size of the lower line, and the effect of assimilation is to increase the perceived size of the upper line. Note that this explanation does not entail either depth perception or constancy.

To test this theory, investigators have used variations of the Ponzo illusion that eliminate a sense of perspective. In one test, they separated the two test lines, each within its own inducing background, since continuity of the inducing lines is not essential to the explanation. All that remains are the appropriate distances between the ends of the test lines and the contours of the inducing pattern, as can be seen in the figure at left. By and large, these experimental variations *do* yield an illusion that is analogous to the Ponzo illusion. But the effect is generally smaller. One possible conclusion is that contrast and assimilation are indeed determining factors in the Ponzo illusion but not the only ones. Thus, it is possible that this illusion is the joint result of both contrast and assimilation *and* depth processing, a possibility to which I return at the end of the chapter.

Assimilation of color. A colored region appears to be darker when black contours are within it than it otherwise would, and lighter than it otherwise would when white contours are within it. These effects imply that, in our perception, the lightness of the contours spreads to the surrounding region. The illusion is the opposite of contrast, in which black regions lighten, and white regions darken, adjacent regions.

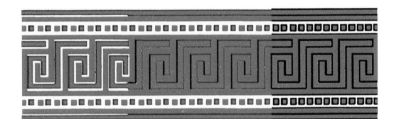

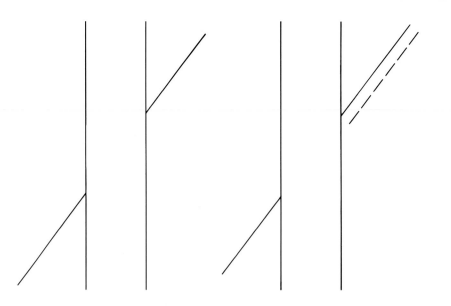

The Poggendorff illusion. The two oblique lines in the figure on the left do not appear to be aligned although they in fact are. The dashed line in the figure on the right represents where subjects typically place a line that they perceive to be aligned with the solid lower oblique line. The separation between the dashed line and the upper solid line is a measure of the illusion.

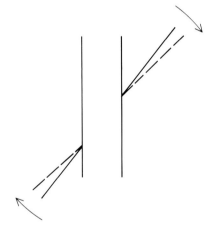

Overestimation of the acute angles in the Poggendorff figure would lead to the illusory misalignment shown by the dashed lines.

The Poggendorff Illusion

In the illustration at left, above, the illusion created by J. C. Poggendorff in 1860 shows two oblique test lines crossing parallel vertical inducing lines. The illusory effect is that the oblique lines, which are in perfect alignment, do not appear to be. The upper line appears raised with respect to the lower one. For the oblique lines to *appear* to be in alignment, a lower oblique line (such as the dashed line in the figure at right, above) would have to be substituted for the upper one.

How can this illusion be explained? According to some investigators, the Poggendorff illusion, as well as many other illusion figures, is best explained by a third theory, one based on a type of contrast termed *angular displacement*. Investigators of illusions have long maintained that we tend to overestimate acute angles—that is, we tend to perceive them to be larger than they actually are. In the case of the Poggendorff illusion, overestimation of the two acute angles would cause the two oblique lines to appear to bend in opposite directions, as shown in the illustration at left. Thus, the oblique lines do not appear to be perfectly aligned.

Several other well-known illusions, such as those shown on the facing page, and the one shown on page 6, illustrate this general principle. Even though the illusory effects appear to be different—parallel lines appear to converge, straight lines appear curved, circles or squares appear distorted—it has been held that they share a common denominator: A single test line appears to bend away from the inducing lines that cross it. The greater the number of crossing points, the more bent the line appears to be.

An experiment by Colin Pitblado and Lloyd Kaufman, then at the Sperry Rand Research Center, supports the theory that the Poggendorff illusion results from displacement of angle contours. They used a stereoscope to present a rectangle against a background of converging lines,

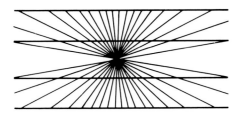
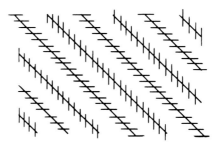

Other well-known illusions are said to have in common test lines that appear to bend away from the inducing lines that cross them.

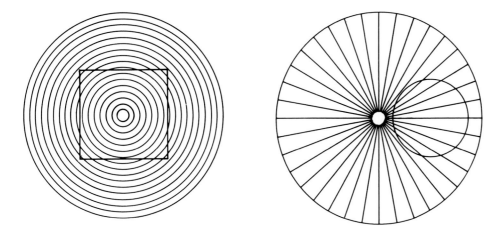

shown in the stereogram at the top of the following page. The rectangle appeared in a vertical plane, separate from the converging lines, which appeared to recede in depth even though the retinal image still contained the crossing of the rectangle's vertical contours and the converging line contours. Observers saw a distorted rectangle. The top edge looked longer than the bottom edge, presumably *because* the sides appeared to slope outward, due to overestimation of the angles at the intersections of the rectangle's sides with the converging lines. Earlier, the same investigators did a variation of this experiment, shown on page 157. They found that the Ponzo illusion disappeared with stereo viewing, suggesting that the original Ponzo effect, unlike the intersecting-lines variation, was the outcome solely of inappropriate depth processing.

Colin Blakemore and his associates at Cambridge University have attempted to test the angular-displacement theory by requiring observers to

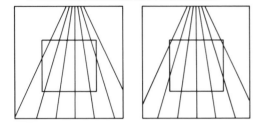

Stereogram used to test the angular contrast theory in a variant of the Ponzo figure. When the two views are fused, one sees a vertically oriented but distorted rectangle in one plane behind a plane formed by the oblique lines.

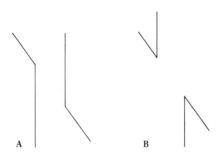

A test of the overestimation-of-acute-angle explanation of the Poggendorff illusion is here accomplished by (A) eliminating the acute angles and (B) eliminating the obtuse angles. As can be seen, doing the former has little if any effect—the illusion persists—whereas doing the latter seems to eliminate the illusion.

set a comparison line parallel to one side of an acute-angle pattern. They assumed that an overestimation of the angle can be demonstrated by measuring the perceived orientation of its sides. When the observers were asked to set the comparison line parallel to one side of the angle, they in fact placed it in a different orientation. The effect was appreciably greater for small angles (those of around 10 degrees) than it was for large angles.

What is the mechanism that explains the angular-displacement effect? The currently favored theory is based on Hubel and Wiesel's discovery of cells in the visual cortex that "detect" contour orientation on the retina. A given contour orientation on the retina—say, a vertical line—triggers activity in a whole population of cortical orientation detectors in the brain, but more so in those most attuned to that retinal orientation (e.g., vertical) and less so in those tuned to different retinal orientations (e.g., plus or minus a few degrees from the vertical). The presence of an adjacent contour of different orientation (e.g., 5 degrees clockwise) would have the effect of inhibiting some of these units from firing. The peak of activity shifts away from the one that would occur without the presence of the second contour (e.g., the peak would now be at 3 degrees counterclockwise). This is an example of the broader category of neural functioning known as lateral inhibition, which was discussed in Chapter 2. In that earlier example, the inhibition concerned intensity (or luminance) based on the rate of firing of neurons, where activity in one fiber had the effect of reducing the rate in an adjacent fiber. Here, it is the contour orientation rather than intensity that is relevant. This physiological theory, then, attributes illusions to the "hardware" of the visual nervous system, a very different explanation from others we have been considering.

When put to a direct test, however, the claim that the Poggendorff effect is based on the overestimation of acute angles is found wanting. In the illustration directly to the left, the Poggendorff pattern is modified in two ways: In A, the acute angles are eliminated; in B, the obtuse angles are eliminated. As can be seen, the former continues to yield the illusion whereas the latter does not. Therefore, if misperception of angle accounts for the illusion, it must be argued that the effect occurs because obtuse angles are underestimated, not because acute angles are overestimated. However, this conclusion is not consonant with Blakemore et al.'s findings, nor does it follow from the lateral-inhibition theory.

A further difficulty for the angular-displacement theory becomes evident when we try to explain why the Poggendorff illusion occurs in a figure such as the one shown on the facing page at right, below. An effect is illustrated here that was discussed in Chapter 5—that of illusory contour. The vertical inducing lines of the Poggendorff illusion have been replaced by irregularly spaced black semicircles. Vertical contours appear

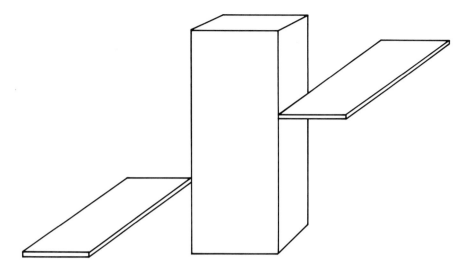

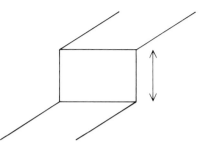

Illustration of the depth-processing explanation of the Poggendorff illusion. The oblique line segment on the right in each figure appears to be in a higher plane than the one on the left and, therefore, the two cannot be aligned perceptually.

to be present, but none physically exists between the semicircles. The oblique lines "intersect" the vertically perceived boundaries at regions where there is no actual vertical contour to form acute or obtuse angles. Thus, although this illusory effect does not rule out the hypothesis that the Poggendorff illusion is based on misperception of angle, such an effect cannot readily be attributed to lateral inhibition of contour-orientation detector cells. No such inhibiting contour is present in this figure.

Most of the facts about the Poggendorff illusion, however, can be explained by the depth-processing theory, as Barbara Gillam has ingeniously argued. She believes that this illusion, like the Ponzo illusion, arises from the tendency of the perceptual system to process the figure as a representation of a three-dimensional scene, not as a pattern in two dimensions. The figure above makes this process abundantly clear. The oblique lines are processed as edges in a horizontal plane. The angles formed between the vertical and oblique lines are interpreted as right angles. According to this theory, *all* angles are misperceived: Acute angles are overestimated and obtuse angles are underestimated. But misperception of angle has a very different meaning here: The misperception is one of perspective representation, not of two-dimensional distortion. In fact, except for the special case of contours in a frontal plane, right angles in the environment will project to the eye as either acute or obtuse angles. Thus, for example, rectangular objects project trapezoidal images, none of the angles of which are right angles. This is one of the major distortions that occurs in the projection of objects in the world to the eye. The reason that the oblique lines in the Poggendorff figure appear misaligned

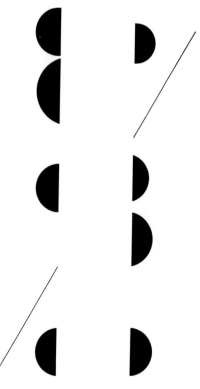

The Poggendorff effect can be obtained even though the vertical contours are illusory.

By modifying the inducing vertical lines in the top figure so that they are part of a plane receding in depth (such as seen in the figure below it), the oblique segments no longer appear to be in differing horizontal planes. The illusion is greatly reduced or abolished.

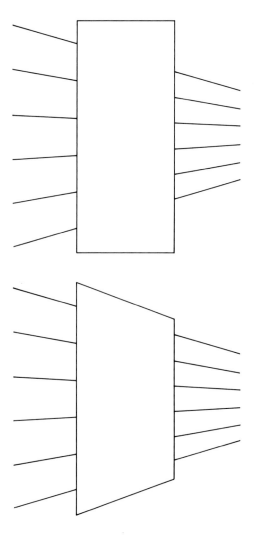

is that they seem to belong to two different planes (i.e., planes at different heights in the scene). In making these planes explicit, the figure at the top right of the previous page creates an even greater illusion of that misalignment than does the original Poggendorff figure.

Impressive support for the depth-processing theory comes from another variation of the Poggendorff figure. If the inducing pattern of lines is modified to look like a rectangle at a slant so that the plane of the surface formed by the vertical lines appears to slant back, as in the figure at lower left, the illusion is much diminished or disappears. In the actual three-dimensional scene that such a drawing represents, the oblique lines would belong to the same plane. Yet other theories, such as the theory of angular displacement, would predict the persistence of an illusion in this example because the angles formed by the vertical and oblique lines remain unchanged.

The depth-processing theory may also explain why, in the illustration on page 162, in which the acute and the obtuse angle components of the overall illusion pattern are separated from one another, the illusion occurs in the case of the obtuse angles and not in the case of the acute angles. Both versions could represent a scene in perspective. In the figure with obtuse angles, however, the two oblique lines appear to represent horizontal lines at very different heights. But in the figure with acute angles, the two oblique lines appear to represent horizontal lines at roughly the same height. For this reason, the theory predicts—correctly—an illusion of misalignment in the first case but not in the second.

Finally, the depth-processing theory accounts for the misalignment illusion obtained with the illusory contour figure. Physical contours adjacent to the oblique components are not necessary because angular misperception is not based on a process such as lateral inhibition. All that is required for the illusion to occur is that the given *perceived* components trigger a perspective interpretation.

The Müller-Lyer Illusion

The best known of all illusions is the one created roughly a century ago by F. C. Müller-Lyer. As can be seen in the illustration at the top of the facing page, the line contained within reversed arrowheads appears appreciably longer than the line of equal length contained within the normal arrowheads. The illustration also shows some of the many variations of this illusion of extent. Hundreds of papers have been published on this illusion, and some interesting facts about it have been uncovered, but in my opinion it has not yet been satisfactorily explained. Several entirely different factors may cooperate to produce it.

Richard Gregory has presented striking illustrations (such as those

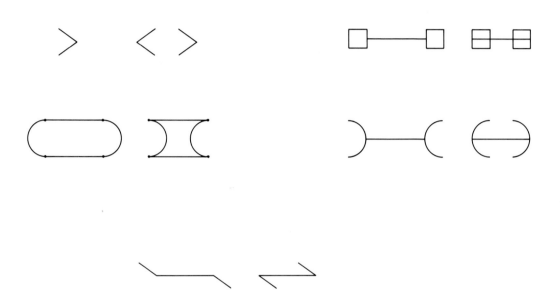

The original Müller-Lyer illusion is shown in the top figure. The other figures are variations of the same illusion.

shown on page 166) of how one might explain this illusion in terms of the depth-processing theory. Consider the two photographs as representations of the junction of several surfaces. The line, or shaft, with the normal arrowheads seems to represent a convex corner with the shaft appearing closer than the shorter lines that form its heads. The line with the reversed arrowheads seems to represent a concave corner, with the shaft appearing farther away than the shorter lines. Gregory argues that the illusion is based on a simple application of Emmert's law: The nearer-appearing shaft should look smaller than the farther-appearing shaft. But nearer and farther than what? The theory requires that the shafts appear nearer and farther *than each other*, but Gregory's argument implies only that one shaft appears to be nearer than its inducing components and that the other appears to be farther than its inducing components. Some students of perception, including myself, have thus concluded that this theory is not applicable to the Müller-Lyer illusion. An exception to this conclusion occurs when the two configurations are embedded in a scene

A depth-processing explanation of the Müller-Lyer illusion suggested by Richard Gregory. The test line in the photograph on the left is processed as the edge of a convex corner and the one in the photograph on the right as the edge of a concave corner.

such as the one shown at the top of the facing page because there each test line has a certain position in the third dimension relative to the other—there they are nearer and farther than each other.

A theory that can plausibly be applied to the Müller-Lyer figure concerns eye movements. The argument initially was that perceived extents are a function of the distance required to move the eyes from one end of the figure to the other. Because of the direction of the arrowheads, it was argued that eye movements would differ for the shaft lengths that were actually equal. No one believes this general principle anymore, and in fact the geometrical illusions occur in exposures much too brief to permit any eye movement at all.

However, a more sophisticated theory proposed about eye movement is that perceived spatial properties, such as the separation (or extent) between points and the orientation or curvature of a contour, are a function of how we "intend" to move our eyes, of what "commands" a higher center in the brain issues to the eye muscles. The theory is based on the fact that the information we obtain about what the eyes are doing derives not from proprioceptive feedback from the eye muscles but from a record of commands *to* the eye muscles. (This topic will be discussed in the next chapter.) Leon Festinger of the New School for Social Research has maintained that such central commands to the eye muscles determine what we perceive.

In the case of the Müller-Lyer figure, the observer may, at first, tend to command the eyes to move inappropriately when attempting to scan from one vertex at the end of each shaft to the other. The reversed arrowheads may lead to a tendency to overshoot, and the normal arrowheads may lead to a tendency to undershoot. Such eye-movement errors have been observed to occur, at least initially. This finding has been regarded

The Müller-Lyer illusion in a realistic setting.

as supporting evidence for the theory: We command our eyes to move too far (or too little). For this reason, the shaft in question appears too long (or too short).

If the observer is required to scan the illusion figure continuously and to judge the lengths of the lines, the illusion tends to diminish and, after hundreds or thousands of judgments, to disappear completely. The eye movements tend to become increasingly accurate, and the overshooting and undershooting tend to disappear.

In my view, this theory is incorrect because it has reversed the cause and the effect. The overshooting and the undershooting of the eyes at the outset do not cause the perceived illusion, they are caused by it. Similarly, the increasing accuracy with continued judgments may be based on the diminution of the perceived illusion, whatever may be the cause. We tend to command eye movements appropriate to *perceived* separations. I do not believe that perceived spatial properties are based on intended or commanded eye movements. Festinger himself has since abandoned this theory because in an experiment in which a new pattern of eye movements was learned, there was no corresponding change in perception. But one important problem that remains to be addressed is why continued scanning of illusion figures tends to diminish the illusions.

An alternative explanation of the Müller-Lyer figure is based on the *incorrect-comparison theory*. It holds that we cannot succeed fully in isolating parts from wholes. Despite a clear understanding of what parts of the line are to be compared, we cannot avoid including other components in our judgments. In the Müller-Lyer figure, we intend to compare only the shafts, but we include the arrowheads. The shaft *plus* the reversed arrowheads is, of course, longer.

The effect of attention and perceptual organization on the Müller-Lyer illusion. If one attends to the magenta lines, the space on the left appears to be larger than the one on the right; if one attends to the blue lines, the opposite is the case.

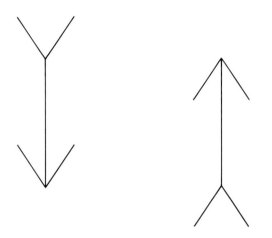

Two identical figures, one being an inversion of the other. The shaft on the left appears to be higher than the one on the right, although both are at equal heights on the page.

The incorrect-comparison theory can be restated as an assimilation process: The shaft within the reversed arrowheads assimilates to the arrowheads and thus its length is perceived as more like the overall length of the pattern. It is not obvious, however, what role contrast plays in the shaft with the normal arrowheads. Experiments have tested each type of figure separately, using an isolated line as a comparison figure. The shaft with the normal arrowheads appears only slightly shorter than an isolated line of equal length. The greater part of the illusion comes from the shaft with the reversed arrowheads. Therefore, an assimilation process is a plausible explanation of much of the Müller-Lyer effect.

Although other factors are probably at work in the Müller-Lyer illusion, I believe that incorrect comparison plays the major role. There is evidence to support this view. The illustration at left contains two identical figures; one is an inversion of the other. Both are hybrids of the Müller-Lyer figure. Although the tops and bottoms of the two shafts are aligned horizontally, the shaft on the left appears to be higher. This effect is based on the observer's inability to separate the shaft's location from the end parts of the figure. Stanley Coren and Joan Girgus, then at the New School for Social Research, have shown that any steps taken to isolate the shaft from its arrowheads, such as using different colors or verbally instructing the viewer, reduce the illusion.

The figure at the top of this page illustrates the assimilation process in another version of the Müller-Lyer figure. Here we have two superimposed patterns. If one concentrates on the magenta lines, the space on the left looks longer than the one on the right. If one directs attention to the blue lines, the space on the left appears to be shorter than the one on the right. Attention here affects perceptual organization, and this in turn creates the crucial impression of connection between the spaces and the end lines. This figure is also evidence against other theories of the Müller-Lyer illusion, expecially those that explain it exclusively in terms of such factors as eye movements, blurred images, or lateral inhibition. The fact is that the stimulus input from the two halves of this figure is identical.

The Corridor Illusion

Each illusion figure that we have considered so far seems tailor-made to illustrate one particular theory. The Ponzo illusion nicely illustrates a misapplied constancy (or depth-processing) theory; the Poggendorff illusion fits a misperception-of-angle theory (although it also can be explained in terms of depth processing); and the Müller-Lyer illusion is a good example of an assimilation (or incorrect-comparison) theory. No one theory seems to do justice to all these illusions. How, then, can we

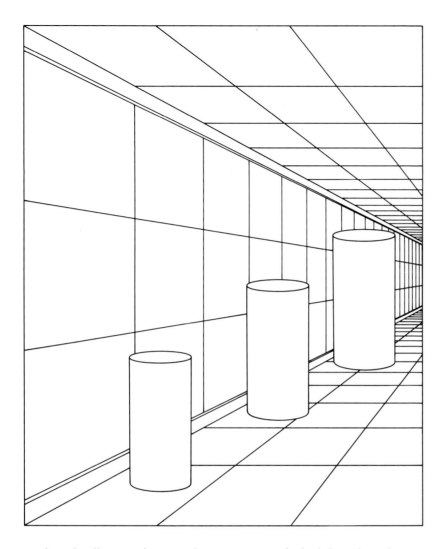

explain the illusion of extent above, versions of which have been known for many years as the perspective illusion and which has lately appeared in many textbooks? This particular version appeared in a book by James Gibson and is now referred to as the corridor illusion. The illusory difference in the perceived size of the cylinders is quite striking, greater than in most geometrical illusions of extent.

The corridor illusion reveals a greater effect of constancy (Emmert's law, to be precise) than can usually be obtained in representational pictures. The illusory effect is usually explained in terms of depth processing. Alternatively, one might want to explain it in terms of contrast and assimilation or, otherwise expressed, in terms of stimulus relations. The proportion of each cylinder to the height of the corridor wall adjacent to it differs appreciably for the three cylinders. This was one explanation we considered for the Ponzo illusion, which is quite similar to the corridor illusion. To test this hypothesis, we can eliminate the overall perspective, as shown in the illustration above right, and simply embed each cylinder

In the corridor illusion (above, left), the three cylinders look unequal in size. In the test of the contrast and assimilation theory of the corridor illusion (directly above), the cylinders appear to be only slightly different in size.

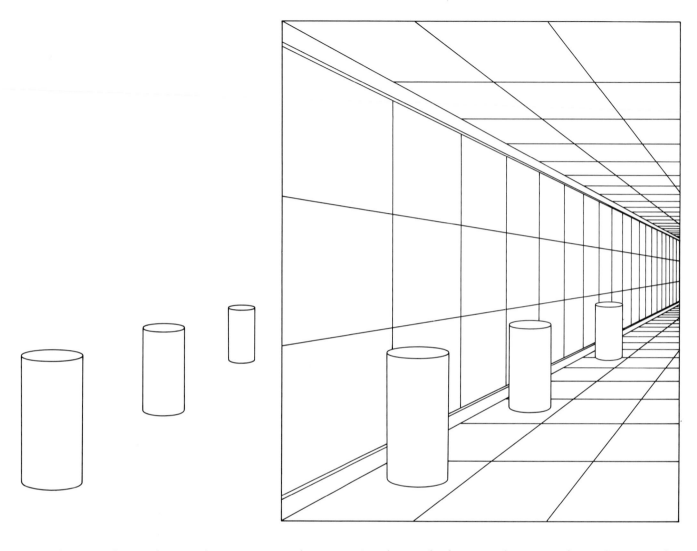

By equalizing assimilation and contrast for the three cylinders in the figure above, right, the effect of depth processing can be isolated. The cylinders there should appear to be equal or less different in size than they are. Whether or not they do can be seen by comparing the way they appear there with the way the cylinders appear in the figure directly above, where they are shown without any background.

in the appropriate frame of reference—that is, in a frame that is equal in size to the projected size of the corridor adjacent to each cylinder. As can readily be seen, the illusory effect is much diminished in comparison with the original figure or is not present at all. Whatever illusory effect remains cannot be attributed to perspective depth processing.

It is not as easy to eliminate the effect of contrast and assimilation on the cylinders in order to see what contribution depth processing per se makes to our perception of the original corridor-illusion figure. However, if cylinders of equal size are replaced by unequal ones (such as would be projected on a picture plane by cylinders of equal size in the real scene), the illusion is much diminished, as can be seen in the figure above. The unequal drawings of the cylinders do not appear to be almost equal, as they would if constancy fully prevailed. They do not look much different in relation to one another than they do in the figure from which

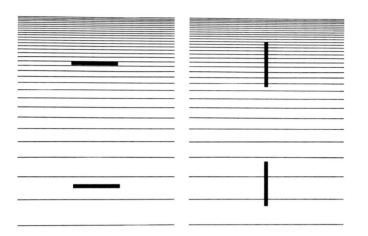

the background is removed. This also demonstrates that constancy is only partially achieved in representational drawings of scenes.

At first, the conclusion one must reach may seem odd. When isolated, neither depth processing nor contrast and assimilation, the two factors that could be producing the large corridor illusion, seems to produce much of an illusion. Even the sum of the effects would not be great enough to explain the corridor illusion. It would seem, therefore, that it is the *interaction* of pictorial cues to depth and a contrast-assimilation pattern that yields such a great effect. Exactly the same reasoning may apply to the Ponzo illusion, which, when rotated 90 degrees, can be seen to be very similar to the corridor illusion. Both depth processing and contrast and assimilation are applicable, but each factor alone is very weak, as can be seen in the illustrations on pages 156 and 158. The main difference between the corridor illusion and the Ponzo illusion is probably the relative excellence of perspective depth in the former and the poorness of it in the latter.

If this conclusion is correct, it may explain a striking effect uncovered by Barbara Gillam. In the illustration above, foreshortening has been isolated from other usual concomitants of perspective. Equally spaced horizontal contours on a ground plane are represented as decreasingly separated vertically. One can achieve an impression of depth from it. Accordingly, one achieves a size illusion in viewing equal vertical extents on it. That this effect is not simply one of filled as against unfilled space or divided as against relatively undivided extents can be seen in the illustration of the Oppel-Kundt illusion, as it is called, at the top of the following page. A vertical line intersects densely packed horizontal lines and another of equal length intersects a sparse array of horizontal lines. The vertical lines look only slightly different because there is no perception of

Foreshortening isolated from other aspects of perspective. The equal vertical bars look different in length but the equal horizontal bars do not.

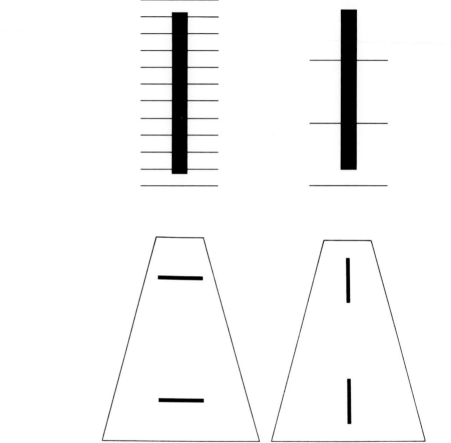

The effect of divided versus relatively undivided space on the perception of vertical extent.

Isolation of linear perspective. The equal horizontal bars look different in length but the vertical ones do not.

depth. That depth is not the whole story, however, is shown by the fact that, in Gillam's display, two equal *horizontal* lines hardly look different at all, although they are embedded in the foreshortening perspective array. Missing here is any contrast effect, because these lines are not perpendicular to the main lines of the display. Thus, it would seem that *both* contrast and depth are necessary to generate a strong illusory effect.

Conversely, if one isolates only linear perspective, as in the illustrations above or in the original version of the Ponzo illusion that appears on page 155, an effect opposite to that in the foreshortening display occurs, as we have seen: Equal horizontal test lines generate an illusion (depth *and* contrast-assimilation), whereas equal vertical lines yield only a miniscule effect (depth but no contrast or assimilation). Therefore, the evidence seems to support the hypothesis that the joint action—or interaction—of perspective and contrast yields a strong illusion of extent, whereas either of these factors alone yields only a slight illusory effect. Precisely why joint action of these two factors is so effective is not clear. Gillam's explanation of the effects just considered is that the inducing perspective patterns create a scale of size, but that the scale only runs in one direction in these different figures, vertically in the foreshortening display and horizontally in the linear-perspective display. Therefore, size illusions only occur for vertical lines in the first case and for horizontal lines in the second case.

Illusions in Children and in Other Cultures

If depth processing of line patterns accounts for some illusions, it has seemed to some investigators to follow that past experience ought to affect an observer's susceptibility to perceiving illusions. There are, however, two meanings of "past experience" to consider. One concerns experience with pictures. If young children or individuals from a stone-age society have never seen pictures, and if, therefore, they are incapable of regarding the drawn illusion figure as *representing* a scene or a three-dimensional structure, one can hardly expect an illusion to occur if it is based on depth processing. We have already considered this issue in the chapter on perception and art. It seems that even very young children and people from diverse cultures perceive pictures as representations of objects or scenes. It is not yet clear whether or not such observers are as sensitive to pictorial cues to depth (such as perspective) as are older observers from technologically more advanced societies.

It is at this point that the second meaning of "past experience" enters in. Some investigators have argued that perspective patterns containing converging lines and representations of right angles abound in the "carpentered" environments of industralized countries but occur only rarely in the forests, jungles, and plains of more primitive societies. Similarly, young children in the former environments have not yet had much exposure to the kinds of scenes suggested by geometrical illusions. In short, the argument is that the less experience observers have had with the scenes that yield perspective projections to the eye—scenes of roads, railroad tracks, buildings, rooms, and the like—the less one can expect them to fall prey to illusions that processing pictures of such scenes allegedly generates.

What are the facts? Children are generally *more*, not less, prone to illusions. For adults of differing societies, the answer depends upon which particular illusion is investigated and, in fact, much the same is true for children. The Ponzo illusion seems to be stronger in adults from a European type of carpentered environment than in children anywhere or in adults from a rural environment. This evidence thus supports the

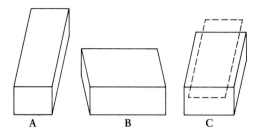

Depth processing (plus some contribution of the horizontal-vertical illusion) leads to the impression that the top surfaces of A and B are quite different in size and shape, although they are congruent. The top of C was drawn to look congruent with that of B, but it is in fact the dashed outline that is congruent with it.

depth-processing theory. But the results are contradictory for the Müller-Lyer illusion. Children are *more* prone to it, but people in less industralized societies are less prone to it. Children are also more prone to the Poggendorff illusion. It should be noted, however, that these trends are not always substantiated by independent studies.

The most one can safely conclude from the developmental and cross-cultural studies currently available is that the depth-processing theory is *not* unequivocally supported by them. With the possible exception of the Ponzo illusion, the developmental data and the cross-cultural data are not consistent with one another in supporting this theory. The tendency of children by and large to perceive illusions of greater magnitude than adults do can perhaps best be explained by their inability to isolate the test lines from the inducing ones in which they are embedded. An illusory effect based on difficulty of this kind is consistent with the incorrect-comparison theory.

A possible explanation of cross-cultural differences that is quite unlike one based on differing visual environments is that of innate differences in the structure of components of the nervous system. Differences in such factors as density of pigmentation of the lens and the central region of the retina, the macula, are even more highly correlated with differences in susceptibility to illusions than are differences in the physical environment. These physiological factors, if proven to be relevant, are rather different from the kinds of explanations of the illusions explored in this chapter. Perhaps there are other as yet undiscovered inherited differences in the structure and function of the perceptual system that might explain the differences in susceptibility to the various illusions among peoples of various societies in the world.

It is evident, then, that investigators in perception have not solved the problem of the geometrical illusions, although progress has been made. Probably no one theory can do justice to all of the known illusions, and it may well be the case that even a single illusion is based on several simultaneously occurring factors. Of the illusions considered here, it seems warranted to suggest that the Ponzo illusion (and the corridor illusion, which is similar to it) is jointly determined by depth processing and by contrast and assimilation, that the Poggendorff illusion is explicable in terms of unconscious depth processing, and that the Müller-Lyer illusion is primarily the result of an inability to isolate the test lines or, otherwise stated, of an incorrect comparison. But these conclusions are put forth only tentatively.

To come back to a point made at the outset, it does seem to be true that we are learning something relevant to the problem of veridical perception in daily life by the exploration of these illusions and, conversely, that what we have learned from the study of nonillusory phenomena has helped us in trying to explain the illusions. But even if we learned nothing of value in investigating illusions, they would still constitute puzzles that curiosity would drive us to unravel.

We have been concerned here with what might be called static illusions—that is, illusions of extent or line direction in stationary patterns. But many of the most striking illusions are those based on motion. While the emphasis in the next chapter is not on illusion but on the search for general principles of motion perception, it will be seen that almost every phenomenon considered there is, in fact, an illusion of motion.

7 THE PERCEPTION OF MOTION

The moon seems to be sailing through the clouds. Most of us have experienced this illusion, but few ask why it occurs. Of course, the moon does change its position in the sky as the earth rotates, but that movement is too slow to detect with the eye. In fact, we perceive the moon to move in a direction opposite to that of the clouds passing in front of it, regardless of the direction in which the clouds happen to be traveling.

Ever since the discovery in the nineteenth century of illusory stroboscopic effects, the predecessors of moving pictures, motion perception has been one of the major areas of investigation in vision. Like form or color, motion is a perceptual property of objects. Although the second hand and the minute hand of a watch both move, the second hand is seen to be moving whereas the minute hand moves at a rate usually below our threshold for detecting its motion. Although it is the clouds that often move at a rate that we can detect, it is the moon that we perceive as moving. The perception of motion, then, is not simply a reflection of the physics of motion, of what is happening in the world. Although in physics one might say that no object moves absolutely but only changes its position relative to some frame of reference, in perception objects do appear to move absolutely or to be stationary.

Our perception of motion is usually veridical, but sometimes it can be highly deceptive, as is the perception of the moon passing through the clouds. In fact, much of the research in motion perception has been designed to explain this and other illusions of motion. Why, for example, do people and things depicted in motion pictures appear to move? When we look at a single star in an otherwise dark sky, why does it appear to drift? Why does a stationary object sometimes give the fleeting impression that it is moving upward after we have been looking at a waterfall? In this chapter, I will discuss the nature of each of these illusions. But understanding the perception of objects that are really moving turns out

The sequence of photographs of a pole-vaulter in action conveys an impression of motion, although not the perception of motion that one obtains from viewing the successive projections of such a scene on a movie or television screen.

to be just as much of a puzzle, and it is well to begin our discussion with those perceptions.

The Perception of Real Motion

If a cat jumps from a chair within our field of vision when we happen to be looking at the newspaper, the cat's image will displace over the retina, and we will perceive its motion. It thus may seem reasonable to suppose that the bases of motion perception are the sensory consequences of a displacing image. The perceptual system must detect the displacement if we are to gain the information that the cat yielding that displacing image is in motion. Physiologists have in fact discovered cells in the retina or in the visual cortex of some animals that discharge rapidly if, and only if, a contour or spot moves over the region of the retina to which such cells are connected. Presumably such cells exist in the human visual system as well. The firing of these cells, which have been called *motion-detector mechanisms*, might be regarded as an explanation of the perception of motion.

There is a problem with this explanation, however. For animals that move their eyes as we do, displacement of contours over the retina is neither necessary nor sufficient for the perception of motion. It is not necessary because we often track a moving object by moving our eyes, thus holding its image more or less stationary on the retina. Nevertheless, we see the object moving. Moreover, in many illusions of motion—the moon in the clouds and the still images in the frames of a movie, for instance—the image of the object seen as moving is stationary. Neither is the displacement of contours over the retina sufficient, because frequently an object's image displaces over the retina without creating an impression of motion. When we move our eyes across a room, for example, the location of chairs and tables appears unchanged, although the images of them on the retina move. Investigators refer to this phenomenon as *position constancy*.

Instead of regarding these motion-detector mechanisms as the immediate cause of motion perception, at least in animals high on the phylogenetic scale, it may be more appropriate to think of them as a source of information about events on the retina. In interpreting what is happening in the world, the perceptual system must take into account other information from other sources as well. For example, if these detectors signal "motion" when only the eyes are in motion, the perceptual system must discount that signal as a sign of object motion. The perceptual system "assumes" it was caused by the observer's own eye movements. However, if the signal occurs when the eyes are stationary, then it *is* interpreted as a sign of object motion.

If the detectors do not signal motion, as when we track a moving object and the retinal image remains stationary, the perceptual system can still infer that the object is moving. For this inference to be made, however, the perceptual system must somehow know that the eyes are in motion.

How does the brain "know" whether or not the eyes are moving and, if they are, in what direction and at what speed? Given what is understood about how the brain gains information about movement of other parts of the body, we might suppose that such information derives from sensory feedback. For example, physiologists believe that, when the arm bends, receptor cells in the elbow joint signal the change. Such proprioceptive information has long been held to come from the activity of muscles as well as joints. Receptor cells in the eye muscles were thus assumed to be the source of similar information about eye movement.

It is unlikely, however, that the information that tells us about eye movement derives from sensory feedback. Consider two countercases. First, there are circumstances in which the eyes remain perfectly still—and thus there is no proprioceptive feedback that they are moving—but nonetheless the eyes are interpreted as moving. If the eye muscles are paralyzed or are otherwise prevented from moving, the observer may still attempt to look at an object in the periphery. Each time this happens, the entire visual field appears to move rapidly in the direction of the intended eye movement. Helmholtz and subsequent investigators inferred from this result that the perceptual system treats the intention or command to move the eyes as equivalent to actual eye movement. Ordinarily the command would be followed immediately by eye movement. Thus the image displacement of a stationary thing would not be improperly interpreted as signifying that the object was in motion. But if the eyes cannot move, the command is still recorded, and the eyes are interpreted as moving. Consequently, the stationary image is incorrectly interpreted as signifying that the object is in motion.

In the second countercase, the eyes are moving—and thus there should be proprioceptive feedback—but they are nonetheless treated by the perceptual system as stationary. If we push our eyes gently to the side with our fingers, presumably there is proprioceptive feedback to that effect, just as there would be if we lifted a limp arm by active movement of the other arm. But we can infer from the fact that the entire scene appears to move that the perceptual system treats such imposed eye movement as no movement at all. Position constancy is not achieved because, with no eye movement registered, the perceptual system does not discount image displacement.

Therefore, it seems that we "know" what our eyes are doing not by what they are in fact doing but by what we command them to do a fraction of a second before they move. The information is efferent (derived from signals flowing *out* to effector organs) rather than afferent (derived from signals flowing *in* from sense organs). Some evidence suggests that a similar mechanism plays a role in the interpretation of other body movements as well.

We have seen that the perceptual system gains information on the displacement of contours (or its lack) over the retina by the firing of motion-detector cells. The perceptual system not only makes use of this information about image motion, but also takes account of information about the movement of the eyes in arriving at an "inference" as to whether or not the object producing such image contours is moving. The general rule of motion perception, it seems, is this: An object that changes its *perceived* direction at a rate fast enough for the eyes to detect will generally be seen to be moving, and an object that does not will generally appear to be stationary.

A brief comment should be made about the perception of rates of motion, or velocity. If the perception of motion depends upon detecting a change of perceived direction, the perception of velocity depends upon detecting the rate of change of perceived direction. One might expect that perceived velocity would decline with the object's distance, because the angular rate of change in direction of an object moving across the field at a constant speed is less the farther away the object is. After all, the farther away the object is, the smaller will be the visual angle traversed by its image per unit of time. Nevertheless, constancy prevails, at least up to a certain distance. The object's velocity is perceived to be roughly the same whether the object is near or far. The explanation of such constancy is still in dispute, since two possibilities exist: Either we take into account the object's distance, as when we achieve size constancy, and thus interpret the visual angle traversed per unit of time accordingly, or we judge velocity in terms of the proportion of the extent traversed by an object per unit of time, relative to the object's frame of reference (for example, a mouse will traverse a corridor in the same amount of time whether it is near or far from us).

The Perception of Motion when We Are in Motion

In many instances, we are the ones in motion, not the objects around us. When we move, all objects change their direction with respect to our position. Thus, according to the general rule of motion perception, they ought to appear to move. Instead, however, our perceptual system attributes the change in the direction of things to our own motion. For any given movement of our own, an object at a particular distance will undergo a particular change in its direction and will do so at a particular rate (motion parallax). As long as the object's distance is perceived correctly, it will appear to remain stationary. Thus, position constancy is achieved. For example, an object seen straight ahead and close by will "go" to the observer's left at a fairly rapid rate as the observer moves to the right. Does this mean that, if the object were perceived to change its direction differently or at a different rate with this same movement of the observer, it would appear to move? It is plausible to believe that it would, and in fact we know that it would. Around the turn of the century, George Stratton, a psychologist at the University of California at Berkeley, performed an experiment that is still being discussed and disputed. For eight days in succession, Stratton wore lenses mounted in a tube in front of one of his eyes that inverted and reversed the images that reached his retina. He was interested in discovering whether or not the scene that appeared upside down would eventually appear right side up if he continued to wear the lenses, an issue we will take up in Chapter 8. What is of interest here is Stratton's observation that objects viewed through the lenses appeared to shift in direction in an abnormal way when he moved. At first, a stationary scene appeared to move in the direction of his own movement and at a faster rate. We can conclude from this fact that, when there is an abnormal change in direction during an observer's movement, things will appear to move. Position constancy is lost. More recent experiments indicate that the same is true if the rate at which things change their direction is altered during the observer's movement, even if the direction of movement itself is not altered.

In experiments such as Stratton performed, observers will adapt to this abnormal change in direction during their movement. After a few days, the scene no longer appeared to Stratton to move when he moved. It was

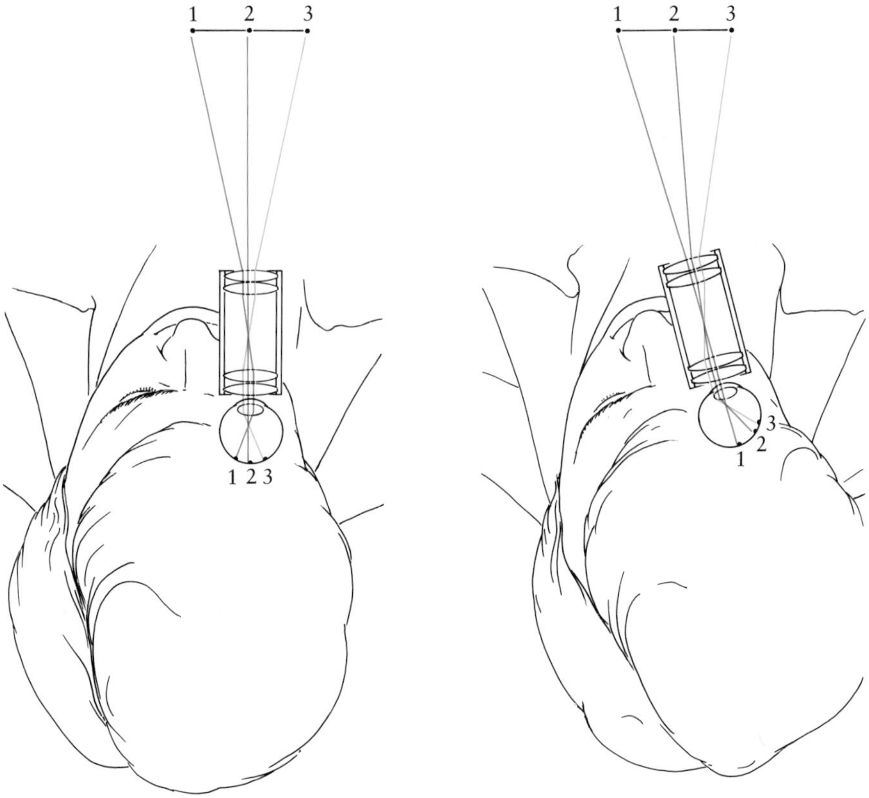

Stratton's inverting lenses yield illusory motion of a scene. When Stratton turned his head from the position shown on the left to the position shown on the right, the retinal images of stationary objects shifted in a direction opposite to their normal direction.

not simply that he grew accustomed to such motion effects and stopped attending to them. The proof is that, on removing the lenses at the end of the experiment, the scene appeared to move whenever Stratton moved and in a direction opposite to the direction in which it appeared to move when he first put the lenses on. This kind of outcome, of perceiving things opposite to the way they appeared when distorting optical devices were worn (generally referred to as a *negative aftereffect*), can be taken as strong proof that an adaptive change has occurred. We can therefore conclude that Stratton's perceptual system learned, while he was wearing inverted lenses, that the change of direction of stationary things during his own movement is toward the direction of his movement, not opposite to it, as is normally the case.

These findings tell us that the specific relations between a change of an object's direction and a change in the observer's position that yield an impression of motion or position constancy can be learned or relearned. They do not necessarily imply that the relations had to be learned in the first place, however. For some animals tested, position constancy is innately determined. In one experiment, the head of a fly was surgically rotated 180 degrees and kept in that position. This had the effect of

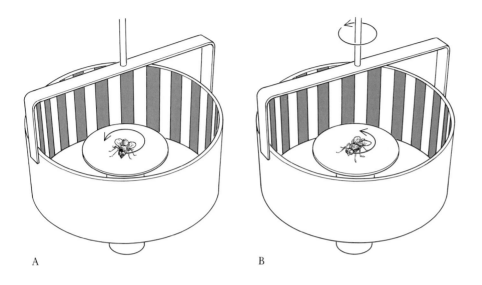

A   B

C

reversing the direction of the motion of the image of the stationary scene during the fly's motion, much as did the lenses in Stratton's experiment. What did the fly perceive when it moved? A simple but ingenious experiment, conducted by Horst Mittelstaedt of the Max Planck Institute, that made use of a known reflexlike effect supplied an answer.

When an animal is placed inside a rotating drum lined with vertical stripes (such as the one shown above), it will rotate its eyes, its head, or its entire body in the direction in which the drum is moving. This reflex action is generally referred to as the *optomotor response;* in humans, in whom only the eyes turn, it is referred to as the *optokinetic response.* Before its head was rotated, the fly was placed on the platform inside the drum. When the drum was stationary and the fly happened to move, no optomotor response was evoked. We can thus presume that, despite displacement of the images of the stripes over the fly's retina, no motion was perceived. The fly achieved position constancy. But after the head was rotated and the fly happened to move, it continued turning indefinitely. Apparently, the stripes in the stationary drum appeared to the fly to move when it moved, for the same reason that the scene initially appeared to move for Stratton. Because the stripes appeared to move, the optomotor effect was generated, and the fly turned precisely as it would if the drum had actually been rotating. Such turning produces further apparent rotation of the drum, and so on. Since a normal fly does not engage in the optomotor response when walking or flying, even soon after hatching, we can presume that the world appears stationary during its motion. Thus it is plausible to infer that, for the fly, position constancy is innately determined.

Experiments on position constancy in flies. A. When a fly that is rendered incapable of flight spontaneously moves inside a stationary drum, no optomotor response is triggered. B. When the drum rotates around the same fly, the fly circles in order to keep pace with the drum (optomotor response). C. When the fly's head is rotated 180 degrees, and the fly spontaneously moves inside a stationary drum, the fly continues circling indefinitely.

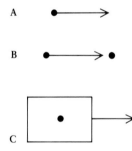

Induced motion of an object. A. An isolated point moving slowly in a homogeneous field may be below the threshold for detecting its motion. B. When a second, stationary point is introduced, the motion is now readily detected, although it may be attributed to either point. C. When the stationary object is surrounded by a moving one, the stationary object will be perceived as moving.

Relative Motion

Ordinarily, a moving object not only changes its direction with respect to us but changes its location with respect to all other stationary things in the scene. This relative change of location can affect the motion we perceive in various ways.

INDUCED MOTION   When the moon appears to move across the clouds, the moon is not changing its direction with respect to us—that is, its *egocentric direction*—but the clouds are doing so. If changing egocentric direction were all there were to motion perception, the moon would appear stationary and the clouds would appear to move. The fact that we see the moon as moving suggests that the change in position of an object relative to background objects must be a strong determinant of perceived motion. This effect is called *induced motion*—·the inducing of motion in a stationary object by a nearby moving object. One might have predicted that this relative change would simply reinforce an impression that the clouds are moving. The clouds ought to appear to move because they change direction with respect to the observer. The presence of the moon might be expected to further support that appearance by the impression of relative change it yields. Why, then, should the introduction of relative change cause us to see the moon rather than the clouds as moving?

At slow rates of change of egocentric direction—as would often be true of slowly drifting clouds—motion detection is poor. But change of relative location is more readily detected. The following experiment makes this point clearly. In a dark room, a single luminous spot can be set in motion at a speed below our threshold to detect its movement. If a second luminous stationary spot is introduced nearby, however, we immediately do see a spot in motion. Apparently, we are very sensitive to the changing distance between the two spots. Although we will tend to see one of the spots moving, we are equally often wrong as right as to which spot it is. In this experiment, the only usable motion information we are receiving is of a relative kind. Because such information is ambiguous, however, we cannot tell which object's motion is producing the relative change.

In the case of the moon and cloud, then, it is reasonable to suppose that the relative change of position between the two is paramount in our perception but that it is also ambiguous. Therefore, half of the time we should erroneously attribute the change to the moon's motion. However, the moon will almost *always* appear to move when a cloud moves in front of it, not merely half the time. There is a further principle of induced motion that is applicable in this case. An object that surrounds another, or is much larger than it is, tends to be seen as stationary. The larger object therefore serves as a *frame of reference* with respect to which the relative displacement of other things is gauged. To prove this point, we have only to change the experiment just described by replacing the moving point by a moving luminous rectangle that surrounds the stationary luminous spot. Now the stationary spot appears to move on every trial.

Students of perception do not entirely agree on why this effect occurs. Karl Duncker, a Gestalt psychologist who investigated induced movement in the late 1920s, believed that the larger or surrounding object serves as a surrogate of the entire visual world. The world as a whole is perceived as stationary, he argued, so that anything representing it tends to be interpreted as stationary. This tendency might be thought of as one based upon an "assumption" or preference on the part of the perceptual system.

This analysis of the induced motion of the moon can be applied to many other situations. Thus, in daily life, when an object moves in front of a stationary background it seems correct to conclude that its perceived motion is overdetermined—that is, determined by more than one factor. If it is moving fast enough, it will be seen to do so on the basis of its egocentric change, even if nothing else is visible. But, given its change relative to the background, it will be seen to move even if its egocentric change is below the threshold of detection. In typical cases of object motion, then, perceived motion seems to be governed by two independent factors.

INDUCED SELF-MOTION   We ourselves sometimes undergo induced motion. When we are in a stationary train and a train on the adjacent track is in motion, for example, we often misperceive which train is actually moving. A similar effect occurs when we stop for a light in a car. If a car alongside ours begins to roll backward, we often perceive our own car to be rolling forward and step on the brakes. When we look down at the water current from a stationary boat or from a pier, we sometimes experience ourselves as in motion.

Induced motion of the self was demonstrated in the Haunted Swing Illusion, an exhibition at an 1894 fair in San Francisco. Observers sat in a large seat suspended by ropes. The seat seemed to swing back and forth in ever increasing arcs until eventually it turned upside down. No one fell off—for the simple reason that the swing only moved slightly. It was the room that swung back and forth. The people on the swing experienced themselves as in motion and the room as stationary. In this example, the induction effect is powerful enough to overcome information based on gravity, which indicates that the observers are not tilting or inverting and that the room *is* tilting from the upright.

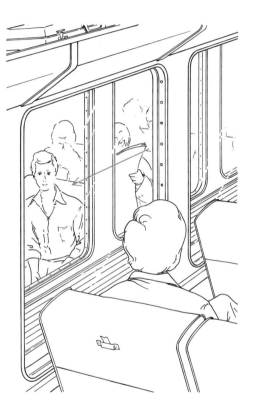

Induced motion of the self. Slow displacement of an adjacent train (designated by the arrow) is often experienced as motion of the train in which we are sitting. The adjacent train then appears to be stationary.

Relative change is clearly the determining factor in these cases. Unless we have clear information as to our own motion, such as when we are walking, information about the change in direction of the surrounding scene will be ambiguous. It could be the result of motion of the outer object or objects, or it could be the result of our own motion. If the moving object fills most of our visual field and no stationary objects surrounding the moving one are visible, the visual experience is essentially what it would be if we were moving in a stable environment.

In the laboratory, induced self-motion is studied by seating an observer inside a rotating drum lined with stripes, as shown at left. Ideally, the stationary floor and ceiling are not visible. If we were in the observer's place under these conditions, how could we tell whether it was the drum that was turning or we that were turning while the drum remained stationary? The visual input would be highly ambiguous.

But what about nonvisual information that tells us about our movement and its direction and rate? Nonvisual information ordinarily derives from the vestibular apparatus of the inner ear and is only available when there is change in the speed, or rapid change in the direction, of our movement. Such signals are lacking when we move at a uniform speed. Therefore, if we are inside the drum, we could interpret the absence of nonvisual signals to mean either that we are stationary or that we are turning at a uniform speed. Given this ambiguity, frame of reference again becomes important. The perceptual system assumes that the drum, as surrogate for the environment, is stationary; thus we interpret the changing direction of the drum's stripes as a sign that we are rotating.

There is usually a brief period before this interpretation occurs, however. At first, the drum does seem to turn. Then it appears to slow down and, if we were typical observers, we would begin to experience ourselves as slowly rotating. Finally, the drum appears to stop entirely, and we see and feel ourselves to have as much rotary motion as, in fact, the drum has. The feeling that one is turning is another example of what in Chapter 5 was termed *visual capture*—the tendency of a visual percept to force nonvisual perceptions, such as those gained through touch, proprioception, or audition, to fall into line with itself. It thus seems that induced motion of the self follows the same principles as induced motion of other objects. Relative change and frame of reference are again the determining factors.

Is there a link between induced self-motion and the optomotor response, since both effects arise when the observer or experimental animal is inside a rotating drum? In the optomotor effect, the animal turns or moves in the direction of the drum's rotation; in the induced-motion effect, observers experience themselves as rotating and do not *do* anything except with their eyes. Unless instructed to fixate a stationary spot

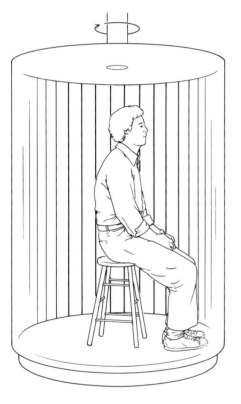

Laboratory arrangement for studying induced self-motion.

in front of the moving stripes, observers will typically rotate their eyes, pursuing the moving stripes until the stripe pursued goes out of the field, at which point they will snap their eyes back in the opposite direction, the two movements being referred to as the slow and fast phase, respectively, of optokinetic nystagmus. This eye movement is sometimes regarded as the equivalent of what is a more complete motor response in animals.

The prevailing view of the cause of these optomotor or optokinetic responses is that they are reflexlike tendencies to stabilize the retinal image. If such responses were absent, it would be difficult to perceive moving objects clearly. The response is analogous to another reflex: When we turn our heads, the eyes automatically swivel in the opposite direction (even if the eyes are closed). These compensatory eye movements enable us to maintain fixation on an object as we move.

If the optomotor response is simply a reflexlike behavior to guarantee a stable retinal image, there is no connection at all between the optomotor effect in animals and the induced self-motion effect as studied in human subjects. However, another interpretation of the optomotor response is possible. Consider, for example, a fish in a current that tends to carry it downstream. The fish will generally resist the current by swimming upstream, so that it remains in the same place. When the current begins to carry the fish along, the visual situation for the fish is exactly like that of an observer inside a rotating drum. That is, the surrounding visual scene—for the fish, the sides or bottom of the river—is moving. Suppose, as seems reasonable to believe, that induced self-motion causes the fish to experience itself in motion, as being carried away from its position. Because the fish had not intended to swim downstream, the motion it perceives in itself is, so to speak, unwanted, so it swims upstream to maintain its position.

Deborah Smith and I performed some experiments with tropical fish to test this hypothesis. We placed a fish in a cylindrical glass tank that was surrounded by a drum lined with vertical stripes. The top was covered except for a small hole in the center through which the fish could be viewed. In one experiment, we rotated the tank about its center, thus generating a current because of friction, while keeping the surrounding drum stationary, as shown in the left-hand illustration on the following page. This essentially simulates the situation of the fish in the river carried downstream by a current. We reasoned that the fish does not directly react to the water current but ordinarily responds to it only by its visual consequences—that is, being carried away from visible objects in its field. To prove this, we first wrapped the tank with white paper so that the fish could not see through the tank. Under these conditions, the fish made no effort to swim against the current going around the tank. When we removed the paper so that the fish could see the stationary stripes,

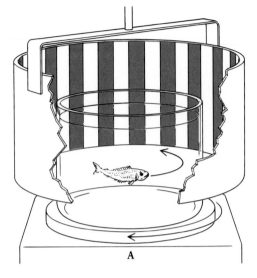
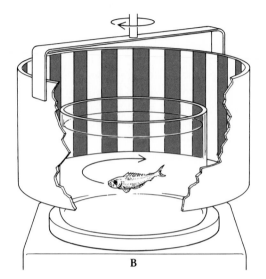
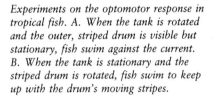

Experiments on the optomotor response in tropical fish. A. When the tank is rotated and the outer, striped drum is visible but stationary, fish swim against the current. B. When the tank is stationary and the striped drum is rotated, fish swim to keep up with the drum's moving stripes.

however, all fish swam vigorously against the current, thus remaining in place opposite any given set of stripes.

In a companion experiment, we kept the tank stationary while rotating the drum, as shown in B, above. Now the fish swam vigorously in the direction of the drum's motion, keeping pace with it, even though there was no current. This condition would be regarded as the optomotor paradigm, whereas the one with the rotating tank and stationary drum would not. But they are psychologically and behaviorally identical. They both illustrate that a surrounding visible structure, when moving, generates or induces an experience of self-motion, while the structure itself appears to be stationary. In an animal such as a fish, *that* experience in turn generates a tendency to compensate for such unwanted movement of the self; the animal attempts to maintain its position in its perceived world. In a human observer, the self-motion seems to be tolerated; it elicits no behavior designed to nullify it, at least in an experimental situation. (In a more natural situation, such as in a river, a person might well react as the fish does, by swimming upstream in order not to be carried away downstream.) The optokinetic response is undoubtedly motivated by the tendency to stabilize the moving image, but, according to the present hypothesis, it has nothing to do with induced self-motion. It occurs both when the drum appears to be rotating and the self is stationary and when the drum appears to be stationary and the self is experienced as moving.

If this interpretation of the optomotor response in fish is correct, induced self-motion may be far more prevalent in the life of animals than we realize. It is perhaps confusing to think of situations in which the observer is in motion as exemplifying induced motion—as in the case of

the transported fish—but the fact is that the perceptual situation is identical here to the one usually defined as yielding induced self-motion, where the surroundings are moving and the observer is stationary. If this is true, then there are many other cases in the daily life of human observers in which induced self-motion is occurring. Whenever we are transported in a vehicle and moving at uniform speed, it is only by induced motion that we see ourselves in our vehicle as moving. With our eyes closed, the only cue to motion would be vibrations, and that is insufficient. Even with our eyes open and, let us say, only a single light visible, we would tend to misperceive *it* as moving if we did not know that we were in a moving vehicle. But with the full scene surrounding the vehicle visible, we do perceive ourselves to be in motion. Therefore, the determinant here is the same as if our vehicle were stationary and the scene contrived to move past us. The underlying factor of great theoretical importance in this entire discussion is the tendency for the surround to be "assumed" to be stationary, to be interpreted as the frame of reference, and thus to yield the various consequences for perceived motion that we have considered. In the next section, we will see certain other consequences of relative motion and the frame of reference.

Illusions of Direction

A reflector on the wheel of a moving bicycle seen on a dark night will appear to move in a peculiar way. When the wheel rolls, the spot of light appears to move along a path that mathematicians call a cycloid curve, as shown in the photograph and the illustration above.

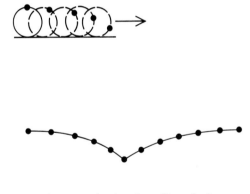

A spot on the rim of a rolling wheel traverses a cycloidal path through space. In the time-exposure photograph, a reflector shows the path traversed by a point on a bicycle's wheel.

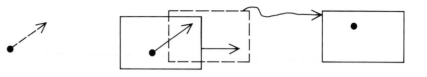

(Left) A spot moving along an oblique path in a homogeneous field is perceived veridically. (Right) When a horizontally moving frame surrounding the spot moves along with it, the spot appears to be moving vertically.

The two components of perceived motion of an object traveling along an oblique path.

The reflector travels this path because it is both revolving around the axis of the wheel *and* being carried forward as part of the wheel. If the eyes are held still, the reflector's image also moves over the retina along a cycloidal path. Therefore, what we perceive in looking at the moving bicycle's reflector at night can be said to be correct and not an illusion. But when we watch the moving bicycle's reflector in daylight—or, for that matter, any wheel rolling—we no longer experience the cycloidal path of motion: All points on the wheel appear to revolve around its axis and the wheel-as-a-whole appears to be rolling along a straight path.

Before trying to understand these perceptions, consider the following example illustrated at the top of the page. If we view a spot of light traveling along an oblique path in an otherwise dark room, we will perceive its motion correctly. If we view the spot traveling the same path, but this time surrounded by a rectangular frame that is moving horizontally along with the spot such that both will reach their rightmost and leftmost positions at the same moment, the spot will no longer appear to move obliquely. Our dominant impression will be that it is moving up and down. However, we will also have the impression, although a less strong one, that the spot belongs to the rectangle and is moving horizontally along with it.

Thus, as has been suggested by Duncker and by the psychologist Gunnar Johansson at the University of Uppsala, under some conditions a path of motion will yield two components of perceived motion, as if the actual path were split into two vectors, as shown in the illustration at left. Some insight into the basis of this kind of effect can be gained by considering an example from daily life. Suppose you watch a friend leaving on a train. Your friend waves at you. You perceive the waving hand moving up and down, although, in fact, as the train moves forward, the hand is moving along a path similar to the one shown on the facing page, above. In this example, perceiving the hand as moving vertically is not an illusion because, relative to the train, it *is* moving vertically.

There are conflicting frames of reference in both examples. Relative to the observer, both the spot in the laboratory example and the hand of the person waving are moving obliquely. But relative to the moving frame of reference—the rectangle or the train—these objects are moving up and down. This latter relation seems to dominate our perception. However, there is a second component to our perception of the movements: We see

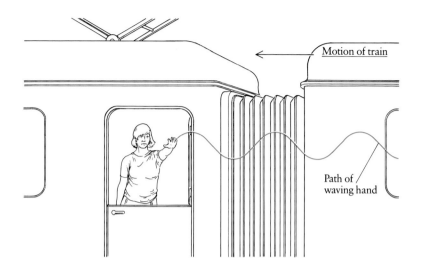

Motion of train

Path of
waving hand

The path of the person's hand waving goodbye as the train leaves a station resembles that of a sine curve, but it is perceived to be moving up and down.

the spot and the hand as partaking of the horizontal motion of the objects that encompass them (frame or train), apparently because we perceive the spot as *belonging* to the frame and the hand as *belonging* to the train. The two components of perceived motion, vertical and horizontal, together fully account for the changing angular direction of the spot or hand with respect to the observer.

Johansson has shown that this kind of perception can occur even when no visible structure serves as a frame of reference. In the illustration at right, one spot, A, moves up and down. Another spot, B, moves along the path of a circle. However, B's motion is linked to A's vertical motion so that B arrives at the top and bottom of its circular path when A arrives at the top and bottom of its path. If A is not visible, B appears veridically to move around a circular path. But when A is visible, B is not perceived to move in a circle. Rather, it appears to move back and forth horizontally, approaching and receding from A. In addition, both A and B appear to move up and down together.

There is some disagreement over how to explain this effect. One explanation is that B's motion is purely horizontal relative to A's, and that such relative change is salient in our perceptual experience. Therefore, we perceive this change. But, in addition, both spots are going up and down together, and we perceive this fact secondarily. An alternative explanation evokes the principle of grouping by "common fate," discussed in Chapter 5: When objects move together in the same direction and at the same speed, we tend to perceive them as belonging together. The spots in our example are moving together in the vertical direction. Once we see both spots as a group, this structure becomes a frame of reference with respect to which the horizontal component of B's motion is noted. In both explanations, however, the net result is that the circular motion of B is divided into two vectors of perceptual motion.

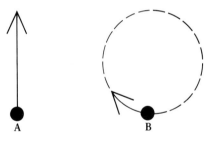

A   B

Spot B, moving in a circular path, is perceived veridically when spot A is not visible. When spot A is visible, spot B appears to move back and forth horizontally while both spots as a group appear to move vertically.

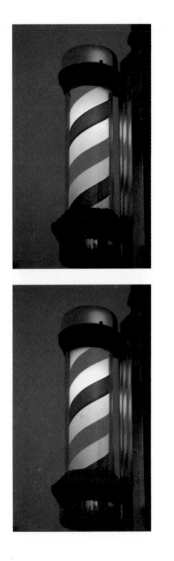

Stripes on a barber pole appear to move vertically although every point in the helical stripe is rotating in a horizontal plane around a vertical axis.

Now we can reconsider the spot on the rim of the rolling wheel. The spot's true path through space is not perceived unless the rest of the wheel is invisible, as in the case of the bicycle seen in the dark. When just a few additional spots on the wheel are visible, the wheel becomes a frame of reference for the spot. The spot is now seen as revolving around its axis. Because it "belongs" to the wheel, it also is seen as partaking of the wheel's horizontal, linear motion. Therefore, there are two components of motion that are perceived.

These examples of directional illusion and those of induced motion suggest the following conclusions: The motion of one object relative to other objects is particularly important in the perception of movement. Under certain conditions, one object in the field will serve as frame of reference with respect to which other objects will be seen to move. The frame of reference is often "assumed" to be stationary so that any motion relative to it is attributed to other objects. When the frame of reference is seen to be in motion, objects seen with respect to it will appear to have different components of movement, one based directly on relative change and another based on their belonging to the frame and partaking of its motion. Finally, under the right conditions, observers may perceive themselves to be in motion when a nearby structure that is in motion is assumed to be stationary.

An illusion of direction of motion that is very different from the kinds thus far discussed is the barber-pole illusion, illustrated at the left. One tends to see stripes moving down (or up), although in fact any region on the colored helical stripe that curves around the barber pole is simply rotating around the pole and not displacing downward or upward. In order to see this motion veridically, however, we would have to distinguish some specific point on the helix. Then we would detect its rotation in a horizontal plane. Without such a distinct point, however, we have no good information as to how the contour of the helix is moving. The stimulus is thoroughly ambiguous, as is shown by the successive views of the pole in the illustration. Under the circumstances, we tend to "assume" that the visible parts of the contour at time 1 are the same as those at time 2—that is, that these regions have the same physical identity. In fact, they are different because the helix is rotating. Thus those visible at time 1 will be occluded by time 2. If the parts were the same, the stripe would have to be moving directly downward, and that is precisely what we perceive.

Another way of stating the barber-pole effect is that we have a tendency *not* to perceive the points constituting a visible contour as moving out of view, or as changing location and being exchanged for new points, when there is no good stimulus information that they are doing so. Under some conditions, this tendency can lead to perceiving moving lines as

stationary. This tendency, in turn, leads to various other illusions, such as the impression that the circles in the stereokinetic display shown on page 69 are not rotating when the display is turning. If they are not rotating, they must be changing their positions by sliding around. In my opinion, the difficulty the perceptual system has in explaining this perception leads it to search for a better solution. The depth solution discussed in Chapter 3, in which the object is perceived to undergo perspective change, is precisely that. The same tendency not to perceive rotation of rotating circular or curved patterns leads to the perception of a rotating spiral as expanding or contracting, since each region of it then appears to be moving only inward or outward, depending upon the direction of the spiral's rotation.

Apparent Movement

Most people realize that moving pictures, including television, are illusions based on a succession of still pictures projected on a screen. But many believe that the illusion results from the eye's tendency to continue to transmit signals to the brain from a frame of film even when it is no

The illusion of motion. Successive shots taken by Eadweard Muybridge of a woman throwing a handkerchief into the air and picking it up. These shots lead to the impression of movement when they are viewed successively at a rapid rate. The apparent-motion effect is the basis of perceiving movement in television and moving pictures.

Arrangement for studying apparent motion.
Objects A and B are alternately flashed,
creating the impression of a single object
moving back and forth.

longer projected on the screen, thus filling the gap between frames. However, such persistence of vision explains only the absence of flicker, not apparent motion.

Students of perception have not done much better in their attempts to explain this illusion of motion. In the laboratory, *apparent motion* (also referred to as *stroboscopic motion* or the *phi phenomenon*) is studied in its utmost simplicity by flashing a single object or line in one place, and then, a short time later, flashing a similar object or line in another place. If the spacing and timing are just right, the observer will see the object or line moving from the first location to the second (from A to B in the illustration at left). Usually, the cycle is repeated and the observer sees the object moving back and forth. Why do we tend to see movement when the stimulus consists of one stationary object followed by another? The presumption is that, if we can unravel this problem, it will provide a key for understanding motion perception in general.

One approach to the problem is to consider apparent motion as a special case of real motion and to explain the perception as the result of motion-detector neurons firing in the visual nervous system. If the successive stimulation of adjacent retinal cells leads to the rapid firing of neurons that are specialized to detect such stimulus motion, then the successive stimulation of retinal cells that are farther apart may cause the rapid firing of neurons that detect the stroboscopic stimulus sequence.

Horace Barlow and William Levick at the universities of California and Cambridge have shown that precisely such a successive stimulation of neighboring, but not directly adjacent, regions of a rabbit's retina will trigger the response of neurons in its visual nervous system.

We might regard this approach as a sensory theory of apparent movement. While a theory of this kind may provide the explanation of perceived movement under stroboscopic conditions in animal species lower on the phylogenetic scale (fish, for example), it is inadequate to explain how we perceive it. First, apparent movement can be seen across a considerable angular distance, far enough for it to be unlikely that the two stimulated regions of the retina would be associated with the same motion-detector neuron in the brain. We can see such motion when a stimulus, *A*, falls on one side of the retina and a second stimulus, *B*, on the other. In fact, this probably occurs often, such as when the eyes are fixating between *A* and *B*. Under such conditions, *A* is projected to one hemisphere of the brain and *B* to the other. As can be seen in the illustration on page 7, the only connection is through neurons that cross in the structure of the brain known as the corpus callosum.

Implicit in the sensory theory of apparent motion is the assumption that what distinguishes apparent from real motion is the extent of separation between *A* and *B* on the retina. But that assumption may be incorrect. *A* and *B* are separate from one another in perceived space, whereas an object in real motion is seen to be located in a series of adjacent positions in space. If we track a really moving object, we perceive it to be moving even though its image remains stationary on the retina. Perhaps, then, an analogous situation prevails in the case of apparent motion. In an experiment Sheldon Ebenholtz and I performed some years ago, observers had to synchronize their eye movements with the flashing on and off first of *A* and then of *B*. As *A* appeared, observers looked directly at it. Thus the image of *A* fell in the central region of the retina, the fovea. As *A* disappeared, observers rapidly shifted their eyes to point *B*; just as the eyes reached that position, *B* flashed. It, too, then projected onto the fovea. The observers perceived apparent motion from *A* to *B*. In this case, a simple sensory explanation will not suffice because only one region of the retina was stimulated, not two. A single retinal region can represent two locations in perceived space because the direction of stimulation is interpreted differently on the basis of the two different positions of the eyes. In that respect, this experiment is analogous to the one in which we track a really moving object.

This outcome suggests an inference theory of apparent movement. According to this theory, apparent movement is a solution to the problem posed when object *A* disappears in one place in the scene and another object, *B*, suddenly appears in another place. After all, this sequence is quite similar to real motion, particularly when it is rapid. If one views a rapidly wagging finger, the conditions are much like those of apparent motion, except that the finger remains visible throughout its path. But Lloyd Kaufman and his associates at New York University have demonstrated that the visibility of the path *between* locations *A* and *B* is essentially a blurred streak and of little use for motion perception. They showed that, if the end positions of *A* and *B* (where, in the present example, the finger is momentarily stationary) are occluded so that only the intervening blurred motion is seen, observers do not perceive apparent motion. Conversely, if the end positions of the wagging finger are visible but its intervening path is not, motion *is* perceived. In this case, we have converted real to apparent motion.

Therefore, real motion and apparent motion are very similar if not identical, at least at fast speeds. This fact solves one puzzle about apparent motion: why we perceive apparent motion when there are few if any circumstances that animals or human beings encounter in the natural environment in which the conditions of apparent movement prevail. If the perception of apparent motion serves no adaptive purpose, why did we evolve in such a way that we could perceive it? The work of Kaufman and his associates suggests an answer: Perception of rapidly moving objects was necessary for survival, and the conditions for such perception

Apparent motion of multiple objects. The three spots in A, designated by the white spots, alternate with the three spots in B, designated by the dark spots. (In an actual experiment, all of the spots would be the same color.)

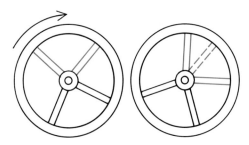

The wagon-wheel effect. In moving pictures, a wheel is often perceived to roll backward when in fact it is rolling forward.

reduce to those for apparent motion. Thus, in an apparent-movement display, when the conditions mimic those of real, rapid motion, entailing sudden disappearance of an object in one place and its reappearance in another, our perceptual system makes the plausible inference that the object has moved.

For apparent movement to be seen, the temporal interval between *A* and *B* must be neither too long nor too short. Although this fact has been known since apparent motion was first discovered, the reasons behind it have never been clear. The inference approach, however, may help to explain it. If the temporal interval is too brief, we tend to perceive both *A* and *B* simultaneously. This fact is based on persistence of vision. If *A* is still visible when *B* appears, the perceptual system can hardly infer that *A* has moved to *B*! If the interval is too long, *A* must be inferred to be moving rather slowly across the intervening space. After all, the object must be assumed to be moving at a speed such that it reaches *B* just as *B* appears. If an object were to be moving slowly, it ought to be visible between *A* and *B*. Only at fast speeds does the perceptual system "expect" the object to be little more than a blur between *A* and *B*. Therefore, if the speed is inferred to be slow and the object is invisible, the inference that the object is really moving is rejected.

So far, we have considered the case of a wagging finger or other single stimulus object. But in moving pictures several things are often moving or different parts of one object are moving simultaneously. For example, when we see a woman walking across the screen, we usually see feet, arms, and the entire body move. Consider the simplified situation in the upper illustration at left, in which the three white spots represent *A* (flashed first) and the three dark spots represent *B* (flashed second). What spot in *A* should we expect will be seen to be moving to what spot in *B*, and why? This issue is referred to as the correspondence problem.

The prediction that a sensory theory of apparent movement should make is one based on proximity. It should be predicted that whatever spot in *B* is nearest to a spot in *A* will be the one to correspond to it such that motion will be seen between them. Proximity is a powerful principle for predicting correspondence in apparent motion displays, and it is a powerful principle of perceptual grouping. We can make use of it to explain a common but curious phenomenon of apparent motion. In movies, the wheels of a vehicle often seem to roll backward as the vehicle moves forward. This effect, which has been called the wagon-wheel effect because it is frequently seen in wagons used in Western movies, can be explained as follows. Consider one spoke of a wheel, that shown in magenta in the illustration in the left margin. In the first frame of the film, the camera records the wheel in the position on left in the figure; in the second frame, the camera records it in the position on right in the figure, the wheel having turned about 50 degrees. We will tend to see the spoke shown in magenta as rotating counterclockwise, the principle of proximity suggests, because, in the second frame, the spoke shown in blue lies closer to the magenta spoke's position in the first frame than does the actual new position of the magenta spoke. Thus, we tend to identify the spoke shown in blue in the second frame as that shown in magenta in the first frame. But all the other visible points in the wheel are recorded in each frame in the same locations relative to one another; thus, the wheel as a whole appears to turn backward.

If proximity were to govern correspondence in all cases, however, we would have to predict that, in the upper illustration on the facing page, the second spot in *A* would appear to move to the position of the first spot in *B*, and the third spot in *A* would appear to move to the position of the second spot in *B*, while the first spot in *A* and the third spot in *B* would not correspond with anything. A sensory theory, or any theory based *only* on stimulus proximity, is "blind" to the content of each stimulus unit and its role in the whole configuration. But an inference theory suggests a very different conclusion. If *A* and *B* each consists of three spots, the most plausible inference is that *A* has moved as a whole to *B*. Thus, we would predict that the first, second, and third spots in *A* would appear to move to the respective positions of the first, second, and third spots in *B*. In general, we perceive this kind of sequence in just this way.

An even more striking correspondence occurs when some of the spots in *A* and *B* actually overlap, as shown in the illustration to the right. In the illustration, *A* consists of spots 1, 2, and 3, while *B* consists of spots 2, 3, and 4. This kind of experiment was done 60 years ago in Berlin by Josef Ternus, a student of Max Wertheimer. Here, we have the option of perceiving some spots as simply "flashing" on and off in place. Under some conditions, however, we see the entire configuration as moving back and forth. Thus, for example, the middle spot in *A* corresponds not with the leftmost spot in *B*, to which it is physically identical, but with the middle spot in *B*, with which it perceptually corresponds, since it is the middle spot in both *A* and *B*. Ternus referred to this as *phenomenal identity*. What governs correspondence is the perceptual (phenomenal) identity or role of a part in a whole, not simply the physical identity or physical proximity of the part in *A* and *B*.

Certain findings that at first seem to challenge the inference theory can in fact be reconciled with it. For example, Paul Kolers and James Pomerantz, then at the Bell Telephone Laboratories, demonstrated that apparent movement is easily seen when the two separate images are different shapes. If *A* is a circle and *B* a triangle, observers will perceive the circle changing shape as it moves, becoming a triangle by the time it reaches *B*. This effect suggests that the sudden disappearance of the object at *A* and the sudden appearance of an object at *B* creates such a strong presumption of movement from *A* to *B* that the movement is

In this apparent-motion display, spots 1, 2, and 3, shown as white, compose A and are shown first, while spots 2, 3, and 4, shown as black, composing B, are shown next. The middle and rightmost spots in A overlap with the leftmost and middle spots in B. Yet the cluster of three spots in A is often perceived to move as a group to the cluster of three spots in B.

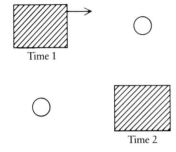

The rectangle alternately covers and uncovers the two spots, which are present throughout the experiment. When the rectangle is not visible, the spots appear to move back and forth. When it is visible, the spots are not perceived as moving.

perceived despite the dissimilar shapes. The perceptual system thus seems to account for the dissimilarity in an ingenious way, by perceiving that the object deforms as it moves.

One final experiment in support of the inference view is worth mentioning. Based upon an earlier finding by Arnold Stoper, then at Brandeis University, Eric Sigman and I performed the experiment illustrated at left. Two spots appeared and disappeared at spacings and intervals that normally would yield an impression of apparent movement. However, this appearance and disappearance was achieved by moving an opaque rectangle back and forth over the spots. When the rectangle itself was not visible, observers perceived the spots moving back and forth, as would be expected. When the rectangle was visible, however, they did not perceive the spots to be moving. Instead, they perceived them to be permanently present but alternately covered and uncovered by the rectangle. Although images of the spots stimulated the retina at the appropriate spacing and timing, the sequence did not yield the illusion of apparent movement. This finding suggests that we ordinarily perceive apparent movement not because it is an inevitable sensory outcome of stimulation but because it is the best explanation of the otherwise inexplicable sudden appearance and disappearance of objects. But in the present experiment another solution is available.

There is now reason for believing that the sensory theory and the inference theory may both be correct. Oliver Braddick of Cambridge University has discovered that there are two different kinds of apparent motion. One is based on very small separations between the images of *A* and *B* on the retina and very short time intervals between them. It is likely that the mechanism observed by Barlow and Levick is responsible for apparent motion perception under such conditions. Braddick calls this the short-range process. The other kind of apparent motion, the long-range process, is based on greater spatial and temporal separations between *A* and *B*. It is unlikely that the sensory motion-detector mechanism can be responsible for apparent motion under these conditions. Consequently, it is plausible that the inference theory applies here and that the findings cited in support of such a theory derive from conditions that favor the long-range process.

The Autokinetic Effect

A striking illusion of motion occurs when a single star seen against an otherwise homogeneous sky appears to drift across the field of vision. This illusion can be recreated in the laboratory by asking observers seated in an otherwise dark room to view a single spot of light. Soon the spot appears to drift slowly in a particular direction. This *autokinetic effect*, as it is called, is highly susceptible to suggestion, the studies of social psychologists show. When "planted" subjects report motion of the spot in a particular direction, a naive subject will often report perceiving the spot to move in just that direction.

What causes the autokinetic effect? Investigators do not know for sure, but certain facts about motion perception already discussed here shed some light on it. We have seen the importance for motion perception of an object's change in location relative to other objects or to a frame of reference. Conversely, the absence of an object's change in location relative to a background must be important information in perceiving an object as stationary. In other words, a stationary spot seen within a stationary rectangle will not appear to move, no matter how long we look at it. But without the rectangle, the spot's location in a homogeneous background (such as a dark room) is not sufficiently anchored to a frame of reference.

Under these conditions, the only basis for perceiving the spot's location is our knowledge of where the eyes are looking. If the eyes were to be slowly drifting when viewing a spot, we could be tracking a spot that was moving slowly. Perhaps that explains why suggestion can be effective. On hearing that the spot is moving, say to the right, we can imagine that we are tracking it to the right when, in fact, the eyes remain stationary.

Some investigators have argued that the autokinetic effect results from actual eye movements. The idea behind this argument is simply that, with eye movement, the image of the spot displaces over the retina and that retinal displacement causes the illusion. Such a theory is inadequate because, as we have seen, stationary objects do not appear to move every time the eyes move. Position constancy is achieved, presumably because retinal displacement is discounted when the perceptual system "knows" that it is caused by eye movement. For an eye-movement theory of the autokinetic effect to be tenable, it would have to be maintained that the eyes move but that the brain does not "know" that they are moving. One difficulty for this theory is that it must also predict that an entire stationary scene will appear to move, not just an isolated spot. I suggest that it is not eye movement that causes the illusion but the illusory misperception of eye behavior. The eyes are stationary but are misperceived to be tracking the (stationary) spot because the perceptual system "believes" for some reason—whether it be suggestion or self-suggestion—that the spot is drifting slowly across the field.

The Aftereffect of Movement

After viewing a continuously moving display such as a waterfall, stationary contours appear to move in the opposite direction for a brief interval.

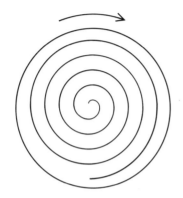

A spiral used in demonstrating the aftereffect of motion.

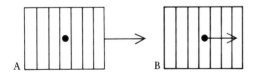

Arrangement for the experiment on the aftereffect of motion. A. When observers fixated the stationary point, they experienced an aftereffect of motion, whereas when they tracked the moving stripes, they did not. B. When observers tracked a moving spot over the stationary stripes, an aftereffect was created.

In the laboratory, a rotating spiral is often used to generate this *after-effect of movement*, which is sometimes called the *spiral*, or *waterfall, illusion*. If the moving spiral shown at left is viewed for 30 seconds or more while the eyes are fixating its center, and if the spiral is then stopped, it will still appear to be moving, but in the opposite direction. The effect is strongest immediately after the spiral stops, and then it gradually disappears. When the spiral is rotating, it will appear to be either expanding or contracting, depending upon the direction of its rotation. When it stops, it will appear to be either contracting or expanding. In other words, the aftereffect is always opposite in direction to the initial direction of motion. By the same token, if another stationary object, even a person's face, is viewed thereafter instead of the spiral, it will appear to be expanding or contracting for a short duration.

What causes this aftereffect? The evidence strongly suggests the theory that it results from sensory adaptation to contours moving over the retina, in a specific location on the retina. Stuart Anstis and Richard Gregory, then at Cambridge University, performed some simple experiments that demonstrate this. In one experiment, illustrated in A, left below, observers either tracked moving stripes or looked at a stationary spot while the stripes passed in front of them. Although the stripes appeared to move in both cases, only in the second, in which the images of the stripes displaced across the retina, was an aftereffect produced. In another experiment, illustrated in B, left below, observers tracked a dot moving across stationary stripes. Although here nothing was seen to be moving, the images of the stripes moved over the retina, creating an aftereffect. Therefore, the effect is misnamed. It should be called the aftereffect of retinal displacement, not the aftereffect of movement.

Why should contour displacement over the retina lead to a motion aftereffect? To answer this, it will be helpful to consider a color aftereffect. If one fixates a point while viewing a colored region, and then views a gray region in the same location, the gray region will appear tinged with the complementary color. This effect is referred to as successive color contrast. The effect is localized within the region on the retina exposed to the particular color (just as the motion aftereffect is localized within the region of the retina exposed to the motion of contours). The explanation is that cells in the visual system most sensitive to, let us say, blue are satiated. For this and other reasons, the normal balance between yellow and blue in this region is upset. In subsequently viewing an achromatic gray region, the cells that signal the sensation "yellow" are more active than those that signal "blue," so that the gray region appears somewhat yellowish.

By the same token, some cells are most responsive to one direction of contour motion. If these are fatigued, the cells responsive to the opposite direction of contour motion are, by comparison, more active. Hence stationary contours stimulating that region of the retina will create an impression of motion in the opposite direction. These adaptation effects, of both color and motion, are clearly sensory in origin. In fact, the motion aftereffect is paradoxical in one respect. A sensation of motion (or of expansion or contraction) does exist, but the contours do not appear to be going anywhere. No doubt this occurs because other information continues to indicate no change in location.

If this kind of explanation of the aftereffect of motion is correct, the phenomenon is different from all the other kinds of motion perception that were considered in this chapter. Whereas it can be explained in terms of localized sensory mechanisms and is not an aftereffect of *motion perception* but rather of a certain kind of sensory stimulation, the other phenomena cannot be explained simply in terms of sensory mechanisms and *do* concern the perception of motion. Contrary to what might seem to be a plausible explanation of motion perception, the displacement of an object's image over the retina cannot account for such perception, although it is relevant information to be taken into account. We have seen that illusions of motion of various kinds—induced, directional, apparent, and autokinetic—as well as the perception of real motion, are based on more complex central processes entailing constancy operations, relativistic comparisons often based on structures serving as reference frames, and unconscious problem solving.

A number of new concepts and principles have thus emerged in connection with the various phenomena of perceived motion that were not relevant in the earlier discussions of static phenomena. In particular, we have seen for the first time how the body of the observer, the visible self, is another object in the field that conforms to the same lawful processes that govern the perception of other objects. Some of these same concepts will come up again in the next chapter, where we consider how we perceive the orientation of objects and ourselves in the world.

8 THE UPRIGHT WORLD

If the retinal images of the scenes we view are upside down, why does the world not appear to be upside down as well? If an observer were floating in space far from Earth, so that the direction of gravity or other indicators of "up" and "down" in relation to the world were unknown and irrelevant, the question of the uprightness of vision from an inverted retinal image could still be posed. For if a second person were floating in space next to the observer, his or her image would be inverted on the observer's retina, yet that person would not appear inverted.

"Upright" and "inverted" are defined *egocentrically* here—that is, in terms of how things appear to be oriented in relation to the self. But there is another meaning of "upright" in perception. "Upright" can refer to the orientation of a thing in relation to the direction of gravity, to how it is positioned in the environment, quite apart from how it is oriented in relation to ourselves. No matter what may be our own body orientation, whether supine or even standing on our heads, we can still ask whether or not an object is perceived to be vertical or right side up in the world. In this sense, an object such as a tree may be perceived to be right side up even if we happen to view it when we ourselves are upside down, thus rendering it egocentrically inverted. Here, "upright" (or "tilted" or "inverted") is therefore defined *environmentally*. As will be seen, there are some intriguing problems to be addressed in understanding both the perception of an object's *environmental orientation* and its *egocentric orientation*.

Observers floating in a gravity-free space will still perceive the orientation of objects in relation to themselves.

The Perception of Environmental Orientation

What determines whether or not an object looks vertical, tilted, or horizontal in the world? One might think that it has something to do

The perceived orientation of things in the environment is independent of their egocentric orientation. Here, the sign is upside down in the environment although right side up in relation to the observer.

with the object's orientation relative to other objects. For example, a picture on the wall may look tilted because it is not aligned with the wall's vertical and horizontal coordinates. As we shall see, this proposition is true. But it leaves unexplained how we perceive the orientation of the coordinates of the wall. To what can we compare *them*? It also leaves unexplained how we can perceive the environmental orientation of a single object more or less correctly, even when it is the only object visible. There must be another source of information about orientation available to us.

GRAVITY INFORMATION AND ORIENTATION CONSTANCY
The obvious answer is that we obtain sensory information about the direction of gravity and that this information, although not itself visual, enables us to perceive the visual orientation of things in the environment. Two experiments show that this is true. In the first, the observer enters a small, dark room that revolves in a circular track, as shown in the illustration at the top of the facing page. Inside the room is a luminous rod that the observer is asked to place in a vertical position. The centrifugal force adds a horizontal component to the existing vertical force of gravity

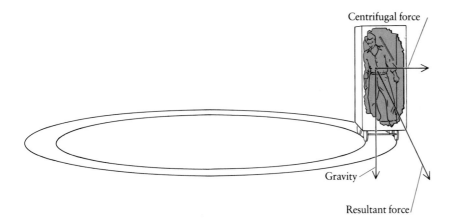

Observers in a dark room revolving in a circular path, given the task of setting a rod to the vertical, set it parallel to the direction of the resultant force acting on them rather than parallel to the direction of the pull of gravity.

so that the resultant force on the observer is now in an oblique direction. On the average, observers place the rod in this oblique direction, perceiving it to be vertical.

A similar conclusion can be drawn from a simpler experiment. Suppose an observer is tilted in a dark room, as shown at right. If asked to indicate when a rod is vertical, the observer can do so with reasonable accuracy. Under these conditions, the vertical rod does not generate an image that is vertical with respect to the retina. Thus, the perceptual system achieves constancy of perceived orientation.

Just as size constancy depends upon taking into account sensory information about distance, constancy here would seem to be based upon taking into account information about body orientation. For example, if observers are tilted 30 degrees clockwise, they will perceive the rod to be vertical only if its image is tilted 30 degrees counterclockwise from the vertical meridian on the retina, as shown in the illustration on the following page. The perceptual system takes body orientation into account in inferring the environmental orientation of objects from their retinal-image orientations. The same inference process undoubtedly underlies perception in the revolving-room experiment. As a result of the centrifugal force, the observer feels tilted and thus perceives the true vertical orientation as tilted and a tilted orientation as vertical.

The direction of gravity is detected by the sensory system in various ways. The pressure on the feet, or on whatever parts of the body take its weight, is a cue. Muscular reactions to maintain balance may also provide cues. But the major source of information about gravity derives from sensory mechanisms inside the inner ear, in the so-called vestibular apparatus. Hair cells in two structures of the inner ear, the utricle and saccule, are embedded in a gelatinous substance. These hair cells bend with the

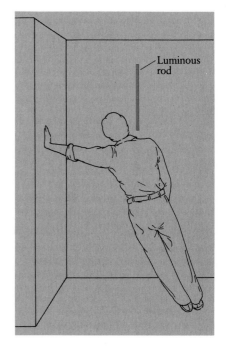

When observers are tilted in a dark room and asked to set a luminous rod to the vertical, they usually do so fairly accurately. Despite the tilted retinal image of the rod, constancy of orientation is achieved.

pull of gravity, causing nerve fibers attached to them to discharge, the rate of discharge being a function of the degree to which the head is tilted. We are completely unaware of this source of information because no conscious sensations emanate from this part of the inner ear.

The visual perception of orientation obviously can be no more accurate than is the body's information about its orientation. If, in the previous example, the signals from the inner ear failed to indicate that the head was tilted 30 degrees, we could hardly expect full constancy to be achieved. This reasoning may explain a rarely experienced but curious illusion that occurs when the body is tilted 60 degrees or more in a dark room. It was discovered by the German investigator Hermann Aubert over a century ago. If an observer lies on his or her side and views a luminous vertical rod in a dark room, the rod will appear tilted from the vertical by 8 degrees or more. If the observer is tilted clockwise, the rod will appear to be tilted counterclockwise. The *Aubert illusion* (or *A effect*) represents a partial failure of the constancy mechanism. The most probable explanation of the illusion is that the vestibular signals triggered by the head's tilt do not correlate perfectly with the actual extent of tilt of the head. The information available to the perceptual system is that the head is tilted, say, only 80 degrees when in fact it is tilted 90 degrees. The computation of object orientation will thus be in error by 10 degrees.

THE VISUAL FRAME OF REFERENCE   Why does the Aubert effect not occur in daily life when the entire scene is visible? If the observer lies on his or her side in a lighted room, the same misinformation from the inner ear is received. Thus, the entire scene ought to appear to be tilted, but it does not. Some source of information other than gravity must, therefore, be available. The same conclusion can be reached when we consider the perceptions we have when we are inside a tilted fun room in an amusement park or an enclosed room of a listing ship or a banking plane. The brain surely registers information about the direction of gravity. But these rooms do not look tilted; they tend to look perfectly upright. Accordingly, we may align our bodies to what seems to be the room's vertical axis and risk either falling over or, at the least, feeling peculiar.

In these instances, we seem to accept the coordinates of the room as *defining* vertical and horizontal and to perceive all other orientations in relation to them. The room becomes a visual frame of reference. Just as a frame of reference is important in motion perception, so it is important in orientation perception. Gravity is not the only information that affects how objects appear to be oriented in the environment.

Ordinarily, the direction of gravity is aligned with a main axis of a structure, such as a room, so that both information about gravity and visual cues cooperate in determining perceived orientation. This also

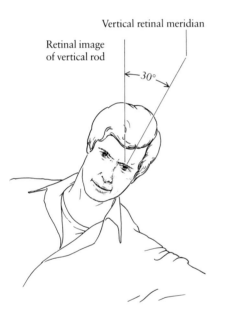

Vertical retinal meridian

Retinal image of vertical rod

←—30°

Because the eyes tilt when the head is tilted, a vertical rod will not produce a vertically oriented image. Thus, veridical perception of orientation requires the taking into account of body position in interpreting the orientation of the retinal image.

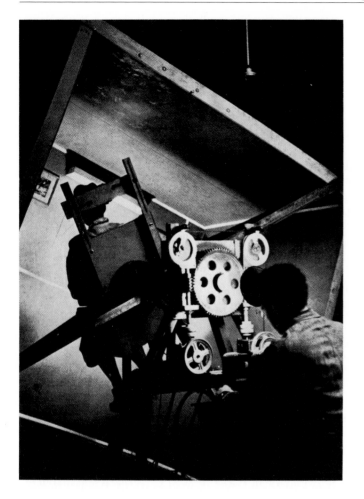

holds true outdoors, where the ground is horizontal and trees, buildings, and the like are truly vertical. But in some cases, such as those of the tilted rooms, a conflict exists between information about gravity and visual cues. One way to explain the outcome of this conflict is in terms of visual capture. Not only do our own bodies *look* like they are tilted if they remain upright when we are inside a tilted room, because the visual information overpowers the gravity-based information, but they *feel* tilted, too. If so, the veridical gravity-based information is not directly taken into account; instead, the perceptual system uses the distorted, proprioceptive perception of body orientation in the computation of environmental orientation. As a result, all information about horizontal and vertical orientation is now congruent rather than in conflict.

In 1949, H. A. Witkin, then at Brooklyn College, performed an important experiment that demonstrates the dominance of visual information over gravity information in perceiving the orientation of the body. Observers seated on an adjustable chair inside a tilted room were required to adjust their chairs to a position in which they experienced themselves as

Wertheimer's method for viewing a scene through a tilted mirror.

upright. They could not see out of the room, as shown in the photograph on the preceding page, and thus had no way to gauge that it was tilted with respect to an external frame of reference. As a result, observers typically set the chair in the direction of the tilt of the room. In such a tilted room, objects other than the observer's own body are perceived in relation to the frame of reference that the room constitutes. A plumb line looks quite tilted despite the fact that we know its direction reflects the pull of gravity.

Does visual information dominate when the observer is not *inside* the frame of reference? Suppose the observer views the tilted structure from outside of it. Max Wertheimer performed this kind of experiment by looking into a tilted mirror at a room, an arrangement illustrated above. He reported that after a short while the scene seemed to right itself, and no longer appeared tilted.

Following this lead, Solomon Asch and Witkin constructed small, tilted roomlike structures that. observers viewed from outside, either through a tube or by simply standing close to them. In a further variation, they constructed tilted luminous rectangular perimeters that the observers viewed in a dark room, as shown in the illustration at right on the facing page.

An important innovation in these experiments was the introduction of a luminous rod, the orientation of which could be varied. The observer indicated when the rod seen inside the room or the rectangle appeared to be vertical. This gave the experimenters a way to measure the relative strengths of the visual frame of reference and gravity-based information as cues to orientation. The illusory effect created by the tilted rectangular perimeter is referred to as the *rod-and-frame effect* and has been the subject of countless experiments.

What is the typical result of these experiments? "Typical" is perhaps not the best term, because individuals differ widely in their responses to these situations. Some observers are able to resist the effect of the tilted frame and set the rod correctly in an orientation close to that of the gravitational vertical. Others cannot resist the effect of the frame and set the rod parallel, or almost parallel, to the edge of the frame that seems to define vertical, the edge that is least tilted in the world.

Witkin and his associates discovered that performance in this task was correlated with performance in other perceptual tasks. For example, those who were strongly influenced by the surrounding frame, the so-called field-dependent observers, also found it difficult to isolate or find familiar figures embedded in a larger pattern. The so-called field-independent observers, who resisted the effect of the frame on the perception of the rod, performed better in the embedded-figure task. The researchers also claimed that the two categories of observers tended to have different kinds of personality.

If experimenters use a rectangle sufficiently large to serve as a surrogate frame of reference for the vertical-horizontal coordinates of the environment, and they place it at, say, a tilt of around 30 degrees, observers, on average, will set the rod at roughly 6 or 7 degrees in the direction of the tilted frame. This result implies that a truly vertical rod seen in the frame would appear tilted by 6 or 7 degrees—a sizable illusion. Quite a few observers do set the rod at this orientation; thus this effect is not simply based on averaging the two extreme types of subject. Such a result has been interpreted as a compromise between the two conflicting determinants: gravity and the visual frame of reference.

How is the frame itself perceived? How it is seen presumably would influence the positioning of the rod. Were it to look upright, as does a tilted room in which the observer is enclosed, we should expect that the rod would be set parallel to its edges. Were it to look tilted, as tilted as it really is, should we expect any effect on the perception of the rod at all? If the frame is veridically perceived as tilted by 30 degrees, presumably information about gravity is not being overpowered or captured by the surrogate frame of reference. In that event, the same information ought to be available to the observer to set the rod to the true vertical.

The rod-and-frame effect. The observer indicates the orientation in which a luminous rod, seen within a tilted luminous rectangle in an otherwise dark room, appears to be vertical.

Oddly enough, few experimenters have paid much attention to how the frame appears in experiments on the rod-and-frame effect. In one experiment in which this question was addressed, Walter Gogel and his associate R. E. Newton of the University of California at Santa Barbara found that the rectangular frame's tilt was perceived accurately. But, in this experiment, a small frame was used, subtending only 10 degrees in visual angle, so that it probably could not have served as an effective world surrogate. The small illusory impression of rod tilt obtained in this experiment might then be interpreted as an illusion analogous to geometrical illusions in which acute angles are misperceived. To put it another way, the angle formed by the rod and an edge of the frame would be overestimated so that the rod, when vertical, would appear to be slightly tilted.

When Joseph Di Lorenzo and I examined this question, therefore, we used a large frame, one subtending a visual angle of 54 degrees. We found that the frame's tilt was then underestimated. That being the case, it is understandable why a strong illusion of rod orientation occurred. If, for example, a frame tilted by 30 degrees appears to be tilted by only 20 degrees, then a vertical rod within it that is displaced by an angle of 30 degrees from the frame must appear to be tilted by 10 degrees in the direction opposite to that of the frame. To appear upright, therefore, the rod would have to be tilted by 10 degrees toward the tilted frame. In fact there was a high correlation between the underestimation of the frame's tilt and the illusory tilt of the rod. Other evidence we obtained consistently supported the conclusion that whatever factor caused the frame to appear less tilted than it was also led to a correspondingly large effect on the appearance of the rod.

This conclusion about the rod-and-frame effect is quite consistent with the strong effect on perceived body and object orientation that occurs when the observer is inside a tilted room. The underlying principle seems to be this: A large structure with rectangular coordinates tends to become the surrogate of the vertical-horizontal coordinate system of space. But to do so, it must surround the observer or, equivalently, it must occupy a large angle of the visual field. However, when the observer is inside the structure, visual capture seems to be more or less complete, with the result that gravity-based information is no longer a conflicting factor. When the observer is outside the structure, some degree of visual capture undoubtedly occurs as well. Experiments have shown that observers then err in their perception of how their own bodies are oriented. But, because the phenomenon of visual capture is not complete, there is a conflict between gravity information and visual structure. The outcome is a compromise. The frame still looks tilted, but less tilted than in fact it is.

The Perception of Egocentric Orientation

How do we manage to perceive veridically the orientations of things, or a scene as a whole, in relation to ourselves? This question is often posed because, as most people know, even though the image of the scene on the back of the eye is upside down and reversed left to right, we see the world as upright in relation to ourselves. This is not the difficult problem that it may first appear to be, however. In fact, the more interesting and puzzling problem is how we would perceive the world if the retinal image were turned around and made upright.

UPRIGHT VISION FROM AN INVERTED IMAGE   Is it really a problem that vision is upright although the retinal image of the scene is inverted? For once, all students of perception agree on an issue: It is not. If it were the case that the scene did appear inverted, a further question would immediately arise: With respect to *what* would it appear inverted? According to the definition of egocentric orientation already given, the scene would have to appear upside down in relation to the observer. But visible parts of one's own body produce images on the retina, and these images are also upside down. In other words, the perceived orientation of one thing relative to another and of all things relative to the visible parts of the self are in no way altered by the fact that the entire retinal image happens to be physically upside down. No one has stated this fact more clearly or eloquently than Berkeley, almost three centuries ago. (Berkeley is talking about the inverted image of another person, but his reasoning would apply just as forcefully to images of parts of the observer's own body.)

> The head, which is painted [by which Berkeley means imaged on the retina] nearest earth, seems to be furthest from it; and on the other hand, the feet which are painted furthest from the earth, are thought nearest to it. Herein lies the difficulty, which vanishes if we express the thing more clearly and free from ambiguity. . . .
>
> If we confine our thoughts to the proper objects of sight, the whole is plain and easy. The head is painted furthest from, and the feet nearest to the visible earth; and so they appear to be. What is there strange or unaccountable in this? Let us suppose the pictures in the fund of the eye, to be the immediate objects of the sight. The consequence is, that things should appear in the same posture they are painted in; and is it not so? The head which is seen, seems furthest from the earth which is seen; and the feet which are seen, seem nearest to the earth which is seen? and just so they are painted.
>
> But, say you, the picture of the man is inverted, and yet the appearance is erect: I ask, what mean you by the picture of the man, or, which is the same thing, the visible man's being inverted? You tell me it is inverted, because the

heels are uppermost, and the head undermost? Explain me this. You say, that by the head's being undermost, you mean that it is nearest to the earth; and by the heels being uppermost, that they are furthest from the earth. I ask again, what earth you mean? You cannot mean the earth that is painted on the eye, or the visible earth: for the picture of the head is furthest from the picture of the earth, and the picture of the feet nearest to the picture of the earth; and accordingly the visible head is furthest from the visible earth, and the visible feet nearest to it. It remains, therefore, that you mean the tangible earth, and so determine the situation of visible things with respect to tangible things: contrary to what hath been demonstrated [earlier]. The two distinct provinces of sight and touch should be considered apart, and as if their objects had no intercourse, no matter of relation to one another, in point of distance or position.

Another way to analyze the issue is to note that we do not see our own retinal images. We see on the basis of the information contained within them. The information about orientation contained within them is no more distorted by the fact that it is in its entirety upside down than is the information about the relative size of things distorted by the fact that the image is a miniature replica of the scene it represents. After all, we do not wonder why things look as *large* as they do simply because their retinal images are so much smaller than the things they represent.

Puzzlement over the fact that upright vision results from an inverted image may derive from adherence to the camera theory of visual perception: The eye sends a picture into the brain where an upright inner "observer" looks at it. If that picture is upside down, it ought to appear so to that inner "observer." However, a sensory stimulus such as the retinal image in the eye should be thought of more as an encoding of the information in the world, not as an exact copy of it. Moreover, as we have seen repeatedly, the resulting perception should not be thought of as an exact copy of the retinal image. Thus, the fact that uprightness of vision is achieved despite an inverted retinal image is a pseudoproblem.

UPRIGHT VISION FROM AN UPRIGHT IMAGE? If we can obtain the same information about the orientation of things relative to one another and to our own seen bodies, will we see the world upright even if we turn the image 180 degrees? This was precisely the question that, as was mentioned in Chapter 7, George Stratton asked around the turn of the century, having absorbed the relativistic analysis given by Berkeley two centuries earlier. He set out (in Berkeley, California, a city named in honor of the philosopher!) to prove that upright vision would be upright even when one views the world through an optical device that inverts the normal retinal image. He also wanted to disprove certain theories of his day that held that upright vision actually *required* an inverted image. According to one such theory, "uprightness" was a result of the direction the eyes move in scanning objects. For example, to gaze directly at an object whose image is in the lowermost part of the retina, one must move the eyes *upward*. In other words, if that image is below the fovea, the eyes must swivel upward before it can fall on the fovea.

Stratton constructed a lens system inside a tube that inverted and reversed the image from its usual orientation, as shown on page 182. He wore this tube over one eye (the other eye being patched) throughout his waking hours, first for three days and later for eight more days. He observed how things appeared and how he behaved during the experiment and carefully recorded his observations.

What were the results? Stratton describes an increasing tendency, over the course of the experiment, for the world to appear upright or normal, and he infers that, in time, it would have looked upright permanently. However, his findings have been in dispute and are often misstated in textbooks. One reason for the confusion is that his description of how scenes appeared varied from day to day as the experiment progressed. Another is that he referred to both egocentric and environmental orientation without distinguishing between them. Suppose that at the beginning of the experiment an object in the scene appeared upside down in the environment whereas at some later point it did not. For example, a chair might at first look as though it were inverted in relation to gravity or the ground, with the floor looking like the ceiling, but might later look as though it were upright in this respect. Still, the chair might have continued to appear to be inverted in relation to Stratton himself. This, indeed, happened. Stratton reports that:

> [If] full attention was given to outer objects, these frequently seemed to be in normal position, and whatever there was of abnormality seemed to lie in myself, as if head and shoulders were inverted and I were viewing objects from that position, as boys sometimes do from between their legs. At other times the inversion seemed confined to the face or eyes alone.

Still another reason for the confusion over Stratton's findings is that his motor performance clearly did undergo successful adaptation. At first, as we might expect, his movements toward visible objects were inappropriate. He reached for an object on the left when it was in fact on the right. But he soon learned to correct for these errors and, in time, such correction became automatic, although occasionally errors recurred. Others who have repeated this kind of experiment over longer time periods have learned to negotiate the environment so successfully that they have even been able to ride a bicycle or ski.

There is also some confusion because the scene appeared increasingly "normal" to Stratton. By "normal," I mean that Stratton became accus-

When subjects wear inverting optical devices, they eventually learn to negotiate the environment successfully. At first, however, they frequently misjudge the location of objects.

tomed to the optical reinversion. He no longer paid much attention to its "peculiar" character. But "becoming accustomed" to something should not be confused with coming to perceive it differently. More telling tests of how an observer perceives things are possible, but Stratton did not attempt them. For example, suppose figures are flashed on a screen and the observer has to identify them. What would be the spontaneous response to a "W"? At the outset, it will look like an "M," but how will it look after prolonged wearing of the inverting lens device? If true egocentric adaptation occurs, the observer will report "W." In order to be sure that it is egocentric orientation that is being tested, one can have the observer lie in a supine position and view the letters overhead, as is shown in the illustration at left. Another test is to require the supine observer to view an overhead spot moving in a horizontal plane. (The horizontal plane would eliminate confusion about gravity-based or environmentally defined orientation.) When the spot moves in the foot-to-head direction, will the observer see it move head-to-foot, as occurs at the outset of the experiment, or will he or she see it move veridically in the foot-to-head direction?

Finally, Stratton's own theory adds to confusion about the outcome. He believed that harmony between touch and sight is the ultimate meaning of uprightness. After a lifetime of experience, he began the experiment with certain touch sensations closely associated with certain visual sensations. Therefore, when he put on the inverting lenses, he found that if he touched an object before seeing it, he did not receive the visual sensation that he expected to have when he looked in that direction. The converse was true for objects seen before they were touched. Over the course of the experiment, new associations between touch and sight gradually supplanted the old ones. This reestablishment of intersensory harmony, Stratton argued, accounted for his increasingly frequent experiences of the world as upright. Thus, to Berkeley's question (With respect to what does the scene appear to be inverted?) Stratton answered, With respect to other sense modalities, such as touch. However, it is not immediately evident why such harmony between the senses should, in itself, restore either egocentric or environmental uprightness of vision.

Unfortunately, the evidence gained from repetitions of Stratton's experiment is not conclusive either. Some investigators were not concerned with the question of visual appearances but only with sensory-motor performance; others changed the apparatus in certain critical respects, making comparison difficult. One study by Theodor Erismann and Ivo Kohler made use of a mirror placed on the underside of the visor of a cap into which the observer looked in order to see the scene. The mirror reversed up and down, but not left and right. The investigators claimed that egocentric adaptation occurred, and, to their credit, they were the

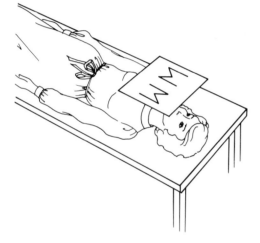

If true egocentric adaptation to an optically reinverted image has occurred, the observer should see the "M" as a "W" and the "W" as an "M" once the inverting device is removed.

Inverting prism apparatus used in a recent experiment on perception of orientation.

first to introduce tests in which objects were presented for identification whose orientation was ambiguous—for example, letters such as "M." But these results were not sufficiently clear-cut to support their conclusion, at least in my opinion.

Moreover, some subjects' introspections in these studies are hard to comprehend. For example, Kohler claimed that his subjects' visual perception underwent a peculiar piecemeal transformation. After 18 days of wearing right-angle prisms that reversed the retinal images right for left without inverting them, one subject reported: "Inscriptions on buildings, or advertisements, were still seen in mirror writing, but the objects containing them were seen in the correct location. Vehicles driving on the 'right' . . . carried license numbers in mirror writing." Kohler notes that "the subject is capable of localizing both sides of, say, a '3' correctly (open to the left, the curves to the right) and still see it mirrorwise." It is difficult to imagine how such inconsistent perceptions could occur.

More recent research, however, may shed some light on adaptation to optical inversion and reversal and on the ambiguities in both Stratton's and Kohler's reports. Charles S. Harris, at the University of Pennsylvania and Bell Laboratories, has confirmed Stratton's report that, when optical devices create a discrepancy between the visually perceived locations of body parts and their felt locations as given by the proprioceptive, or position sense, the position sense is actually recalibrated to conform with the visual information. Not only does visual capture occur, but with longer exposure to a more extreme discrepancy—mirror reversal of the image of the observer's moving hand—proprioceptive perception ultimately is drawn into line with the reversed visual perception, even though at first the observer is acutely aware that the seen direction of hand movement is the opposite of the felt direction. This recalibration of touch and sense of position persists even when the distorted visual information that caused it is no longer present, as was mentioned in Chapter 5.

Harris argues that analogous changes in position sense underlie Stratton's and Kohler's adaptation and make comprehensible their otherwise puzzling reports. For example, Stratton says that when he first donned inverting lenses, ". . . the parts of my body were *felt* to lie where they would have appeared had the instrument been removed; they were *seen* to be in another position. But the older tactual . . . localization was still the *real* localization." As the experiment progressed, however, ". . . the limbs began actually to feel in the place where the new visual perception reported them to be."

Harris argues further that although a sensory harmony between the visual scene and Stratton's feet and lower extremities was achieved, it did so only because the feet were visible. Such harmony was achieved because the felt position of his feet came to match the seen position, not because of any change in visual perception. As Stratton put it, "I could at length *feel* my feet strike against the *seen* floor, although the floor was seen on the opposite side of the field of vision from that to which at the beginning of the experiment I had referred these tactual sensations."

By contrast, Stratton asserts that "shoulders and head, which under the circumstances could never be directly seen, kept the old localization they had had in normal vision." If legs and torso were felt to match the perceived orientation of the scene while head and shoulders did not, would not that imply a misperception of the orientation of the head on the body? Thus Harris is here offering an explanation of Stratton's frequent experience that he was viewing an upright scene from an inverted position of his head and shoulders. Similarly, Harris argues that, if Kohler's subjects adapted to reversal by coming to feel that their hands were actually where the reversed visual information reported them to be, the subjects could correctly judge that the curves of a 3 were closer to their right hand than to their left, while nonetheless continuing to see the 3 as backward.

What, then, does Stratton's experiment demonstrate about upright vision? We can grant that sensory-motor coordination can adapt to inverted images and that tactual and proprioceptive perception are sufficiently malleable that these sensations will, with time, be "captured" by vision, thus abolishing the intersensory disharmony that occurs at the outset. We also can grant that the optically altered scene will become increasingly "normal" in appearance and that the environmental scene can ultimately appear upright with respect to gravity, but still not necessarily grant that a change in perceived egocentric orientation occurred.

My own reading of Stratton's report is that the scene continued to appear upside down in relation to himself (or at least to his head) throughout the experiment.

Consider this report of the last day of the experiment:

> As long as the new localization of my body was vivid, the general experience was harmonious, and everything was right side up. But when, for any of the reasons already given—an involuntary lapse into the older memory-materials, or a willful recall of these older forms—the pre-experimental localization of my body was prominently in mind, then as I looked out on the scene before me, the scene was involuntarily taken as the standard of right directions, and my body was felt to be in an inharmonious position with reference to the rest. I seemed to be viewing the scene from an inverted body.

While admittedly this statement is open to different interpretations, I take it to mean that the scene had by this time righted itself—that is, appeared as an upright world. But the orientation of its image on the retina, upright rather than inverted as it ordinarily is, continued to yield an impression of egocentric inversion. It simply did not look upright in relation to Stratton himself. The solution to these two facts had to be that he himself somehow must be viewing an upright world from an inverted position. I am here suggesting a different explanation of Stratton's peculiar experiences from the one suggested by Harris.

The critical test is what happened when the tube was removed. Had the scene viewed through the tube come to look upright, we should expect that the scene viewed without the tube should look inverted (being an example of a negative aftereffect), but it did not. Yet other negative aftereffects did occur, including Stratton's impression that the scene moved rapidly whenever he moved his head. Thus, adaptation to the lens-induced "swinging of the scene" occurred during the experiment, as noted in Chapter 7, but not egocentric adaptation.

Why did visual adaptation to a reinverted image not occur readily in Stratton's experiment or in subsequent repetitions of it (assuming that it did not)? If, following Berkeley's logic, one can see that visible objects retain their proper orientation relative to ourselves—for example, treetop to tree-trunk is in the same direction as is our head to our feet—why should adaptation be necessary at all? Why doesn't the reinverted image immediately convey the same impression of an upright scene that the normally inverted image does?

The most plausible answer to these related questions is that some linkage exists between the inverted image and upright vision, either innately or through a lifetime of experience. It may be that *only* from an inverted image can one achieve upright vision. It may be that the direction from top to bottom of the retina is either an innately given or irre-

A camera eye's view of how a scene appears to subjects wearing an inverting optical device when they tilt their heads slightly.

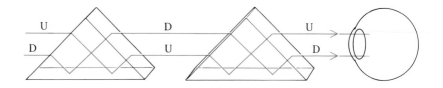

Arrangement of prisms used in studying adaptation to a tilted retinal image of a scene. When one of the prisms is tilted around its horizontal axis, the scene will appear tilted by twice the angle of the prism's tilt.

versibly learned indicator of the egocentric direction "chin to forehead" and that the direction from left to right over the retina is an irreversible indicator of the egocentric direction "right to left." If true, it is at present a mystery as to why this should be the case.

We can investigate the same issue by examining the effect of lesser degrees of altered orientation. For example, using a right-angle (or Dove) prism or, even better, two of these in tandem, one can rotate the retinal image by, say, 30 degrees. These prisms, illustrated above, can be mounted in goggles, and an observer can wear them for any desired period of time. There are several advantages in doing this kind of experiment rather than one with 180-degree rotation, such as Stratton's. First, the change is less drastic, so that there is the greater likelihood of successful adaptation. Second, the effect can be quantitatively measured.

At various intervals, the experimenter can bring the observer into the laboratory, turn the lights out, remove the prisms, and ask the observer to indicate when a luminous line appears vertical. If the observer has completely adapted to a prism system that causes the scene to appear tilted by 30 degrees clockwise, that orientation will now appear vertical. A truly vertical line should look tilted counterclockwise by 30 degrees. If only partial adaptation has occurred, the scene may still look tilted when viewed through prisms, but it may look less tilted than it did at the outset. The experiments that have been done reveal increasing degrees of adaptation over time. In some experiments by Richard Held and his associates, then at Brandeis University, complete adaptation has been obtained over a period of only hours.

It may seem that these data finally can give us an answer to Stratton's question. The image need not be inverted for upright vision to occur; it can be oriented in a different way than it ordinarily is. There is, however, an important reason why this conclusion may be incorrect. Is adaptation to a tilted image egocentric? Suppose, as in Stratton's experiment, the visually altered scene, over time, begins to look like one that is environmentally upright—that is, *not* tilted with respect to the direction of gravity. Suppose, further, that this is the only kind of adaptation that occurs. Because the image is tilted 30 degrees on the retina, observers would have to experience themselves or just their heads as tilted for that image to represent a vertical line in the environment. The kind of adaptation that is occurring thus may be an adaptation to the direction of the scene in relation to gravity, but not in relation to the self. In the latter instance, there may be no egocentric change, just as may have been the case in Stratton's experiment. But the evidence on this question is not yet sufficient to resolve it.

While the two kinds of orientation perception have been discussed separately in this chapter to avoid confusion of issues, the fact is, of course, that they are both simultaneously occurring aspects of perception in daily life as well as in the experiments described. For example, when upright observers enter a tilted room and tend to perceive the room as upright, they necessarily must perceive themselves as tilted. What was not made explicit earlier in the discussion of this experiment is that they perceive themselves as tilted because they immediately detect that they are not aligned with the room—that is, they perceive that they are tilted with respect to it. This is based on perceiving the egocentric orientation of the room. Since its image is tilted on the retina, it appears tilted from the main axis of the body. Integrating all this information, the perceptual system arrives at the overall "solution": room upright, body tilted from upright. The two aspects of the perception of orientation, therefore, work hand in hand.

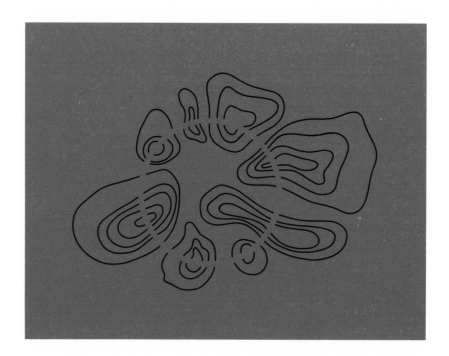

9 THE INTELLIGENCE OF PERCEPTION

Now that we have surveyed the major topics in perception, it is time to see what general principles have emerged. In doing so, it will be useful to consider what, if anything, has survived of the three major traditions of thought about perception. What kinds of controversies are going on today? How do contemporary theorists attempt to answer Kurt Koffka's famous query, Why do things look as they do?

Why Do Things Look As They Do?

THE THREE TRADITIONS As we have seen, the answer to this question for the major traditions of thought would be: for the *inference theory*, things look as they do because of the inferences we make about what given stimuli (or sensations) most likely represent in the world; for the *Gestalt theory*, because of the spontaneous interactions in the brain to which the components of the stimulus give rise; for the *stimulus* (or *psychophysical*) *theory*, because of the sufficient information we receive from the stimulus.

In examining the current scene in psychology, one hardly finds a controversy raging among defenders of these differing viewpoints. For the most part, one finds an eclectic approach to theory in which features of each of the major traditions are incorporated into a more or less *unin*tegrated set of beliefs. Thus, for example, many acknowledge that past experience plays at least some role in perception, but they do not believe that past experience takes the form of unconscious inference or that it derives from the sense of touch. Many acknowledge the role of organization and of configurational or holistic effects not reducible to the sum of parts, but nonetheless feel that these phenomena remain unexplained. And, of course, all acknowledge the necessary role of the stimulus and of

The light red ring that one perceives so clearly in this figure is not physically present. This illusory contour percept can be regarded as an intelligent solution to the problem posed by the stimulus pattern.

In the pattern on the left, one tends to perceive spontaneously the red regions as figures, and in the pattern on the right, the white regions as figures. The basis of this perceptual preference would seem to be symmetry, because each red region on the left and each white region on the right is symmetrical. Advocates of each of the major theories would explain this phenomenon differently. The Gestaltists, who uncovered the effect, believed that spontaneous processes of organization in the brain were reflected by a preference for perceptions that were simple, regular, and symmetrical. Inference theorists would say that the preference for symmetry is based on the likelihood that the ambiguous pattern represented symmetrical objects in the scene rather than asymmetrical ones. For Stimulus theorists, the phenomenon poses a difficult problem since the same stimulus pattern can yield more than one perception; thus some factor other than the stimulus must be governing the perception. They would argue that line drawings such as this are not representative of perception in daily life, where ambiguity is rarely if ever encountered.

certain information contained within it that may not be simple or obvious, although they would not maintain that perception can be fully explained by the stimulus.

In other words, most investigators today believe that innately determined, bottom-up processing leads to some degree of organized pattern vision. Thus, the earlier belief that perception in its entirety is learned is disavowed. However, many investigators also believe that past experience plays some role in perception. Such experience might take many forms, from mere exposure to a normal environment very early in life to ensure the proper maturation of the visual nervous system, to learning to make fine discriminations among members of the same category, to enrichment effects. Many students of perception also accept the claim of stimulus theory that there is information in higher-order dimensions of the stimulus, such as texture density or motion-perspective gradients.

The conclusions drawn by students of perception about almost any topic discussed in the earlier chapters illustrate this eclecticism. Much depends upon the particular phenomenon under study. Nowadays there is a tendency to consider each type of perception separately and to sift out the evidence concerning it in arriving at a theoretical conclusion.

PERIPHERALISTS AND CENTRALISTS   Apart from particular theoretical perspectives, investigation in visual perception is characterized by dispute over the question of whether a particular phenomenon can be explained in terms of a peripheral mechanism or requires a more central explanation. By "peripheral" is meant a mechanism that can be localized in the eye or the movements of the eye; by "central" is meant a process that must occur deeper in the brain and thus often cannot even be specified in "hardware language" because we do not know enough about the brain.

For example, suppose the phenomenon in question is the constancy of lightness of a surface despite variations in illumination on the surface. Ewald Hering, a contemporary and a theoretical opponent of Helmholtz, suggested several possible explanations. Although Hering advanced other, more central explanations, one was based on the well-known fact that the iris surrounding the pupillary opening of the eye automatically alters the pupil's diameter as a function of the amount of light reaching the eye. If the illumination on a surface increases, the pupillary opening decreases, and this has the effect of offsetting the increased level of illumination. Thus, the intensity of light reaching the retina from a surface of a given reflectance could conceivably remain constant. If it did, perceptual constancy would be explained. This peripheral explanation turns out to be incorrect because, among other reasons, while the area of the pupil can change only by a factor of about 17, illumination can change by a factor of 100,000. By way of contrast, Helmholtz's view that the perceptual system takes account of the level of illumination and allows for it in judging sensations of intensity is a central theory. As has been seen, however, it is quite probable that this theory is also incorrect.

Often, peripheral explanations are the first to be proposed. In my opinion, at least, they are usually wrong and they die hard. Because such an explanation will generally be simpler than a central one, it is good science to begin an investigation by testing it. But it is bad science to cling to that explanation in the face of strong evidence to the contrary. Explanations in terms of eye movements have always been popular. Thus, in the domain of motion perception, such phenomena as apparent motion, induced movement, and the autokinetic effect (see Chapter 7) have all been held to be caused by eye movements at one time or another. Max Wertheimer, in his famous research on apparent movement that launched the Gestalt approach, found it necessary to perform a special experiment to demonstrate that such motion could not be explained by eye movements. He arranged for one object to appear to move leftward simultaneously with another object appearing to move rightward. The eyes cannot move in opposite directions at the same time. Eye movements have been invoked as the explanation of the origin of form perception, of depth perception based on retinal disparity, and of the perceived direction of all regions in the field, an example of which is the uprightness of vision despite the inverted orientation of the retinal image.

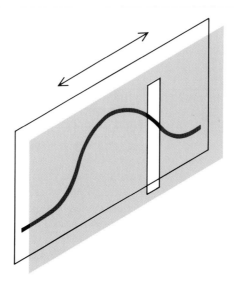

Anorthoscopic perception display. A figure moving back and forth behind the front panel is viewed successively through a narrow slit.

As a contemporary example of this controversy, consider a phenomenon not yet mentioned. If a figure is moved behind a narrow, stationary slit in an opaque surface so that all but the segment behind the slit is occluded at any given moment, one still tends to perceive the entire figure. Helmholtz and others studied this effect in the last century, and Theodore Parks of the University of California at Davis rediscovered it in this century. It is now referred to as *anorthoscopic perception*—an abnormal way of presenting something. How is such perception possible? Isn't an extended, simultaneous retinal image of a figure necessary for the perception of its shape?

One explanation is based on eye movements and the resulting retinal image thereby created. Suppose the eyes move back and forth in synchrony with the moving figure. The result would be that an image of the slit would be spread over the retina. Because the figure behind the slit is moving, different portions of it would be successively visible through the slit. Therefore, an extended image of the figure would be spread over the retina. So the explanation of the anomalous effect is simple. As in normal form perception, an extended image is present on the retina. True, it is not present *simultaneously*, but, given the known fact of visual persistence after a stimulus is no longer present, if the figure (and eyes) move fast enough, the extended image would be equivalent to a simultaneous extended image. The effect would be rather like that seen when a glowing cigarette is moved rapidly in a dark room. Its entire path is perceived simultaneously. This then is the peripheral theory.

There are many difficulties with this view (although there is also some evidence supporting it). Why, for example, should the eyes move back and forth, unless possibly because the figure is perceived and the eyes seek to track some region of it. In that case, however, the eye movement is a consequence, not a cause, of the figure perception.

In any event, we have been able to show in our laboratory (as have others) that the anorthoscopic effect occurs without any eye movement. Thus, the effect is indeed anomalous, a succession of differing contours all falling on a narrow column of the retina somehow leading to the veridical perception of a moving figure. A central theory seems to be required here. First, the perceptual system must detect, or otherwise have a preference to perceive, a figure moving at right angles to the slit rather than contour elements moving up and down the slit, as in the barber-pole effect (Chapter 7). The figure must possess certain characteristics before perception of an extended figure will occur. A straight line will not do. Once the perceptual system interprets the event appropriately, as an occluded object moving at right angles to the slit, it can reconstruct the figure from the set of successive directions that constitute it. The process might run as follows. In the illustration at right, region A is first seen moving to the left at the bottom of the slit. It is followed by B, which is higher. Region B, in turn, is followed on the same level by C. Therefore, B is described by the perceptual system as higher and to the right of A, and C is described as on the same level as B but to the right of it, and so forth. This yields the full configuration shown in the margin. Here we obviously have an example of a central theory.

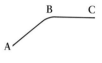

Shape that would be perceived by integrating spatial information from the successive locations of the moving figure's parts in an anorthoscopic perception display.

MECHANISTS AND NONMECHANISTS   If there is a real controversy today in the field of perception, it is not so much among followers of different theories as it is between those who hold a different philosophy about explanation in perception. Some believe that we have already reached a point where explanation of perceptual phenomena is possible in terms of known neural mechanisms. More particularly, I am referring to such mechanisms as the activity of neurons in the retina or the brain that respond to the presence of certain features of the stimulus on the retina, described by what is now known as feature-detector theory. Another example would be lateral-inhibition theory. The guiding philosophy of these approaches is that, once the appropriate stimulus impinges on the appropriate region of the retina, the appropriate cell or cells in the brain will be triggered to discharge. These explanations can be thought of as mechanistic, which simply means that a mechanism is posited that will lead automatically and inexorably to a particular perception. The process is generally assumed to be bottom-up. There is thus no need to invoke explanations that entail past experience, "hypotheses," "decisions," "inference," or "problem-solving." Therefore, effects such as those of preferred perceptions, of holistic organization, and those based on attention pose difficulties for this approach. For a nonmechanistic theory, these very processes and effects are often central to the explanation. Here there is some degree of flexibility. The process is often in part top-down.

Feature-detector theory holds that we can explain the perception of object properties or events by the discharging of neurons in the brain sensitive to (tuned to) certain characteristics of the stimulus on the retina. We have discussed contour or edge detectors (Chapters 5 and 6), motion detectors (Chapter 7), and disparity-depth detectors (Chapter 3). It is of interest to note that, for this theory, the critical sensory information is peripheral: the orientation or motion of an image on the retina. The brain cell that does the detecting is simply responsive to that peripheral fact. However, because the determining physiological event is the discharging of a neuron in the *brain*, it would not be appropriate to designate this theory as peripheral.

Consider, for example, the Poggendorff illusion. According to one theory, it is based on a contrast effect in which the acute angle between each vertical line and the oblique line is overestimated. That occurs because the orientation detector tuned to the orientation of the oblique line is no longer the cell with the strongest activity. Lateral inhibition enters in (see Chapter 6). This is an example of a mechanistic theory of a perceptual phenomenon. Note that it is a thoroughgoing bottom-up theory, and, despite the fact that neural events deep in the brain are posited as explanatory, these events are simply those triggered by the state of affairs on the retina.

According to a different theory, as we have seen, the Poggendorff illusion is caused by depth processing that occurs because oblique lines are cues of horizontal contours receding into the third dimension. Here we obviously have a central theory, because it entails depth processing from pictorial information as well as past experience with certain kinds of objects in the world. In any event, something stored in memory is added into the process that leads to the percept.

Another example that illustrates the two approaches is the illusory-contour effect, discussed briefly in Chapter 5 (see page 132). According to one theory, the root cause of this effect is lightness contrast. The black fragments lighten the regions around them, in this case making them whiter than the rest of the page. Lightness contrast is thought to be governed by lateral inhibition. Obviously, the theory as stated is inadequate because only *some* regions adjacent to the black ones appear very white. Special explanations must be invoked to explain such *selective* contrast. At any rate, if a contrast theory could explain why the inner triangular region appears whiter than the surrounding white page, it can account for the illusory contour. It is simply the contour of this very white region. Following my suggested classification, this is a mechanistic theory.

Another theory reverses the argument, in a manner of speaking. It assumes that the first step in processing is the creation of the illusory figure. The lightness effect occurs secondarily. The stimulus pattern leads initially to the perception of the black fragments as figures on a white ground. That is what we should expect from bottom-up processing based on principles of figure-ground organization. This stage can be easily observed with a pattern such as the one at right because the black regions are each surrounded by white. Moreover, the figure is deliberately drawn so as to be a poorer pattern for producing illusory contours than those illustrated earlier. To perceive the white triangular region, figure-ground reversal is necessary, and that does not always occur with this pattern if the observers remain naive—that is, if they do not know about the possibility. If reversal does occur, it is probable that it does so because it is cued by such factors as the incompleteness of the circular fragments, suggesting that something is occluding them, or by the perfect alignment of the edges of the triangular gaps across the dividing space. Whatever triggers the reversal, the fact is that it entails the perception of a white triangle even though no contours are visible except at its corners. It is possible, therefore, that the perceptual system "invents" the extra whiteness so as to "explain" why one perceives contours where none exist. Following the suggested classification, this is a nonmechanistic theory, since the process entails perceptual reorganization based on the detection of cues. The outcome can be viewed as the preferred solution to the problem of what the stimulus pattern most likely represents. Once the illusory figure is perceived, it is difficult to perceive the pattern in any other way.

An important fact in favor of the problem-solving theory is one already mentioned, that naive observers will not at first perceive the illusory contours if a pattern such as the one illustrated above is presented. If contrast were the explanation, the perception should be immediate and automatic. If, moreover, the pattern is embedded in a larger "noisy" array, observers not looking for it will not perceive the illusory figure at all. One more fact against a contrast theory is illustrated at the top of the following page. The pattern with four crosses does not generate an illusory contour figure because these corner figures are "complete." Therefore, they are not consistent with the hypothesis that there is an occluding yellow figure in front. These findings are difficult to reconcile with the mechanistic approach.

So much for a survey of the present scene in the field of perception. In what follows, I take up some difficult general problems that have only

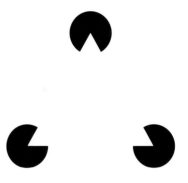

This stimulus pattern can lead to an illusory contour percept. But observers unaware of the possibility of an illusory percept may not see it immediately.

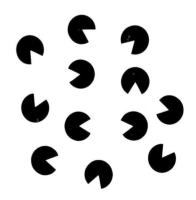

When the pattern seen in the figure at the top of the page is embedded in a "noisy" array, observers who are not searching for an illusory contour figure are not likely to perceive it.

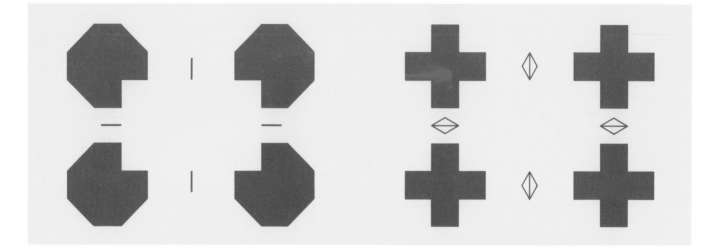

In the pattern on the left, where the corner fragments look like incomplete figures, the illusory contour percept is likely to occur. However, when the corner fragments are familiar, complete figures, such as the crosses shown in the pattern on the right, perception of an illusory contour figure is unlikely to occur spontaneously.

been touched upon in the previous chapters and that, therefore, have not been adequately discussed. I then offer a brief outline of my own view of why things look the way they do and why one can regard perception as intelligent.

Perception, Knowledge, and Past Experience

Beginning students of perception soon learn that what we perceive is independent of what we know about the objects and events in the scene. Illusions do not disappear or diminish simply because we know they are illusions. Conversely, achieving veridicality is not based on knowing what is there in the world. An airplane high in the sky looks small despite our knowledge of its large size, whereas an unfamiliar object on the distant ground will generally be seen in its true size despite our lack of knowledge of what it is. A single black surface will never look black when only it is illuminated in a dark surround, as shown on the facing page, no matter how often we are allowed to see that it is black by turning on the room lights. The dark gray rock of the moon will always look highly luminous to us when seen in the dark night sky, whether or not we are conscious of its true reflectance.

Virtually every phenomenon discussed in this book illustrates the autonomy of perception from cognitive processing on a conceptual or linguistic level. We can only speculate about the reasons for this independence. But one of them surely is that perception is *stimulus bound*. By its very definition, perception is based upon—even if not entirely determined by—the stimulus. Therefore, if a particular stimulus pattern falls upon the retina—a triangle, for example—it stands to reason that the perception will in some sense conform to it—in this case, to a triangular configuration—even if we find out that the three contours derive from object contours that are in entirely different planes in the world or from contours that are curvilinear but happen to be viewed head-on. Or, to give another example, if a stimulus cue informs us that one object is behind another, knowing it is actually in front will have no effect.

A second reason is that lawful processes of perception must have evolved to allow us to achieve veridicality. An animal can hardly be expected to find out about what is actually present or happening in the world by asking someone or by reading a book. Nor can it wait to find out by exploring the situation. Perception must be capable of yielding accurate information immediately and through the senses. It is understandable that the laws of perception that allow us to gain such information will also, under certain conditions, lead to misperception. We can hardly expect such lawful processes to be suspended simply because we find out that, for example, two lines that we perceive to be unequal in length are in fact equal or that the moon, which we perceive to be larger at the horizon, is in fact equal in size and distance from us whatever its position in the night sky.

Still another reason for the insulation of perception from conceptually based knowledge may be this: Perception is sometimes based on inference from rules, but the rules seem to be "known" on an unconscious level. For example, it is probable that the perceptual system "knows" the law of the visual angle, that the visual angle is inversely proportional to an object's distance. This law is invoked and employed unconsciously when it enters into the processing of size at some distance. Therefore, the process underlying perception will run its course on the basis of unconscious "knowledge"; it is thus not influenced by consciously available information. Consequently, when one inspects one's own afterimage projected on surfaces at differing distances, it matters little that one consciously knows it is an image of unchanging size. It will still appear to change its size because of the unconscious application of the corollary of the law of the visual angle, Emmert's law, that the size of objects yielding a constant visual angle is directly proportional to their distance.

In earlier chapters, however, we have seen some cases in which conscious knowledge *can* affect perception. Knowing about a figure's reversibility will make reversal more likely, and not knowing may eliminate it; knowing what a fragmented figure is may lead to its recognition, whereas not knowing may prevent recognition. A disoriented figure will be perceived differently and not recognized unless we happen to know that it is

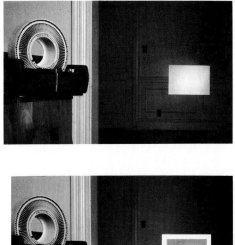

When only a black surface is illuminated in an otherwise dark room, it will continue to appear to be white or light gray despite our knowledge that it is black. But when a white surface is behind the black one, the latter will be perceived as black in that same illumination.

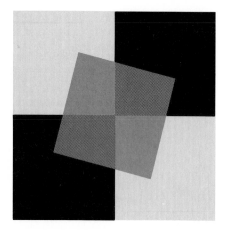

Knowledge on the part of the observer that this display can be perceived as a transparent square in front of a background of differing lightnesses can play a role in how it is perceived.

disoriented. Perceiving illusory contours may sometimes depend upon awareness of this possible perception. The same is true of the perception of transparency, in which one has the impression of looking through a surface at another surface or object behind it. Conscious knowledge plays such an important role in these instances that sophisticated observers give different responses than do naive ones in experiments. Investigators thus often take steps to eliminate one type of observer or the other.

Are these exceptions not enough to vitiate the thesis that perception is autonomous with respect to knowledge? I think not, because they all seem to have in common one characteristic: The stimulus input in each case is ambiguous and capable of leading to two (or more) percepts. One percept is initially achieved by bottom-up processing and is a sufficiently satisfactory "solution" to endure, unless other information enters in to change the equation. Finding out about the alternative percept then makes its occurrence possible or probable. The stimulus will just as well support that percept—indeed, there may be reasons why that percept will be preferred once it occurs. In these examples, knowledge does not oppose a good match between stimulus and percept or overturn lawful or rule-based perceptual processes. Rather, the role of knowledge is simply to alert us to a perception that the stimulus is perfectly capable of yielding even without such knowledge. After all, some observers do achieve it without being told about its potential presence.

In this discussion, I have been referring to knowledge in the sense of knowing something about the external state of affairs being viewed, and I have been arguing that such knowledge only affects perception under special circumstances. However, knowledge in the sense of stored memory of prior experience is another story. In previous chapters, we have seen many examples in which memory of prior experience affects perception. The successful organization and recognition of fragmented figures (e.g., the Dalmatian figure), the preference to perceive the white region as figure in the illustration in the margin on page 131, and, possibly, the tendency to perceive certain line drawings (such as those of cubes) as three-dimensional—all are instances in which perception is enriched by past experience.

In these cases, I would argue that the relevant past experience must be in the form of *visual perceptions* that have left behind visual memory traces. Prior perceptions via other sensory modalities will not be effective, nor will prior nonperceptual experiences. But a visual memory of a cubelike structure can be effective because of its partial similarity to the initial stage of perception of the line drawing seen later. Such similarity is crucial for the accessing of the appropriate memories and does not obtain between the initial *visual* percept and memories in other sense modalities or in the form of nonperceptual stored knowledge. Perceptual enrichment based on such visual memories is not incompatible with what I am saying here about the limitations of the effects of knowledge on perception. Past-experience effects of prior visual memories can occur because they in no way do violence to the role of the stimulus or to other laws of perception. Rather, they are perfectly compatible alternate perceptions of a stimulus that, logically speaking, is ambiguous.

An Outline of a Theory of Perception

What are the general characteristics of perception with which any theory must deal? An adequate theory must be able to account for the achievement of constancy and veridicality, for preferred perceptions given an ambiguous stimulus, for the effect of context and frame of reference, and for enrichment and completion effects. Each of the traditional theories deals with some of these features but not with all of them. For example, stimulus theory has particular difficulty with the fact that the stimulus is often ambiguous and that more than one percept can arise from it. The necessity of perceptual organization also raises grave difficulties for this approach, as does the fact of perceptual enrichment. Gestalt theory has difficulty with those cases of constancy that seem to be based on an inferential process (the taking-account explanation).

Moreover, both of these theories have difficulty with a very important fact about perception. Often one perception seems to depend upon another. Earlier I suggested that the stereokinetic depth effect occurs if, and only if, the circles are no longer perceived to rotate—that is, they must first be seen to maintain their orientation before they appear to slide around with respect to one another. If at first the circles are seen to rotate, the depth effect will not occur. So it is not simply the stimulus transformation that leads to the depth effect, it is a certain prior perception that does so. There are many examples of this sequence of events, but this one will suffice. We see, then, that perception is more than a direct consequence of a stimulus and more than a consequence of the organization of stimulus components.

The limitations of these approaches, and of peripheral and mechanistic approaches as well, lead me to attempt to formulate a cognitively oriented theory. It builds on the kind of inference theory that Helmholtz proposed but departs from it in certain important respects.

In this book, I have suggested that perception is the result of a series of stages of processing that occur between reception of a visual stimulus and achievement of a percept. My answer to Koffka's query—Why do things look as they do?—would be: because of the cognitive operations performed on the information contained within the stimulus.

Light reflected from objects is propagated in all directions, but some is intercepted by the eye and images of objects are focused on the retina. This much is consistent with a camera theory because the image is very similar to the picture a camera takes of the same scene. But the "picture" on the retina, the stimulus, is nothing more than a mosaic of varying intensities and frequencies of light and is therefore thoroughly ambiguous with respect to what it represents in the world. It must be organized into discrete and separate units. Some degree of organization occurs at the level of the retina because cells farther along in the visual system are responsive to the nature of the stimulation of an entire group of the light-sensitive retinal cells, those constituting the receptive field of that higher cell. We do not know how more complex organization occurs, such as that which leads to figure-ground differentiation and other larger figural units, but it may conform to some or all of the laws of grouping and figure-ground organization uncovered by the Gestalt psychologists and a few of their predecessors. Following such organization, the structure is described by the perceptual system on the basis of its geometry, orientation, and other factors.

The resulting perceptions that occur at this stage are highly correlated with the organized stimulus thought of as a two-dimensional array. For example, the interposition pattern that appears on page 88 may look like a meshing of a rectangle and an L in one plane, the transparency pattern that appears in the margin looks like several separate regions of differing lightnesses, and a distant object may look small, or a circular one like an ellipse. However, these percepts are fleeting, and often we are unaware of them. One might refer to them as perceptions in the *proximal* or *literal mode.*

Such fleeting percepts are immediately superseded by perceptions that more veridically represent the world and that therefore might be referred to as perceptions in the *world* (or *constancy*) *mode.* However, the literal or proximal mode percepts remain, although they inhabit the background of our awareness and are not so easily brought to the center of attention. The world-mode perceptions are based upon, among other things, further processes of organization. For example, in the case of an interposition pattern, figure-ground organization *within* the pattern leads to the impression of one unit overlapping another. Or, to give another example, the pattern in the transparency illustration at left, which at first may have looked like four rectangles of differing lightnesses, tends to look like a small transparent rectangle through which one is looking at another larger, black-and-gray rectangle. The latter (transparency) percept is preferred, much as is the overlapping percept in the previous example. These perceptions refer to structures arranged in three-dimensional space. Moreover, as we saw in Chapter 5, if more than one object

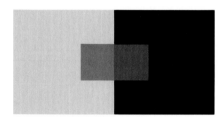

Before this figure is perceived as a transparent rectangle in front of a gray and black background, it may be fleetingly perceived as four regions of different lightnesses in the same plane.

is encountered, it is the one to which we attend that will undergo the description processing that leads to the perception of a distinct shape.

Because these world-mode perceptions seem to be preferred, the organization at this stage must be based upon some underlying principle that governs preference, such as simplicity, stabilization resulting from recognition, or the selection of those percepts that explain certain regularities or simultaneously occurring events in the stimulus. By this I mean that those perceptions are preferred that account for co-occurences or regularity in the stimulus that would remain purely coincidental were the alternative perception to occur. For example, in the kinetic depth effect, the retinal image of a line rotating in the third dimension simultaneously changes its length and orientation. Were one to perceive the line literally as doing just that, the two co-occurring changes would be coincidental—that is, they would have no particular relation to one another. But when one perceives the line rotating in depth, these two transformations are both the result of a common cause, the perspective representation of such a rotating line. Or, to give another example, perceiving literally several regions of differing lightness in the figure on page 230 or the one on page 232 would not explain the fact that the lightness values in the smaller regions change along the same straight line as in the larger regions. But this regularity in the pattern is fully explained by the transparency percept. Therefore, I suggest that a general principle of perception is the preference for "solutions" that account for such stimulus regularities or co-occurrences.

With the emergence of shaped, segregated units in perception, stored representations of prior visual experience enter into the story. Most typically, this step is merely a continuation of the sequence of bottom-up processing, consisting simply of an enrichment of perception, in the sense that the object, if familiar, can be recognized and identified. In some instances, however, the representation from memory can influence the very shape and organization achieved. We have seen several examples of such top-down processing in previous chapters, one of which was the reorganization of fragmented figures that occurs prior to, or at the moment of, their recognition. Even in these instances, however, the effect of past experience depends upon the bottom-up achievement of some degree of organized shape perception. Only then is access to the appropriate memories possible.

Once we have achieved organized form perception, we must integrate it with other relevant information. For example, a triangular shape may be perceived (and recognized) but perception of its size depends upon cues to its distance. Without a determinate location in the third dimension, its size, logically speaking, must remain ambiguous. Thus, size perception and constancy of size depend upon an inference type of process, a computation, albeit unconscious, in which distance is taken into account. A similar process of computation may be presumed to occur in such cases as the perception of shape at a slant and the perception of orientation in the environment for varying orientations of the observer. A somewhat different kind of process occurs when we make use of information given via stimulus relations, as in the case of motion and object orientation. Here, certain principles of organization seem to be at work such that we accept the outermost visible structure as defining or establishing the stationary or upright world and gauge the motion or orientation of things in relation to these frames of reference. We also make use of stimulus relations in reconstructing the world of lightnesses and illuminations.

As far as perception is concerned, then, the mind is hardly a tabula rasa upon which experience writes. It imposes organization on the incoming stimulation, exhibits certain rules of preference, and is particularly sensitive to stimulus relations. It infers and computes, predicating such inference on certain "assumptions," taking account of one kind of sensory information in assessing the significance of another kind. Yet perception is affected by past experience—although the relevant experience that is effective in vision is *not* derived from touch.

The Intelligence of Perception

Although perception is autonomous with respect to such higher mental faculties as are exhibited in conscious thought and in the use of conscious knowledge, I would still argue that it is intelligent. By calling perception "intelligent," I mean to say that it is based upon such thoughtlike mental processes as description, inference, and problem solving, although these processes are rapid-fire, unconscious, and nonverbal. "Description" implies, for example, that a perceptual property such as shape is the result of an abstract analysis of an object's geometrical configuration, including how it is oriented, in a form like that of a proposition, except that it is not couched in natural language. Such a description of a square, for example, might be "a figure with opposite sides equal and parallel and four right angles, the sides being horizontal and vertical in space." "Inference" implies that certain perceptual properties are computed from given sensory information using unconsciously known rules. For example, perceived size is inferred from the object's visual angle, its perceived distance, and the law of geometrical optics relating the visual angle to object distance. "Problem solving" implies a more creative process of arriving at a hypothesis concerning what object or event in the world the stimulus might represent and then determining whether the hypothesis accounts adequately for, and is supported adequately by, the stimulus. An example would be the perception that occurs in an apparent-movement display in

When the two figures are presented successively so as to yield apparent motion, the preferred perception is of the figure flipping over in the third dimension.

which alternating figures of the same shape but differing orientations are presented, as in the illustration on the facing page. Observers tend to perceive an object moving up and down and rotating during its motion. Rotation—that is, flipping over—in the third dimension is preferred.

Of course, one might take the opposite view, that perception is quite unintelligent, because it adheres rigidly to its "conclusions" despite knowledge to the contrary. After all, flexibility is one of the hallmarks of intelligence. However, as we have seen, there are good reasons why perception is more or less impervious to the influence of conscious knowledge about the actual state of affairs in the environment. Perception is intelligent because its operations are like those of thought, not because it is flexible or interwoven with the domain of conscious thought. Its "conclusions" are logical within its own domain.

The intelligence of perception should not be regarded as equivalent to the utilization of past experience in what we perceive. Although experience often does affect perception, it does not always do so, and even when it does, its scope is limited. The thoughtlike operations of perception should be distinguished from the *content* of thought. The capability of reasoning is not synonymous with the use *in* reasoning of certain knowledge gained from past experience.

Perhaps this argument can be reversed. Perhaps perception arose in evolution before conscious reasoning ability, arose out of the necessity for achieving veridicality from the ambiguous, inadequate stimulus input. Inference would then first have the form I have suggested it has in perception. Once this kind of process had evolved, it eventually underwent further modification until it assumed the form that characterizes conscious thinking in human beings. If so, we might conclude that thought is perceptionlike.

SELECTED READINGS

SENSORY PROCESSES

Cornsweet, Tom N. *Visual Perception.* New York: Academic, 1970.

Harris, Charles S., ed. *Visual Coding and Adaptability.* Hillsdale, N.J.: Erlbaum, 1980.

Held, Richard, and Richards, Whitman, eds. *Perception: Mechanisms and Models.* San Francisco: W. H. Freeman and Company, 1972.

Kaufman, Lloyd. *Sight and Mind: An Introduction to Visual Perception.* New York: Oxford University Press, 1974.

Levine, M. W., and Shefner, J. M. *Fundamentals of Sensation and Perception.* Reading, Mass.: Addison-Wesley, 1981.

THE NEUROPHYSIOLOGY OF PERCEPTION

Blakemore, Colin. *Mechanics of the Mind.* New York: Cambridge University Press, 1977.

Frisby, John P. *Seeing.* New York: Oxford University Press, 1979.

Held, Richard, and Richards, Whitman, eds. *Perception: Mechanisms and Models.* San Francisco: W. H. Freeman and Company, 1972.

Hubel, David H., and Wiesel, Torsten N. "Brain Mechanisms of Vision." *Scientific American,* 241(1979)45–53.

Kuffler, S. W., and Nicholls, J. G. *From Neuron to Brain.* Sunderland, Mass.: Sinauer, 1976.

Levine, M. W., and Shefner, J. M. *Fundamentals of Sensation and Perception.* Reading, Mass.: Addison-Wesley, 1981.

AUDITION

Moore, Brian C. J. *Introduction to Psychology of Hearing,* 2d ed. New York: Academic, 1982.

Pierce, John R. *The Science of Musical Sound.* New York: Scientific American Books, 1983.

Plomp, Reinier. *Aspects of Tone Sensation.* New York: Academic, 1976.

Yost, William A., and Nielson, Donald W. *Fundamentals of Hearing.* New York: Holt, Rinehart and Winston, 1977.

THE FIELD OF PERCEPTION

Davidoff, Jules B. *Differences in Visual Perception: The Individual Eye.* New York: Academic, 1975.

Gregory, Richard L. *Eye and Brain,* 3d ed. New York: McGraw-Hill, 1978.

Haber, Ralph, ed. *Contemporary Theory and Research in Visual Perception.* New York: Holt, Rinehart and Winston, 1968.

Held, Richard, ed. *Image, Object and Illusion.* San Francisco: W. H. Freeman and Company, 1974.

Held, Richard, ed. *Recent Progress in Perception.* San Francisco: W. H. Freeman and Company, 1976.

Rock, Irvin. *An Introduction to Perception.* New York: Macmillan, 1975.

Wallach, Hans. *On Perception.* New York: Quadrangle Books, 1976.

CHAPTER 1: THE WORLD OF PERCEPTION

Berkeley, George. *An Essay Towards a New Theory of Vision.* New York: E. P. Dutton, (1709) 1910.

Boring, Edwin G. *Sensation and Perception in the History of Psychology.* New York: Appleton-Century-Crofts, 1942.

Gibson, James J. *The Perception of the Visual World.* Boston: Houghton Mifflin, 1950.

Helmholtz, Hermann von. *Treatise on Physiological Optics* Vol. 3 (1856). James C. P. Southall, ed. New York: Dover, 1962.

Köhler, Wolfgang. *Gestalt Psychology.* New York: Liveright, (1929) 1947.

CHAPTER 2: CONSTANCY

Bower, T. G. R. "The Visual World of Infants." *Scientific American,* 215(1966)80–92.

Epstein, William, ed. *Constancy and Stability in Visual Perception: Mechanics and Processes.* New York: Wiley, 1977.

Kaufman, Lloyd, and Rock, Irvin. "The Moon Illusion." *Scientific American,* 207(1962)120–130.

Rock, Irvin. *An Introduction to Perception.* New York: Macmillan, 1975.

Wallach, Hans. "The Perception of Neutral Colors." *Scientific American,* 208(1963)107–116.

CHAPTER 3: THE MANY PATHS TO THE THIRD DIMENSION

Braunstein, M. L. *Depth Perception Through Motion.* New York: Academic, 1976.

Gibson, Eleanor J., and Walk, Richard D. "The 'Visual Cliff.'" *Scientific American*, 202(1960) 64–71.

Hochberg, Julian. "Perception. II Space and Movement." In J. W. Kling and L. A. Riggs, eds. *Woodworth and Schlossberg's Experimental Psychology*, 3d ed. New York: Holt, Rinehart and Winston, 1971.

Julesz, Bela. *Foundations of Cyclopean Perception*. Chicago: University of Chicago Press, 1971.

Wheatstone, Charles. "Contributions to the physiology of vision: On some remarkable, and hitherto unobserved phenomena of binocular vision. Part I." *Philosophical Transactions*, (1838) 371–394. Reprinted in William N. Dember. *Visual Perception: The 19th Century*. New York: Wiley, 1964.

Wheatstone, Charles. "Contributions to the physiology of vision. Part II." *Philosophical Transactions*,(1852)1–17.

CHAPTER 4: PERCEPTION AND ART

Arnheim, Rudolf. *Art and Visual Perception: A Psychology of the Creative Eye*. Berkeley, Calif.: University of California Press, 1974.

Gombrich, E. H. *Art and Illusion: A Study in the Psychology of Pictorial Representation*. Princeton, N.J.: Princeton University Press, 1960.

Pirenne, M. H. *Optics, Painting, and Photography*. Cambridge, England: Cambridge University Press, 1970.

CHAPTER 5: FORM AND ORGANIZATION

Ellis, Willis D. *A Source Book of Gestalt Psychology*. New York: Humanities Press, 1950.

Hochberg, Julian. "Nativism and Empiricism in Perception." In L. Postman, ed. *Psychology in the Making*. New York: Knopf, 1964.

Kanizsa, Gaetano. *Organization in Vision*. New York: Praeger, 1979.

Köhler, Wolfgang. *Gestalt Psychology*. New York: Liveright, (1929) 1947.

Kubovy, Michael, and Pomerantz, James T. *Perceptual Organization*. Hillsdale, N. J.: Erlbaum, 1981.

Rock, Irvin. *Orientation and Form*. New York: Academic, 1974.

Rock, Irvin, and Harris, Charles S. "Vision and Touch." *Scientific American*, 267(1967)96–104.

Senden, M. von. *Space and Sight: The Perception of Space and Shape in the Congenitally Blind Before and After Operation*. P. Heath, transl. New York: Methuen, 1960.

CHAPTER 6: GEOMETRICAL ILLUSIONS

Coren, Stanley, and Girgus, Joan. *Seeing Is Deceiving: The Psychology of Visual Illusions*. Hillsdale, N.J.: Erlbaum, 1978.

Gillam, Barbara. "Geometric Illusions." *Scientific American*, 242(1980)102–111.

Ittelson, William H. *The Ames Demonstration in Perception*. Princeton, N.J.: Princeton University Press, 1952.

Minnaert, M. *The Nature of Light and Color in the Open Air*. New York: Dover, 1954.

Robinson, J. O. *The Psychology of Visual Illusion*. London: Hutchinson, 1972.

Wade, Nicholas. *The Art and Science of Visual Illusions*. Boston: Routledge and Kegan Paul, 1982.

CHAPTER 7: THE PERCEPTION OF MOTION

Duncker, K. "Induced Motion." In Willis D. Ellis, ed. *Source Book of Gestalt Psychology*. New York: Humanities Press, 1950.

Johannsson, Gunnar. *Configurations in Event Perception*. Uppsala: Almbuist and Wiksell, 1950.

Kolers, Paul. *Aspects of Motion Perception*. Elmsford, N.Y.: Pergamon, 1972.

Michotte, Albert. *The Perception of Causality*. New York: Basic Books, 1963.

Rock, Irvin. *An Introduction to Perception*. New York: Macmillan, 1975.

Ternus, J. "The Problem of Phenomenal Identity." In Willis D. Ellis, ed. *Source Book of Gestalt Psychology*. New York: Humanities Press, 1950.

Wallach, Hans. "The Perception of Motion." *Scientific American*, 201(1959)56–60.

CHAPTER 8: THE UPRIGHT WORLD

Dolezal, Hubert. *Living in a World Transformed: Perceptual and Performatory Adaptation to Visual Distortion*. New York: Academic, 1982.

Harris, Charles S. "Perceptual Adaptation to Inverted, Reversed, and Displaced Vision." *Psychological Review*, 72(1965)419–444.

Howard, Ian. *Human Visual Orientation*. New York: Wiley, 1982.

Rock, Irvin. *The Nature of Perceptual Adaptation*. New York: Basic Books, 1966.

Stratton, George. "Some Preliminary Experiments on Vision Without Inversion of the Retinal Image." *Psychological Review*, 3(1896)611–617.

——— "Upright Vision and the Retinal Image." *Psychological Review*, 4(1897)182–187.

——— "Vision Without Inversion of the Retinal Image." *Psychological Review*, 4(1897)341–360; 463–481. Reprinted in William N. Dember. *Visual Perception: The 19th Century*. New York: Wiley, 1964.

Welch, Robert E. *Perceptual Modification: Adapting to Altered Sensory Environments*. New York: Academic, 1978.

Witkin, H. A. "The Perception of the Upright." *Scientific American*, 200(1959)50–56.

CHAPTER 9: THE INTELLIGENCE OF PERCEPTION

Gregory, Richard L. *The Intelligent Eye*. New York: McGraw-Hill, 1970.

Haber, Ralph, ed. *Contemporary Theory and Research in Visual Perception*. New York: Holt, Rinehart and Winston, 1968.

Rock, Irvin. "Anorthoscopic Perception." *Scientific American*, 244(1981)145–153.

———*The Logic of Perception*. Cambridge, Mass.: M.I.T. Press, 1983.

SOURCES OF ILLUSTRATIONS

PAGE 1: Edward Hopper, *Sunlight in a Cafeteria*, Yale University Art Gallery. Bequest of Stephen Carlton Clark. PAGE 2 (top): Photography by Andrew Brilliant © 1983. PAGE 3: Photography by Kaiser Porcelain Ltd. PAGE 5: Courtesy of Hale Observatories. PAGE 6: From *Optical Illusions and the Visual Arts* by Ronald G. Carraher and Jacqueline B. Thurston. Copyright © Litton Educational Publishing, Inc. By permission of Van Nostrand Reinhold, Co., Inc. PAGE 10: Photography by Joel Meyerowitz. PAGE 11: From Asahi Shimbun's Museum of Fun Exhibition, 1979. (Collection of Jin-ichi Suzuki.) Courtesy of The Asahi Shimbun. PAGE 13: Photography by Hans Wallach. PAGE 14: Courtesy of The Burndy Library. PAGE 16: The Library of the Boston Athenaeum. PAGE 18: Photography by Joel Meyerowitz. PAGE 19: Photography by John Zoiner/Peter Arnold, Inc. PAGE 21: Adapted from "The Processes of Vision," by Ulric Neisser. Copyright © 1968 by Scientific American, Inc. All rights reserved. PAGE 22: Photography by Andrew Brilliant © 1983. PAGE 26 (right): Photography by David Hiser/The Image Bank. PAGE 29: Adapted from *An Introduction to Perception* by Irvin Rock. Macmillan Publishing Company. Copyright © 1975 by Irvin Rock. PAGE 30 (top): Adapted from "The Moon Illusion," by Lloyd Kaufman and Irvin Rock. Copyright © 1962 by Scientific American, Inc. All rights reserved. PAGE 33: Photography by Harry Callahan © 1983/Zabriski Gallery. PAGE 34: Reprinted with permission from Macmillan Publishing Company. From *An Introduction to Perception* by Irvin Rock. Copyright © 1975 by Irvin Rock. PAGE 35: Adapted from "The Effect of Inattention on Form Perception," by I. Rock and D. Gutman, *Journal of Experimental Psy-*

chology: Human Perception and Performance 7 (1981) 275–285. PAGE 37: The Bettmann Archive, Inc. PAGE 45: The Metropolitan Museum of Art, Bequest of Isaac D. Fletcher, 1917. Mr. and Mrs. Isaac D. Fletcher Collection. PAGE 48: Courtesy of Private Collection. PAGE 50: Photography by Andrew Brilliant © 1983. PAGE 52: Moonrise, Hernandez, New Mexico (1941). The Ansel Adams Publishing Rights Trust. PAGE 58: Courtesy of The Burndy Library. PAGE 60 (top right): Courtesy of The Boston Public Library, Print Department. PAGE 60 (bottom): From Asahi Shimbun's Museum of Fun Exhibition, 1979. Courtesy of Vlajimir Tamari. PAGE 61: Photography by Paul M. Churchland, The University of Manitoba. PAGE 62: Courtesy of Bela Julesz. PAGE 72: The Milwaukee Art Museum Collection. Gift of Mrs. Harry Lynde Bradley. PAGE 73 (top): Adapted from *An Introduction to Perception* by Irvin Rock. Macmillan Publishing Company. Copyright © 1975 by Irvin Rock. PAGE 74 (top left): Photography by © Peter Arnold. Adapted from "Figure Organization and Binocular Interaction," by M. Zanforlin, in *Organization and Representation in Perception*, J. Beck(ed.), Erlbaum, 1982. PAGE 75: Photography by Eric Simmons/Stock, Boston. PAGE 76: Courtesy of The University Museum, University of Pennsylvania. PAGE 77: Canaletto, *View in Venice*. National Gallery of Art, Washington. Widener Collection. PAGE 80: From "The Construction of a Plane from Pictorial Information," by I. Rock, D. Wheeler, J. Shallow, and J. Rotunda, *Perception 11*(1982) 463-475. PAGE 86: Photography by William Vandivert and Scientific American. PAGE 87: Adapted from "Psychologische Untersuchungen über die Wirkung Zweidimensionaler körperlicher Gebilde," by H. Kopfermann, *Psy-*

chologische Forschung 13(1930)293–364. PAGE 89: Adapted from "Contours without Gradients or Cognitive Contours," by G. Kanizsa, *Italian Journal of Psychology 1*(1974)93–122 and "The Role of Regularity in Perceptual Organization," by G. Kanizsa, in *Studies in Perception: Festschrift for Fabio Metelli*, G. F. d'Arcais (ed.), Martello-Gianti, 1975. PAGE 90: Scala/Art Resource. PAGE 92: Photography by Madeline Grimoldi. PAGE 93: Kunstwerke der Bayerischen Staat Gemäldesammlungen, Neue Pinakothek/Art Resource. PAGE 94: Henri Fantin-Latour, *Still Life*. National Gallery of Art, Washington. Chester Dale Collection. PAGE 96: World Wide Photos. PAGE 97: Camille Pissarro, *The Artist's Daughter, Jeanne*, Yale University Art Gallery, John Hay Whitney Collection, B.A. 1926. PAGE 98: FPG International. PAGE 99: From *A Psychology of Picture Perception* by John M. Kennedy, Jossey-Bass, 1974. PAGE 100: Master of the Life of Saint John the Baptist, *Madonna and Child with Angel*. National Gallery of Art, Washington. Samuel H. Kress Collection 1943. PAGE 101 (top): From *Land of Black Gold (The Adventures of Tintin)* by Herge. Art copyright by Casterman. Text copyright by Methuen/Little Brown. PAGE 101 (bottom): Photography by Farrfli Grehan/FPG International. PAGE 102 (top): Courtesy of Carol Palmer. PAGE 103 (top): Photography by Andrew Brilliant © 1983. Drawing from "Speed of Perception as a Function of Mode of Representation," by T. A. Ryan and C. B. Schwartz, *American Journal of Psychology 96* (1956)66–69. PAGE 103 (bottom): From "Pictorial Perception and Culture," by Jan B. Deregowski. Copyright © 1972 by Scientific American, Inc. All rights reserved. PAGE 104 (top): Courtesy of The Boston Public Library,

INDEX